The Elizabethan Theatre VIII

The Elizabethan Theatre VIII

Papers given at the Eighth International
Conference on Elizabethan Theatre held at the
University of Waterloo, Ontario, in July 1979

Edited and with an introduction by
G. R. HIBBARD
Department of English
University of Waterloo

Published in collaboration with the
University of Waterloo

P. D. Meany
Port Credit

Canadian Cataloguing in Publication Data

International Conference on Elizabethan Theatre
(8th : 1979 : University of Waterloo).
The Elizabethan theatre VIII

"Published in collaboration with the University of Waterloo."
Includes bibliographical references and index.
ISBN 0-88835-010-4

1. Theater—England—History—16th century—
Congresses.   2. English drama—Early modern and
Elizabethan, 1500-1600—Congresses.   I. Hibbard,
G. R., 1915-   II. Title.

PN2589.I5 1979   792'.0942   C82-094607-9

This book has been published with the help of a grant from the Canadian Federation for the Humanities, using funds provided by the Social Sciences and Humanities Research Council of Canada.

Printed and bound in Canada by
T. H. Best Printing Company Limited
Don Mills, Ontario
for
P. D. Meany Company Inc.
Box 534, Port Credit
Ontario, Canada L5G 4M2

Acknowledgments

The Eighth International Conference on Elizabethan Theatre, held at the University of Waterloo in July 1979, was made possible by generous grants from the Social Sciences and Humanities Research Council of Canada and the Research Grant Subcommittee of the University of Waterloo. The English Department of the University gave invaluable help of a practical kind with the organization and administration of it all. Moreover, this book has been published with the help of a grant from the Canadian Federation for the Humanities, using funds provided by the Social Sciences and Humanities Research Council of Canada. To these agencies and bodies I express my most sincere thanks, as I do also to Carlo E. Bestetti and Aldo Martello for permission to reproduce the illustrations on pages 170-173.

Among the many individuals who contributed to the success of the Conference, Mrs. Diane Mew deserves a special word of thanks for her work in copy-editing this volume, as do Gabrielle Bailey and Sheryl Loeffler for their help in looking after the day to day business while the Conference was going on. I am also much indebted to Warren U. Ober, Chairman of the Department of English at Waterloo, to Robin Banks, the Dean of Arts, and to J. F. Willms, the Assistant Dean. In 1979, as in previous years, Walter Martin presided over the Business Meeting with a tact and good humour that made it easy for me to get my own way. I owe him much.

Richard Martin compiled the index.

G. R. H.

Contents

Introduction

The name of Edmund Spenser appears both in the chapter on play-wrights in E. K. Chambers' *The Elizabethan Stage* and in the Index of English Playwrights included in Schoenbaum's revision of Harbage's *Annals of English Drama*; but, although we have Gabriel Harvey's word for it that the poet's "Nine Comoedies," to which he gave "the names of the *Nine Muses*," had much in common with "Ariostoes Comoedies," it is by no means clear that these lost works, belonging to the years before 1580, ever achieved a final form. Had they done so, they would almost certainly have been either closet dramas or plays intended for Queen Elizabeth and her court. It seems highly unlikely that their author, ambitious both for fame as a poet and for the social advancement that such fame ought, he considered, to bring with it, could possibly have destined them for public performance by the Earl of Leicester's Men at the recently opened Theatre in Shoreditch. Nevertheless, although his "Comoedies" failed to see the light of day either in the theatre or in print, and although the rest of his work does not suggest that Spenser had a truly dramatic imagination, his influence on the popular as well as the courtly theatre was profound and far-reaching. He stimulated and fed that interest in romance, in the past, and in pageantry, which the dramatists were to exploit so fully and effectively; and, even more important, he affected the very medium in which they worked. For, as T.S. Eliot so acutely observed some sixty years ago, in his essay on Christopher Marlowe, it was from Spenser, the "great master of melody," that the writer of *Tamburlaine* learned how to infuse a lyrical note into blank verse and how to release that measure from the stiffness and restrictions of the couplet structure by which it had been dominated ever since its first appearance. Thus blank verse began, at last, to sing and to move with grace and flexibility. Verbal enchantment, "the ravishing sound of the melodious line," became the instrument with which the poetic dramatist built "the walls of Thebes" on the bare Elizabethan stage. The consequences for all that was to follow remain immeasurable. So does the effect of the publication of the *Shepeardes Calender* in 1579. The vogue for pastoralism which it established affected not only lyrical poetry and prose romance but also dramatic writing of every kind, from city pageant to royal masque, from courtly comedy to popular history. Moreover, as J. M. Nosworthy, generously giving Polonius the benefit of the doubt, points out later in this volume, pastoral lent itself readily to a union with other dramatic forms. Promiscuous in this respect, it also had the charm of the paradoxical. Ostensibly simple, "being both so base for the matter, and homely for the manner," as E. K. has it, it was, in fact, highly artificial, a Janus of genres, presenting the face of Audrey and the face of Phebe under one hood. Its essential nature admits no easy definition; and the appeal it made to the world for which it was written is hard to explain. Yet there it is, a challenge to both the literary and the historical imagination.

It seemed fitting, therefore, that a conference on Elizabethan theatre meeting in 1979, the quatercentenary of the appearance of Spenser's poem, should devote its deliberations to the subject of pastoral drama, and seek to take up the challenge that it holds out. A. C. Hamilton's fresh assessment of the nature and the achievement of *The Shepheardes Calender* provides the indispensable foundation for such a response. Arguing that Spenser found himself as a poet in the actual writing of this poem, the essay goes on to demonstrate how the choice of the calendar form enabled him to give unity to his twelve eclogues and endow them with significance by bringing out the correspondences between the seasons of the year and the inevitable vicissitudes of human life. The central concern of the poem, Hamilton suggests, is with time, measured first by the natural calendar and then, more hopefully and consolingly, by the Christian calendar. It is a most pregnant suggestion, for, as more than one of the other contributors to the volume make plain, time was to become a recurring theme in pastoral drama.

In the epilogue to his poem Spenser predicts that it will triumph over time because, to use Hamilton's words, "it applies to each year until the end of time." He does not prophesy, because he could hardly have foreseen, that for many years to come it would also triumph over time by doing what Shakespeare so often urges the "friend" of the Sonnets to do: begetting heirs. Yet this is what happened; and many of those heirs took the form of pastoral dramas. John Lyly, who, Anne Lancashire claims with every justification, is the most pastoral of all Elizabethan playwrights, seems to have realized very quickly that the style he had perfected in the writing of *Euphues* was ideally adapted to the needs of the pastoral play, the taste of a courtly audience, and the capacities of boy players. Adding several other cogent reasons to this in order to explain the attraction the pastoral mode had for Lyly, Dr. Lancashire proceeds to point out that thoroughly pastoral though so many of the comedies are, they do not attempt to recapture the spirit of the golden age. On the contrary, their endings can, for the reader, prove disturbing. But, she continues, it was not for readers that they were designed. To see precisely what Lyly is doing, it is necessary to connect his pastoral plays with their native predecessors, the royal entertainments offered to Elizabeth during the course of her progresses through the land. In these shows the Queen herself was the central figure; in essence, what Lyly did was to move these outdoor entertainments indoors. It is the royal presence at the performance which provides the ultimate resolution of dramatic conflicts and makes the final comic effect.

Lyly leads naturally to Shakespeare who learnt so much from him; and Shakespeare's pastoralism, in its Protean manifestations, is the subject of the three essays that follow. The monster, which has its place and function both in *Gallathea* and in *The Faerie Queene*, is used by James Black to make some connections between two unexpected bedfellows, *A Midsummer Night's Dream* and *King Lear*. Relating the temporary metamorphosis of Bottom into a comic monster to the promise, made at the end, that the offspring of the three marriages will not be monstrous in any way, he goes on to suggest that the same concern with genetics surfaces again in *King Lear*. There are, it is true, no monsters of the Bottom kind in the tragedy; but the notion of human monstrosity pervades it from start to finish, and brings with it the profound question of whether the parents are in any way responsible for the aberrations of the child. The play's answer is, characteristically, double and realistic: monsters may occur in the natural course of generation; but so also, as Lear eventually comes to recognize, may angelic beings such as Cordelia.

This same question, posed within a wider context, also finds its place in G. M. Pinciss's "The Savage Man in Spenser, Shakespeare and Renaissance English Drama." Tracing this wild and ubiquitous figure back to his origins in classical mythology and European folklore, the essay demonstrates how conveniently he met the requirements of both "hard" and "soft" primitivism. Spenser, in *The Faerie Queene*, avails himself of both possibilities; and so do the anonymous author of *Mucedorus* and the creator of Caliban, a veritable embodiment of the great issue of Nature versus Nurture. There is, however, another side to the matter. In its concluding pages the essay neatly reverses itself by moving from the subject of the savage, who may or may not be capable of becoming civilized, to that of his obverse, the civilized man who, under the pressure of adverse experience, reverts from civilization to savagery.

In its concern with change as a dramatic motive, Pinciss's essay prepares the way for J. M. Nosworthy's "Shakespeare's Pastoral Metamorphoses." Reminding us that 1579 also saw the publication of North's *Plutarch*, this paper emphasizes that Shakespeare's pastoralism was classical in conception and, consequently, much preoccupied with the idea of metamorphosis. After briefly restating a view he has already set out in detail in *Shakespeare Survey 32*, to the effect that *Love's Labour's Lost* is about the defeat of Cupid (the "Love" of the title) by Apollo and Mercury (Marcade), Nosworthy proceeds to examine the influence of *The Golden Ass* on *A Midsummer Night's Dream* and to describe that play's debt, especially evident in the names of the characters, to Plutarch. Then, turning his attention to *As You Like It*, he brings out the extent to which this comedy is dominated by the idea of time. In this respect, he concludes, it looks forward to *The Winter's Tale*, where, incidentally, *The Golden Ass* again contributes significantly to the total effect.

The use of a park as the setting for *Love's Labour's Lost*, and, even more insistently, the truncated masque and the outrageously interrupted and unfairly damned pageant that are put on in that setting, invite speculation. Was Shakespeare recalling and adapting memories of 1575, when he could so easily have been a fascinated spectator watching the Princely Pleasures at Kenilworth? That question prompts another: is there a connection between the Hock-Tuesday Show, "whearat her Maiestie laught well" when it was presented before her "by certain good harted men of Couentree, my Lordes neighboors" as part of the same entertainment, and the performance of "Pyramus and Thisby" by Bottom and his fellow mechanicals? If only it could be proved that a strong affirmative is the right answer to both questions, no one would be more delighted than R. W. Ingram, who has devoted so much time and energy to the study of the drama's history in Coventry. For him, as the title of his paper shows, 1579 has melancholy associations, for it was in that year that the city's famous Corpus Christi plays were performed for the last time. Their decline and fall were due less, he thinks, to the decay of the textile trade on which Coventry's earlier prosperity had rested—a bread-and-butter aspect of pastoralism which the poets and dramatists chose to ignore—than to the opposition religious drama met with from church and crown, and from the city's own puritans. Yet so strong and enduring was the tradition of civic drama that even 1579 did not mark its end. For another thirty-five years some of the citizens strove to keep their dramatic heritage alive. The final flicker from the dying embers came with the presentation, in 1614—the year of *Bartholmew Fair!*—of an exciting military tattoo which seems, very appropriately, to have had much in common with the old Hock-Tuesday Show that had been banned for decades.

Political and religious considerations, almost inseparable from each other in sixteenth-century England, doomed the traditional civic drama of Coventry to extinction. But in London, where the prime occasions for pageantry were the royal entries into the City and the annual inauguration of the new Lord Mayor, these same considerations ensured approval for what were, in effect, demonstrations of loyalty to the crown and to the government of the capital. In complete agreement with those who see pastoralism as very much an urban phenomenon, David M. Bergeron describes the large part which it played, both visually and aurally, in the two kinds of entertainment, and how it functioned as a means of asserting the interdependence and unity of town and country. It is no accident, he claims, that there are numerous and striking similarities between the shows which London put on for the entry of James I in 1604 and those with which Edinburgh greeted Charles I in 1633, since the purpose was in each case the same: to welcome a king who was a stranger, and to enlist support for him. In the Lord Mayor's Show, however, there was an additional reason for an extensive use of pastoral, because most Lord Mayors came from guilds that were closely connected with the wool trade. Seemingly innocent, pastoral could readily be converted into an instrument of propaganda, serving economic as well as political ends.

Making a similar point to Bergeron's, Eugene M. Waith and James J. Yoch, each in his own way, widen the scope of the inquiry by extending it from England to Italy, the home of Renaissance pastoral, and by connecting pastoral to the evolution of the court masque, for it is in the masque that the resort to pastoral, as a means of pleasing and complimenting the sovereign, reaches its height. The court masque, Waith contends, took over some of the functions traditionally assigned to comedy, including the triumph of "good" characters over obstacles and ridicule of common defects. Making Angelo Poliziano's *Orpheo* of 1480 his starting point, he suggests that this piece, in its use of classical myth, led on to Cinthio's *Egle* of 1545, the true predecessor of pastoral tragicomedy. At much the same time, elaborate *intermezzi* accompanied the comedy which Antonio Landi composed for the wedding of Cosimo I in 1539, and these provided a precedent for the masque. The crucial shift comes, however, with the production, in 1581, of the *Ballet Comique de la Reine* to celebrate the marriage of the sister-in-law of Henry III of France; for in it the "acts" and the *intermèdes* become closely involved and integrated with each other in what is essentially a comic action. Here we are very close to the English court masque as written by Ben Jonson, where the forces opposing the desired ending are satirized and held up to ridicule in the antimasque.

James J. Yoch approaches pastoral and masque along a route rather similar to Waith's. But his objective is a different one: to consider how spectacle was used in a carefully calculated manner for purposes that were wholly political. Divided into two parts, his paper shows how the *intermezzi* worked to this end, and then sketches the changes the English court made in the Italian formula in order to adapt it to English conditions. So far as Italy is concerned, Yoch bases his findings largely on "the extensive descriptions of the *intermezzi* published with Antonio Ongaro's pastoral play, *L'Alceo*," published at Ferrara in 1614. These *intermezzi*, like the play proper which is itself a parody of Tasso's *Aminta*, show emotions contained within a plot which leads from turmoil to serenity and makes plain the advantages of a settled life under the rule of a powerful prince. In a rather similar fashion, he goes on to claim, the court masque in early seventeenth-century England teaches its audience how to be good subjects of their gracious king. The lesson is at its clearest in *Salmacida Spolia*, the last court masque to be performed before the outbreak of the Civil War; but so also is the difference between English methods and Italian methods. In *Salmacida Spolia*, as in most English court masques, power is literal and explicit, whereas the Italian courts used pastorals and *intermezzi* to provide "alternatives to facts by presenting dreams and fantasies." As a result, the English court antagonized its opponents still further, instead of anaesthetizing them by skilfully diverting their attention elsewhere as the Italian courts did.

"The grene path way to lyfe" was merging rapidly with that other and much-travelled way which was to lead so many "to dusty death," and might have disappeared completely from view but for the genius of John Milton and Andrew Marvell, directing it towards "fresh woods, and pastures new," and especially towards "that happy garden-state" where the creative mind exerts its power of "Annihilating all that's made / To a green thought in a green shade."

G. .R. Hibbard
Department of English
University of Waterloo

"The Grene Path Way to Lyfe": Spenser's *Shepheardes Calender* as Pastoral

A. C. HAMILTON

It is fitting for this 1979 conference on the theme of pastoral in Elizabethan drama to open with a paper on Spenser's *Shepheardes Calender*. The outstanding calendar poem in our language merits such recognition to mark the four hundred years since it was introduced to the world with the poet's modest plea, "Goe little booke, thy selfe present," but concluded with his superb confidence that he had constructed a work which "shall continewe till the worlds dissolution." At least it has continued for four centuries and remains the one poem through which we may relate our lives directly to the natural cycle of the year. As such an almanac, it should be popular; and, as it began Spenser's poetical career, it should begin our literary education. That it serves neither of these ends presents a challenge to us. The poem is a brilliant, major achievement by a major poet, and requires only a little effort of the historical imagination to be possessed freshly and fully by the modern reader.

Since each generation of readers of English poetry after the Renaissance stands at an end of the literary tradition, it is difficult to share the perspective of one who saw himself, as Spenser did, at its beginning. One of the most significant moments in the history of English poetry came when he conceived the "idea or fore-conceit" of *The Shepheardes Calender*. It occurred—one may only surmise—some time in 1578 when he was about 26, for two years an M. A. of Cambridge, now secretary to the Bishop of Rochester, and about to enter the service of the Earl of Leicester. Nine years earlier his first poetic pieces, translations of Petrarch and Marot, had appeared in *A Theatre for Voluptuous*

1

Worldlings; and in the interval he had composed many works now lost and of considerable variety, or so their titles indicate: *My Slomber, Dreames, Dying Pellicane, Legendes, Court of Cupide, Pageaunts, Nine Comoedies,* and *Sonnets.* Instead of publishing a selection of these poems—eclogues in the etymological sense, or *rime sparse*—as did his contemporaries (for example, Breton in his *Smale Handfull of Fragrant Flowers* [1575], and Richard Edwards and others in *The Paradyse of Daynty Devises* [1576]) Spenser discovered a way of combining separate eclogues into a unified pastoral poem. Such a longer unified poem would serve two purposes. It would publicly announce that he was no poetaster, as were the others, but the "new poet" who now succeeds the "old poet" Chaucer; and it would demonstrate his ability to undertake an heroic poem, one which would relate him to England as Homer to Greece and Virgil to Rome.

In his Epistle, E. K. spells out this double purpose. He explains that his anonymous poet, Immerito, is "following the example of the best and most auncient Poetes": "So flew Theocritus, as you may perceive he was all ready full fledged. So flew Virgile, as not yet well feeling his winges. So flew Mantuane, as being not full somd." After naming others, he continues: "So finally flyeth this our new Poete, as a bird, whose principals be scarce growen out, but yet as that in time shall be hable to keepe wing with the best."[1] These discriminating judgments recognize that Theocritus wrote his *Idylls* at the height of his powers ("all ready full fledged"), and that Virgil, "not yet well feeling his winges," derived "the whole Invention of his Aeglogues" from him. E. K. links Mantuan and Spenser, as the one wrote his eclogues "not full somd" and the other when his principal feathers "be scarce growen out." Since every schoolboy knew that "good old Mantuan" did not attempt higher flight, he singles out Spenser as the future English Virgil, one whose lowly pastoral promises flight to higher things. Accordingly, the *Calender* is delivered to the public with the full scholarly trappings of epistle, glossing and commentary that accompanied the similar endeavours of Virgil, Petrarch, Mantuan and Ronsard. Since Spenser writes his pastoral in order later to transcend it, he presents a full and final statement of the genre that reveals his rejection of it. We know that in the year the poem appeared, he promised to send Gabriel Harvey some part of *The Faerie Queene*. One may surmise, now with some assurance, that he began writing his heroic poem immediately upon completing the pastoral.

---

1. References to *The Shepheardes Calender* are from *Spenser's Minor Poems*, ed. Ernest de Sélincourt (Oxford, 1910).

2

Besides baptizing him into the role of the English Virgil, writing a pastoral appealed to Spenser on other grounds. As a youthful genre—Mantuan called his eclogues *Adolescentia*—pastoral allows him to project himself into the centre of his poem as its subject. Writing the poem becomes for him (as reading it may become for us) a quest for identity, a search for the self, which he discovers in three ways: by relating himself to a major poetic tradition, by defining his role in society and by examining human life on the order of nature. Being a highly conventional genre, pastoral serves to transform the man into the poet, the personal into the impersonal. At the time Spenser was writing the poem he appeared to his friend Harvey as a "young Italian-ate signor and French monsieur"; but he portrays himself in his poem as the demented and afflicted English rustic, Colin Clout. The genre allows a major individual talent to absorb an extended classical and medieval tradition, and so seem most natural by being most artificial, and most original by being most imitative.

Pastoral serves also to transform content into form by rendering particular historical events in their universal significance. Fact is so disguised as fiction, and fiction as fact, that events in the poem which seem to allude to events outside the poem instead become exemplary. Topical allusions often serve much the same obfuscating purpose as Pompey's allusion to the fact that Master Froth's father died at Hallowmas: "I hope here be truths." Even as the poem is presented as a coterie work whose meaning is open only to insiders, it becomes a public work to be understood by any reader, then as now, as William Webbe noted in 1586: "there is . . . much matter uttered somewhat covertly . . . yet so skilfully is it handled, as any man may . . . picke out much good sence in the most obscurest of it."[2]

The two other appeals of pastoral to a young poet need only mention. First, it is the primary literary mode, almost the inevitable means of expression when, in Bacon's terms, the mind of man raises imagination above reason and submits the "shows of things to the desires of the mind" in order to give some satisfaction "in those points wherein the nature of things doth deny it, the world being in proportion inferior to the soul." Secondly, a major poet may rightly feel that he invents the pastoral mode, as did Theocritus in his *Idylls*, Virgil in his *Eclogues*, and Mantuan in his *Adolescentia*. The explanation may be that pastoral is more a mode than a genre, one that may be adapted to many genres and freshly to any society. While pastoral poems were

2. "A Discourse of English Poetry," in *Spenser, The Critical Heritage*, ed. R. M. Cummings (London, 1971), p. 58.

written earlier in England—for example, by Barclay and Googe out of Mantuan—only with the publication of *The Shepheardes Calender* in 1579 does the pastoral become established centrally in the English poetic tradition.

Even from our perspective four hundred years later, it is astonishing that Spenser dared to project such a poem in the 1570s, astonishing both for what it is and as a pledge for England's heroic poem. One wonders at times if there were not some forcing of his talent. It was well known through Servius that Virgil was 29 when he was completing his *Eclogues*; and since Spenser was shaping his literary life after the pattern of Virgil, he would have been only 27 in 1579. That is, if he were born in 1552: for all we know, he may have been born two years earlier. Such shaping of early literary life lasted at least until Milton: that Edward King drowned in 1637 was an accident, but it need not have been an accident that Milton, who was 29 in that year, decided to write a pastoral elegy on his death. A recent critic, Richard Helgerson, has argued that the *Calender* "for all its pretension and real accomplishment . . . is rife with intimations of failure, breakdown, and renunciation" because Spenser adopts the common convention of the 1570s, the poet as a youth beguiled by love. He concludes that "it is difficult to imagine how the promised emergence of the New Poet was to be accomplished."[3] In effect, Helgerson accepts Cuddie's claim that Colin could attempt the higher flight of the heroic poem "were he not with love so ill bedight" and does not allow Piers's correcting response: "Ah fon, for love does teach him climbe so hie, / And lyftes him up out of the loathsome myre." One may add that there is no need to imagine how England's new poet could have emerged. It is clear that the *Calender* provides the means for Spenser's emergence and shows just how he became England's heroic poet.

The "intimations of failure, breakdown, and renunciation" in the *Calender* express in part the conventional humility of the pastoral poet. Such humility may be Spenser's response to a strong personal fear of envy throughout his career. In the prologue to the *Calender*, he urges his "little booke" to flee to the protection of his patron "if that Envie barke at thee, / As sure it will," and in the closing lines of *The Faerie Queene*, Book VI, he laments the ravaging of his poem by the envious Blatant Beast. Yet such fear is also conventional (though no less felt) and expressed by any poet who seeks to rise above others.

3. "The New Poet presents himself: Spenser and the idea of a literary career," *PMLA*, 93 (1978), p. 898. David R. Shore offers a cogent defence of the place of love in pastoral, in "Colin and Rosalind: love and poetry in the *Shepheardes Calender*", *SP*, 73 (1976), pp. 176-88.

In the Renaissance, the great enemies of the poets were not the humanists—those literary rednecks of the age—but "the rakehellye route of our ragged rymers," whose envy E. K. fears. That Milton shared the same fear is indicated by the title page of his first collection of poems in 1645, with its inscription from Virgil's *Eclogue* VII in which Thyrsis urges the shepherds of Arcady to crown their new poet, causing Codrus to burst with envy and so stop his malicious tongue from harming the future bard.

What is not conventional is that Spenser's humility is accompanied by exuberant self-confidence. In a letter Harvey complained that Spenser was "hobgoblin runne away with the Garland from Apollo"; and in the June eclogue, as Hobbinoll, he says to Colin:

> I sawe Calliope wyth Muses moe,
> Soone as thy oaten pype began to sound,
> Theyr yvory Luyts and Tamburins forgoe:
> And from the fountaine, where they sat around,
> Renne after hastely thy silver sound.
> But when they came, where thou thy skill didst showe,
> They drewe abacke, as halfe with shame confound,
> Shepheard to see, them in theyr art outgoe.

Colin responds humbly, "I never lyst presume to Parnasse hyll." As he notes in the December eclogue, however, if he won't join the Muses, they will join him:

> And for I was in thilke same looser yeares,
> (Whether the Muse so wrought me from my birth,
> Or I tomuch beleeved my shepherd peres)
> Somedele ybent to song and musicks mirth.
> > A good olde shephearde, Wrenock was his name,
> > Made me by arte more cunning in the same.
>
> Fro thence I durst in derring doe compare
> With shepheards swayne, what ever fedde in field:
> And if that Hobbinol right judgement bare,
> To Pan his owne selfe pype I neede not yield.
> > For if the flocking Nymphes did folow Pan,
> > The wiser Muses after Colin ranne.

While Spenser may sign himself "Immerito" and employ the persona of a bumpkin, Colin Clout, he projects himself in the poem as Orpheus.[4] A similar conjunction of abject humility and soaring pride

4. See Thomas H. Cain, *Praise in The Faerie Queene* (Lincoln, Neb., 1978), pp. 14-15.

in poetic powers is found elsewhere in the Renaissance only in Shakespeare's sonnets.

The Calendar Form

The literary consequence of this conjunction led directly to *The Shepheardes Calender*. Spenser's confidence in his craftsmanship made him ambitious to write a definitive pastoral poem in the tradition of Virgil's *Eclogues* as modified by Mantuan, and his humility—the hobgoblin in him—led to the "idea or fore-conceit" of his pastoral, its calendar form, which he took from a popular and sub-literary French work, englished in the early sixteenth century as *The Kalender of Shepherdes*. The resulting combination of matter and form—of sophistication and simplicity, the learned and the vulgar, the civilized and the primitive, art and nature—expresses exactly the idea of pastoral itself. The calendar measures life on the level of nature, symbolized by the life of shepherds in their pastoral world. In the unfallen state before there were the seasons, the identification of man and nature was ideal; but in the fallen state, as the calendar shows, man is bound to a meaningless and endless cycle, one without beginning or end but simply change in a process that leads only to death.

The twelve eclogues are shaped by the calendar form into one poem. As the title page declares, they are "proportionable to the twelve monethes." In his Epistle, E. K. says that they are "proportioned to the state of the xii monethes"; and in the General Argument he says more exactly that they are "every where answering to the seasons of the twelve monthes". But the poem's idea is expressed most exactly in the Argument to the December eclogue, which declares that Colin Clout "proportioneth his life to the foure seasons of the yeare."

The seasons of the year in relation to man's life provide only the most obvious manifestation of the poem's form. There is much popular calendar lore which Spenser uses to unify his eclogues. For example, under the Ptolemaic system, each month is related to a guardian deity, either the sun or moon or one of the planets. That July is ruled by the sun, whose course is traced by the calendar year, supports Isabel MacCaffrey's observation that the July eclogue "lies at the centre of the *Calender* and in many respects is its pivot."[5] June is ruled by the Moon, and June and July are flanked in symmetrical order: May and August being ruled by Mars, April and September by

5. "Allegory and Pastoral in *The Shepheardes Calender*," reprinted in *Essential Articles for the Study of Edmund Spenser*, ed. A. C. Hamilton (Hamden, Conn., 1972), p. 560. For pertinent comments on Spenser's use of the calendar, see S. K. Heninger, jr., *Touches of Sweet Harmony: Pythagorean Cosmology and Renaissance Poetics* (San Marino, 1974), pp. 309-15.

Venus, March and October by Mercury, February and November by Jupiter, and January and December by Saturn. Such ordering may explain why March and October are linked in their treatment of love: in the one its origin, and in the other its effect on man's aspirations. In March, falling in love marks man's fall from innocence into the world of time; in October, when winter is about to begin, man must choose whether to remain fallen or seek to rise. Also there is considerable astrological lore connected with each month. For example, according to William Lilly's *Christian Astrology* (1647), under the zodiacal sign of Pisces, which belongs to February, when the planet Jupiter is well placed, man will reverence old age. A contemporary reader would have expected, then, that the February eclogue "specially conteyneth a discourse of old age" (Argument).[6]

Spenser also uses numerological lore to unify the eclogues into one poem. Ever since E. K. observed that the December eclogue "even as the first beganne is ended with a complaynte of Colin to God Pan," readers have been aware of the connection between December and January. Each is a complaint sung by Colin alone, telling much the

---

6. One of the few points where Spenser inserts astrological lore directly into his poem occurs in the November eclogue where Colin observes that the sun has "taken up his ynne in Fishes haske." Yet in this month the sun is in the astrological sign Sagittarius, not Pisces, as the woodcut to the eclogue correctly shows. Following W. L. Renwick, William Nelson suggests that "Spenser decided for some reason to make a February eclogue do for November and carelessly failed to change the text accordingly" (*The Poetry of Edmund Spenser: a Study* [New York, 1963], p. 36). Yet this is not true. November marks the death of Dido because it is the eleventh month, the number associated with death, as in Milton's poem "On the Death of a Fair Infant" with its eleven stanzas. The astrological reference cannot be an error because Spenser, being a Renaissance poet, knew his astrology; in fact, he boasts in December that during his wasted life he has "learned . . . the signes of heaven to ken." Paul E. McLane finds a cryptic allusion to Elizabeth's mooted marriage to Alençon in 1579: Elizabeth is the Sun, being the Queen; she is said to be in the fish's hask or basket because she is being captured by Alençon who is the fish as he is the Dolphin of France and a Catholic who observes fast days or "fish days" (*Spenser's 'Shepheardes Calender': a Study in Elizabethan Allegory* [Notre Dame 1961], p. 54). Astrological lore suggests a simpler and more significant explanation. November and February are ruled by the same guardian deity, Jupiter, and mark the beginning and end of winter. In referring to the sun taking up his inn in the fish's hask, Spenser refers to the season rather than the month, as he says in the next line: "thilke sollein season sadder plight doth aske." The first month of winter is the fit season to mark Dido's death but the astrological reference to the end of winter in February points to her resurrection, which is celebrated in the four concluding stanzas after the 11 stanzas on her death. For my observation on the significance of the number 11, I am indebted to H. Neville Davies, "Elaborate song: conceptual structure in Milton's 'On the Morning of Christ's Nativity' ", in Maren-Sofie Røstvig, ed., *Fair Forms: Essays in English Literature from Spenser to Jane Austen* (Totowa, N.Y. 1975), p. 94. I comment only briefly on this important subject because it is being treated by J. M. Richardson. See his "Astrology in *The Shepheardes Calender*," in *Spenser at Kalamazoo, 1979*, where he argues that "an astrological rationale underlies Spenser's handling of character, circumstance, and theme" throughout the poem.

same story in the same stanza form. The linear sequence from January to December turns back to January and another cycle. Maren-Sophie Røstvig has noted that December is exactly twice the length of January, which gives the ratio 2:1, or the diapason, which denotes the closing of the circle.[7] Alastair Fowler has suggested that May is "by far the longest eclogue, since the sun was known to stay longer in Gemini than in any other sign."[8] No one seems to have noted the possible significance of line lengths throughout the poem. For example, except for June, Colin's songs are related multiples of 13: in January, 13 x 6; in April, 13 x 9; in August, 13 x 3; in November, after an introduction of 13 x 4 lines, there are 13 x 12 lines of complaint with Thenot's comment; and in December, also 13 x 12.

The use of the number 13 may be connected with its significance in the Platonic lambda in which 1 (itself no number) is flanked by 2 and 3, and their squares 4 and 9. Four and 9 represent respectively the corporeal and incorporeal parts of man. That their sum is 13 and their "mean" is 6 may lie behind Spenser's use of thirteen line lengths and the six-line stanza. When Spenser praises the bee "working her formall rowmes in Wexen frame" (December, 68), he may be wittily connecting the bee's hexagonal room to his six-line stanza. That 13 is the sum of the nine Muses and the four Graces is surely not sufficiently arcane for any respectable numerologist. Possibly 13 refers to the number of weeks in each season. My own guess is that it is the number of the annual lunar cycle, which associates the lover with the moon, and so with the point of escape through love from the twelve encircling zodiacal signs.[9]

7. "*The Shepheardes Calender*—a structural analysis," *Ren & Modern Studies*, 13 (1969), p. 64.
8. *Edmund Spenser, Writers and their Work* (London, 1977), p. 12.
9. As befits the climactic recreative eclogue, August is more complex than the others: after an introduction of 13 x 4 lines, the "mery thing" sung by Willye and Perigot is followed by 13 x 2 lines of an interlude before Colin's "heavy laye" of 13 x 3 lines. Such patterning disposes of Nelson's speculation (p. 36) that Colin's sestina was interpolated after the editorial work had been completed.
I am not going to attempt to explain why other line lengths correspond, but only note that February has 101 lines of dialogue before the concluding tale; that in May after a formal debate in patterns of four 18-line exchanges, the verse form shifts to an exchange of 59+32+8+2, or 101 lines before the tale; and in September, there are 101 lines of dialogue before Diggon turns from his tale to plain speaking. June and October are each 120 lines. The only eclogue without any correspondence in line length to another is July, and the explanation may be the one suggested above, that the month is ruled by Apollo. Of course, line numbers allow only a crude insight into Spenser's structuring of his poem, and it is more profitable to attend to the elaborate and witty patterning of stanzas in almost any eclogue; for example, the reflecting pattern in the 13 stanzas of January, or the 15 stanzas of June built around the central stanza with its vision of the Muses who attend Colin. Cain's analysis of April (pp. 14-24), needs to be extended to other eclogues.

Through its calendar form, Spenser's poem becomes radically pastoral in two ways. First, in its comprehensiveness. As Dryden realized and Pope agreed, the *Calender* "is the most complete work of this kind which any nation has produced ever since the time of Virgil."[10] As the twelve eclogues are proportionable to the changing seasons and activities of the year, the poem allows various kinds of pastoral, in fact, all kinds. In March and August, for example, there is the simplest kind of pastoral—contented shepherds minding their sheep, playing their pipes and telling tales. This is the native pastoral that preceded Spenser: "Hey ho, jolly shepherd sitting on a hill, hey ho!," to which we are tempted to respond with a "ho hum." In June, Hobbinoll is the spokesman for classical pastoral which escapes into an idyllic, wish-fulfilling natural state:

> Lo *Colin*, here the place, whose pleasant syte
> From other shades hath weand my wandring mynde.
> Tell me, what wants me here, to worke delyte?
> The simple ayre, the gentle warbling wynde,
> So calme, so coole, as no where else I fynde:
> The grassye ground with daintye Daysies dight,
> The Bramble bush, where Byrds of every kynde
> To the waters fall their tunes attemper right.

In his reply, Colin is the spokesman for a Christian attitude to pastoral which does not allow fallen man to return to Eden:

> O happy Hobbinoll, I bless thy state,
> That Paradise hast found, whych Adam lost.
> Here wander may thy flock early or late,
> Withouten dreade of Wolves to bene ytost:
> Thy lovely layes here mayst thou freely boste.
> But I unhappy man, whom cruell fate,
> And angry Gods pursue from coste to coste,
> Can nowhere fynd, to shroude my lucklesse pate.

In July there is pastoral in Empson's sense, the process of putting complex urban life into the simple rural life. Finally, in December there is "hard" pastoral which shows an untamed nature hostile to man and his art.

According to Paul Alpers, pastoral seeks to come to terms with reality: "the great pastoral poets are directly concerned with the extent to which song that gives present pleasures can confront, and, if not transform and celebrate, then accept and reconcile man to the stresses

10. A Discourse on Pastoral Poetry," in Cummings, *Spenser*, p. 235.

and realities of his situation."[11] This sense of pastoral applies to Thenot in the February eclogue:

> Selfe have I worne out thrise threttie yeares,
> Some in much joy, many in many teares:
> Yet never complained of cold nor heate,
> Of Sommers flame, nor of Winters threat:
> Ne ever was to Fortune foeman,
> But gently tooke, that ungently came.

But it applies only to Thenot (whom Spenser makes 90 years old: no wonder he has learned to accept "the stresses and realities of his situation"), and not at all to any of ten other spokesmen of pastoral attitudes in the poem.

In reply to earlier critics who defined the *Calender* as pastoral in terms of its historical or biographical matter, Hallett Smith argued—rightly, I believe—that "there is not a core of something wrapped up in a covering of pastoral, but that the pastoral idea, in its various ramifications, *is* the *Calender*." He defines that idea as "an ideal of the good life, of the state of content and mental self-sufficiency which had been known in classical antiquity as *otium*."[12] Yet Spenser's pastoral displays and supports Colin, the poem's central spokesman, in his radical discontent.

No paradox is involved in saying both that almost any definition of pastoral may be illustrated in *The Shepheardes Calender* and that by almost any definition the poem is anti-pastoral. In its comprehensiveness, Spenser's pastoral involves its own transcendence. Through its calendar form, it becomes radically pastoral as it shows the state of

11. "The eclogue tradition and the nature of pastoral," *College English*, 34 (1972), p. 353.
12. *Elizabethan Poetry: a study in Conventions, Meaning, and Expression* (Cambridge, Mass., 1952), pp. 46, 2. Nelson's comment that "the dialogue of a pastoral poem is not a Socratic demonstration but a valid disagreement in which the speakers explore what may best be said on either part" (p. 46) is extended by Patrick Cullen in his claim that "the overall concern of the Calender [is] to explore the values and limitations of various forms of pastoral experience and moral vision" (*Spenser, Marvell, and Renaissance Pastoral* [Cambridge, Mass., 1970], p. 121). It does not follow, of course, that the best that may be said by any antagonist in a moral eclogue is true even in part. Modern liberalism would like to find any debate ambivalent, as Cullen (p. 47) says of the debate between Piers and Palinode in the May eclogue and so judges the latter to be "at least [a] partially comic and human figure." However, there is a strong polarizing force in pastoral, and Palinode is simply wrong in what he says. Milton responds correctly when he refers to "that false shepherd Palinode" as one of the prelates "whose whole life is a recantation of their pastorall vow, and whose profession to forsake the World, as they use the matter, boggs them deeper into the World" (*Animadversions*, cited in Cummings, p. 163).

man in relation to nature as one bound upon a wheel of time, caught in
a cycle which allows no escape except through death. Yet this pastoral
vision of life is shown so clearly that by the end the reader may see
beyond it.

Structure

In the three framing eclogues—the first, sixth and twelfth—the
poem shows the tragic vision of man living in time as a creature born to
die. The opening eclogue seems deliberately placed to counter the use
of pastoral as a retreat into the golden age. In the external landscape of
winter, Colin finds a close reflection of his inner wintry state:

> Thou barrein ground, whome winters wrath hath wasted,
> Art made a myrrhour, to behold my plight:
> Whilome thy fresh spring flowrd, and after hasted
> Thy sommer prowde with Daffadillies dight.
> And now is come thy wynters stormy state,
> Thy mantle mard, wherein thou maskedst late.
>
> Such rage as winters, reigneth in my heart,
> My life bloud friesing with unkindly cold:
> Such stormy stoures do breede my balefull smart,
> As if my yeare were wast, and woxen old.
> And yet alas, but now my spring begonne,
> And yet alas, yt is already donne.

These two concluding lines, which collapse life into a moment
between birth and death, present an emblem of man's brief state.
Colin's state is Richard II's before his murder: "Now hath time made
me his numb'ring clock"; or Macbeth's, when his life is reduced to the
meaningless chronicity of "tomorrow, and tomorrow, and tomorrow."
In January, rejected by Rosalind, Colin all but despairs; in June,
betrayed by her, he does despair; and in December, his earlier
correspondence with the state of winter—"As *if* my yeare were
wast"—becomes one of identity:

> So now my yeare drawes to his latter terme,
> My spring is spent, my sommer burnt up quite:
> My harveste hasts to stirre up winter sterne,
> And bids him clayme with rigorous rage hys right.

Caught in the cycle of the seasons, he may never escape from the
winter of his discontent. As his correspondence with fallen nature
defines his fallen state, his identification with it becomes absolute in

death. Before the concluding stanza of farewell, Colin's lament ends with the simple, powerful line: "And after Winter commeth timely death." "Timely" reinforces what any reader expects to hear, that after winter comes spring. And so it does—except for man. Spenser's final vision of man's state shares precisely the bleakness of Wordsworth's final vision of Lucy as a thing "rolled round in earth's diurnal course / With rocks, and stones, and trees."

Man's life on the order of nature provides the framework within which Spenser explores the nature of poetry, specifically the power of pastoral song to control love and provide "solace through utterance."[13] Hence his purpose in writing the *Calender*, according to E. K., was to seek the consolation of song: "His unstayed yougth had long wandred in the common Labyrinth of Love, in which time to mitigate and allay the heate of his passion, or els to warne (as he sayth) the young shepheards .s. his equalls and companions of his unfortunate folly, he compiled these xii Aeglogues." This statement suggests that Spenser shows how Colin may escape from the labyrinth of love through his ordering the twelve eclogues into the calendar year.

The eclogues are divided into three kinds—the recreative, the moral and the plaintive—illustrating respectively the three ends of poetry— to delight, to teach and to move.[14] Together they explore the power of pastoral song to represent, contain, order and (if possible) purge the paralysing force of love. Here Colin's English ancestor is Chaucer, the love poet whom he praises in June as one who "well couth . . . wayle hys Woes, and lightly slake / The flames, which love within his heart had bredd." By controlling the force of love, Chaucer was able to "tell us mery tales, to keepe us wake, / The while our sheepe about us safely fedde." Colin's mythological ancestor is Orpheus, the singer who could move trees to sympathize with his plight and then calm the hellish passions to release his beloved from imprisonment.

In praising the poet for his power to move the reader's will, Piers compares him to Orpheus as "the shepheard, that did fetch his dame / From Plutoes balefull bowre withouten leave: / His musicks might the hellish hound did tame" (October 28-30). But concupiscence

13. On this function of poetry, see Rosemond Tuve, *Elizabethan and Metaphysical Imagery* (Chicago, 1947), p. 171. For the pastoral genre, the origin of this convention is Theocritus, Idyll XI, which argues that "there is no medicine so sovereign against love as is Poetry" (*Sixe Idyllia*, 1588).
14. *Cf.* Sidney, *The Countess of Pembroke's Arcadia (The Old Arcadia)*, ed. Jean Robertson (Oxford, 1973), p. 56. While the three kinds of eclogues are distinct in their conventions, functions, and even in such counters as the relation to time—the recreative tends to treat the past, the plaintive the present and the moral the future— there is often very witty mingling.

betrayed Orpheus, as love for Rosalind has betrayed Colin. In June he yearns for Orpheus's power: if he were baptised by Chaucer, he "would learne these woods, to wayle my woe, / And teache the trees, their trickling teares to shedde." Yet pastoral song has lost its power, as he complains in the opening eclogue:

> Wherefore my pype, albee rude Pan thou please,
> Yet for thou pleasest not, where most I would:
> And thou unlucky Muse, that wontst to ease
> My musing mynd, yet canst not, when thou should:
> Both pype and Muse, shall sore the while abye.
> So broke his oaten pype, and downe dyd lye.

Colin's breaking the pastoral pipe is the introductory and major symbolic action in the poem.[15]

As the bagpipe is an emblem of lechery, breaking it marks Colin's failure as a lover. As it is his pastoral instrument, breaking it marks his sense of failure as a poet. While his songs may please the shepherds, they fail to please Rosalind. But more significantly, they fail to "ease / My musing mynd." Evidently the way out of the labyrinth of man's grief is not through pastoral song.

The failure of pastoral song suggests Spenser's impatience with the pastoral genre. Colin's three love complaints—the three plaintive eclogues, January, June and December—offer only negative exempla as they are self-regarding, solipsistic and essentially private. In January, Rosalind "of my rurall musick holdeth scorne"; by June, since the Muses themselves "holden scorne of homely shepheards quill," he resolves to "play to please my selfe, all be it ill," believing he lacks the power to move others. "I am not, as I wish I were" sums up his state at this mid-point of his odyssey. His relation to his landscape shows a steady descent: in January, he absorbs Nature as it mirrors his state; in June, Nature's beauty mocks his inner agony and he becomes an exile "whom cruell fate / And angry Gods pursue from coste to coste"; and in December, he is absorbed by Nature, dying with the

---

15. Hence it is shown in the woodcuts to the three framing eclogues, January, June and December, and referred to in April, 14-16. John W. Moore, jr. points to the significance of this action in "Colin breaks his pipe: a reading of the 'January' eclogue," *ELR*, 5 (1975), pp. 3-24. Unfortunately, he radically misreads the poem, in my judgment, by arguing that the pipe symbolizes Colin's understanding of divine service, so that in breaking it he renounces his public mission as a divine poet. The text provides no support for such a reading. Rosalind's disdain of Colin—she rejects him, his pastoral music and songs, and his occupation—marks her as a Petrarchan mistress, except that her disloyalty marks her as a heroine of romance, specifically Montemayor's *Diana*. More simply, however, she is a function of Spenser's pastoral theme, which requires her disdain and infidelity.

year. Within this context, the three recreative eclogues serve to recall that he once belonged to an idyllic landscape in which his songs pleased himself and others. Yet he cannot return, for his fall cannot be reversed. Time past cannot be recalled so that to his loss of her, which he laments in January, is added "yeeres more rype" in June. His failure as lover and poet leads to his failure as a shepherd: as he complains in the opening eclogue, the weakness of his sheep "mayst witnesse well by thy ill governement / Thy maysters mind is overcome with care."[16]

The function of pastoral song in relation to love, and the relation of love to man's care, become the basis for an elaborate structuring of the eclogues. Most apparent to any reader is the interlocking distribution of the three kinds of eclogues, single and in pairs.

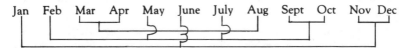

Jan   Feb   Mar   Apr   May   June   July   Aug   Sept   Oct   Nov Dec

The numbers of each are carefully chosen to reflect their importance: three recreative, five moral, and four plaintive as their mean.[17] The first half of the year has the simpler movement: from plaintive to

16. The failure of pastoral to provide "solace through utterance" extends to the moral eclogues. In the first three (February, May and July), Spenser employs the usual devices of allegorical speech in order to attack ecclesiastical abuses. In the climactic September eclogue, much of the earlier matter is reviewed in Diggon Davie's story of the corruption he encountered in his visit to foreign coasts, that is, London. Hobbinoll urges him to tell his tale of grief for

> sorrow close shrouded in hart
> I know, to kepe, is a burdenous smart.
> Eche thing imparted is more eath to beare:
> When the rayne is faln, the cloudes wexen cleare.

When Diggon tells his tale in elaborately allegorical terms, Hobbinoll objects because it is too dark to understand. Then Diggon speaks plainly, but neither kind of speech consoles him and he remains in despair: "Ah but Hobbinol, all this long tale, / Nought easeth the care, that doth me forhaile" (distress).

17. Since Spenser is imitating Virgil's *Eclogues*, one may assume that he would have been aware of their simpler symmetry, noted by Brooks Otis in *Virgil: a Study in Civilized Poetry* (Oxford, 1964) and developed by Paul Alpers, *The Singer of the 'Eclogues': a Study of Virgilian Pastoral* (Berkeley, 1979), pp. 107-13. Eclogue 5 is seen as the centre around which corresponding eclogues, 1 and 9, 2 and 8, 3 and 7 gather, and is the middle of a triad: the prophetic vision of the golden age in 4 and the cosmology and Orphic powers of Silenus's song in 6. Eclogue 5, representing Daphnis as Caesar, is an imitation of Theocritus's best-known idyll. One suspects that Spenser was aware of such symmetry because he imitates the same idyll in November, his pastoral elegy on the death of Dido, which leads to the resolution of his whole poem in the December eclogue, the pastoral elegy on his own death. On Spenser's use of the complaint to structure the *Calender*, see Hugh Maclean, " 'Restlesse anguish and unquiet paine': Spenser and the Complaint, 1579-1590," in *The Practical Vision: Essays in Honour of Flora Roy*, ed. Jane Campbell and James Doyle (Waterloo, 1978), pp. 37-38.

moral to two balanced recreative eclogues (private and public concern), and then a return to moral and plaintive. The second half is altogether more complex: July is a moral eclogue but treats a recreative theme, August is recreative in the singing match but becomes plaintive in Colin's sestina; then follow two moral eclogues and the two final plaintive eclogues.[18] In the absence of narrative, significance is gained chiefly through parataxis, either through paired or companion eclogues, as January and February, or a dialectical juxtaposition, as June and July. It is gained through the distribution of speakers in differing contexts, as Piers serves as the spokesman for true religion in May and for true poetry in October. Also through symbolic landscape, for example, a hill: in June, Colin on the wasteful hills "can nowhere fynd, to shroude my lucklesse pate"; in July, the proud Morrell occupies the hill, and Algrind is wounded by a "shell-fish" while sitting on a hill; and in August, Perigot is wounded by love "sitting upon a hill so hye." (Spenser assumes that the reader will recognize the different but related meanings to be attached to a hill: as it denotes ambition; as it is associated with Eden and therefore a place of pleasure forbidden to man; and as a place for goatherds, not shepherds.) Significance is also gained through structuring within an eclogue: as in the differing relationships between the debate and tale in the moral eclogues; or two kinds of song, in a recreative eclogue such as August. Obviously Spenser places an enormous burden on any critic who would dare spell out the complex significance achieved by the various devices he uses in the *Calender*, but happily not at all on the reader from whom is asked only an imaginative response to the essential facts about man's life.

Resolution

In pastoral, the care of sheep is a complex metaphor that ranges in meaning from the proper use of one's talents to one's relation to nature, both internal and external. The first four moral eclogues, in relating the shepherd-pastor to his landscape, treat man's proper care in the world. In February, Thenot accepts his fortune in the world for "ever my flocke was my chiefe care." In May, Piers urges Palinode to

18. Fowler, pp. 14-15, argues that "the first half of the *Calender* . . . forms a circle, a subsidiary 'world', which may be interpreted as the mundane world of natural life," while the second half "becomes increasingly dark, the secular idyll more and more plainly illusion." He concludes that "this marvellous intellectual structure unfortunately no longer quite succeeds as poetry." I endorse the first half of this concluding sentence but reject the second half because it ignores the final roar of triumph in "Lo, I have made a Calender for every yeare."

withdraw both from the joys and the cares of the world, for the one makes him neglect his sheep and the other tempts him to lose his rightful heritage in order to care for his offspring. In July, Thomalin forgoes worldly ambition: to do so, however, leaves the world to the ambitious goatherd Morrell who neglects his goats. In the September eclogue, Diggon Davie yielded to ambition when he sought plenty elsewhere, only to find idle shepherds who neglected their sheep "all for they casten too much of worlds care, / To deck her Dame, and enrich her heyre." He returns a ruined man with his flock "all served with pyne and penuree." While each eclogue centres upon the pastoral metaphor of care, the three concluding eclogues are climactic as they treat the proper care of the shepherd-poet. In so doing, they resolve the poem as a pastoral.

The October eclogue, the debate between Piers and Cuddie on the place of the poet in society, is grouped by E. K. with the moral eclogues because it treats the "contempt of Poetrie and pleasaunt wits." By its summary account of Colin as a poet wounded by love, however, it includes the scope of the plaintive eclogues. As the religious spokesman for the good shepherd in May, Piers rightly serves as spokesman for the good poet whom he describes as one who may

> restraine
> The lust of lawlesse youth with good advice:
> Or pricke them forth with pleasaunce of thy vaine,
> Whereto thou list their trayned willes entice.

Yet Cuddie prefers to "feede youthes fancie." Piers argues that the poet should seek fame but Cuddie wants material reward. (At this point in their debate one recalls that in the February eclogue Cuddie won his love by a gift.) Piers urges him to forsake pastoral poetry for the heroic:

> Abandon then the base and viler clowne,
> Lyft up thy selfe out of lowly dust:
> And sing of bloody Mars, of wars, of giusts,
> Turne thee to those, that weld the awful crowne.

Yet Cuddie complains that he lacks a wealthy patron and heroic matter: "all the worthies liggen wrapt in leade, / That matter made for Poets on to play." Yet he is ready to allow that Colin would be capable of higher flight if he were not restrained by love. This prompts Piers to extol love's powers to raise man:

16

> Ah fon, for love does teach him climbe so hie,
> And lyftes him up out of the loathsome myre:
> Such immortall mirrhor, as he doth admire,
> Would rayse ones mynd above the starry skie.
> And cause a caytive corage to aspire,
> For lofty love doth loath a lowly eye.

"Above the starry skie" is the key phrase in these lines, in the eclogue and in the whole poem. For the first time there is the suggestion that something lies beyond the enshrouding constellations, the encircling zodiac which confines man to the cycle of seasons and the poet to the pastoral. Yet Cuddie finds inspiration in wine which only serves him for a while until his courage cools and he returns to the humble shade of the pastoral, presumably to nurse a hangover. For all his powers, he is the failed poet who has no role in society and therefore no identity.[19] The pathos registered in his closing words,

> But ah my corage cooles ere it be warme,
> For thy, content us in thys humble shade:
> Where no such troublous tydes han us assayde,
> Here we our slender pipes may safely charme

only reinforces the harshness of his dismissal.

The clash between Piers and Cuddie is a clash between what the poet should be and what he is, between Sidney's "right poet" and the poet of the 1570s. It is expressed in Piers's judgment, "the prayse is better, then the price," which expresses the motto of the whole poem: *Merce non mercede*, that is (roughly), "for reward but not for hire," "for praise or fame but not for personal gain or material payment."[20] The moral eclogues especially show how the moral claims on man are opposed by his desire for personal gain, "What's in it for me, Jack?" In February, Cuddie yearns to enjoy the delights of love; in May, Palinode wants to live "at ease and leasure" enjoying the good things sent by God; in July, Morrell condemns Thomalin for blaming wealth, claiming that "when folke bene fat, and riches rancke, / it is a signe of helth"; and in September, Hobbinoll rejects Diggon's claim that

19. See Richard F. Hardin, "The resolved debate of Spenser's 'October' ", *MP* 73 (1976), pp. 257-63. In *Spenser Newsletter*, 7 (1977), p. 26, Donald Cheney suggests that E. K.'s statement that "in Cuddie is set out the perfecte paterne of a Poete, whiche finding no maintenaunce of his state and studies, complayneth of the contempte of Poetrie" may be read: "in Cuddie is set out a perfect example of the kind of poet who . . ."

20. See Judith M. Kennedy, "The final emblem of *the Shepheardes Calender*," in *Spenser Studies*, I (1980), pp. 95-106. The motto is a pledge that Spenser will never be the courtly poet who praises the Queen for reward.

shepherds should not play or sleep all day for "we bene of fleshe, men as other bee. / Why should we be bound to such miseree?" The pastoral poet is self-regarding, being both *in* this world, and *of* it: he is, as Piers says of Palinode, "a worldes childe."

The November eclogue answers Cuddie's complaint in October. Cuddie's unwillingness to "abandon . . . the base and viler clowne" because " all the worthies liggen wrapt in leade, / That matter made for Poets on to play"is answered by Colin's willingness to lament the daughter of "the greate shepehearde" who is "Dead and lyeth wrapt in lead." For the first time, Colin sings his own song. No longer paralysed in self-regarding lament, he agrees to express Thenot's "wofull tene" for the death of Dido. Dido is, of course, pure fiction: the name seems chosen because the elegy to her balances the encomium to Elisa in the April eclogue—Virgil's Dido was called Elissa. (The allusion becomes unmistakable in the conclusion: Colin's Dido, that "blessed soul" who "walke[s] in Elisian fieldes so free," is not that offended dame who wanders in Dis's gloomy forest.) Like Donne, Spenser writes best when he has least truth for his subject; and most readers agree with E.K.'s judgment that the November eclogue is "farre passing [Colin's] reache, and in myne opinion all other the Eglogues of this booke." It is "farre passing" Colin's reach elsewhere in the poem because its apocalyptic vision of the resurrected Dido breaks through the encircling zodiac.

Death is the greatest challenge to the pastoral—as the ending of *Love's Labour's Lost* shows. Death boasts "*Et in Arcadia ego*" because he should have no place in a landscape of eternal spring. Dido is such a landscape, as "the sonne of all the world," "the fayrest floure our gyrlond all emong," whose death undoes "Dame natures kindly course." While spring may renew Nature, "thing on earth that is of most availe, / As vertues braunch and beauties budde, / Reliven not for any good."

At the beginning of the elegy, Colin's grief is so great that he urges "breake we our pypes." Yet he continues the elegy in its proper sequence until the sight of Dido's bier shows him the vanity of human life:

> O trustlesse state of earthly things, and slipper hope
> Of mortal men, that swincke and sweate for nought,
> And shooting wide, doe misse the marked scope:
> Now have I learnd (a lesson derely bought)
> That nys on earth assuraunce to be sought:
> For what might be in earthlie mould,

18

> That did her buried body hould,
>   O heavie herse,
> Yet saw I on the beare when it was brought
>   O carefull verse.

This is the most dramatic moment in the poem: it involves "breaking" of another kind. The sight of death, of its reality, forces Colin—as it forces Milton at the same point in his elegy to Lycidas, as it forces us all at some time in our lives—to recognize that this dead body is not the person whom we have loved. A dramatic reversal follows in the eclogue and in the whole poem:

> But maugre death, and dreaded sisters deadly spight,
> And gates of hel, and fyrie furies forse:
> She hath the bonds broke of eternall night,
> Her soule unbodied of the burdenous corpse.

Here the poem reaches its polar opposite to April's vision of Elisa decked in flowers, particularly in the line, "Now rise up Elisa, decked as thou art, in royall aray." Dido's resurrection, patterned after Christ's, reminds us almost with the force of revelation, that through Christ's death, death has been made, in E. K.'s words (which he attributes to Chaucer), "the grene path way to lyfe." Now Colin may follow Piers's injunction to "rayse [his] mynd above the starry skie," and there follows the vision of Dido in a heavenly pastoral landscape walking in "fieldes ay fresh, the grasse ay greene." At last the pastoral song affords solace and the elegy ends in triumph: "Ceasse now my song, my woe now wasted is. / O joyfull verse."

With its assurance that there is a life beyond nature, Colin's elegy for Dido provides the context for the December eclogue, the elegy for his own death. Colin traces his descent as love, after it destroys his timeless spring, brings the seasons in their order until he reaches the state of winter and death. As one has come to expect, the eclogue is carefully patterned: three stanzas of introduction, the first for the setting and the next two for the invocation; and three stanzas of conclusion which reverse that arrangement, the first two for general exhortation and the third for a final farewell. As the whole eclogue is a formal retraction of youthful vanities, the last stanza is Colin's farewell to the pastoral.

The twenty-four stanzas of lament would seem chosen to measure the twelve months of the year; however, they open in March, the first month of the natural year, and end with December. There is no return through January and February to another spring. Since the stanzas are patterned on the seasons and progress through the ten months, in reading the eclogue, one rereads most of the poem. Three stanzas, 4-6, show the innocent pastimes of young shepherds, as in March; 7-8 refer to Colin's poetic powers, which are displayed in April; 9-10 show his wounding by love, as Palinode in May is subject to desire; 11-12 trace his wanderings provoked by love's wound, as in June; 13-14 note his wisdom in the ways of the world, as in July; 15-16 declare his inability to cure love's grief, as in August;[21] 17-18 show him left desolate by the world's corruption, as Diggon Davie in September; 19-20 declare his rejection of pastoral life as vain, as Cuddie complains in October; and finally three stanzas, 21-23, treat his death, as November treats Dido's death. By forgoing ambition, the pastoral life may escape the turning of the wheel of fortune but not the wheel of time marked by the seasons and the months of the year.

The six times repeated "Adieu" in the final stanza would seem to conclude the poem. But again there is a dramatic reversal. In a triumphant epilogue, Spenser prophesies life for his poem throughout all time:

> Loe I have made a Calender for every yeare,
> That steele in strength, and time in durance shall outweare:
> And if I marked well the starres revolution,
> It shall continewe till the worlds dissolution.
> To teach the ruder shepheard how to feede his sheepe,
> And from the falsers fraud his folded flocke to keepe.[22]

Many poets have claimed that their verse will outlast time, as Horace

---

21. The correspondence for August is strained, in part because the month is the least integrated eclogue as it turns inward to contrast the old-fashioned "mery thing" sung by Perigot and Willye and Colin's very modish "heavy laye" in sestina form. A more important reason is that Spenser turns the December eclogue on two unanswered questions, the first double question occurring in these stanzas, "Why livest thou stil, and yet hast thy deathes wound? / Why dyest thou stil, and yet alive art founde?" and the second, "Ah who has wrought my Rosalind this spight / To spil the flowres, that should her girlond dight?." (My tentative answer to the first double question is suggested by E. K.'s comment on the Emblem of November: "by course of nature we be borne to dye"; and to the second: time.)

22. In these lines the humble imitator of Virgil indicates an ambition to "overgo" his master. While Virgil "earst had taught his flocks to feede" (October 57), he teaches the shepherd himself both how to feed his flock and how to guard it in the fold. Such ambition comments on the woodcut to the January eclogue which shows Colin as a shepherd in a Janus-pose with the broken pastoral pipe at his feet and his sheep behind him as he looks "forward" to a group of buildings. In "The illustrations to *The Shepheardes Calender*," in *Spenser at Kalamazoo*, 1979, Ruth Luborsky suggests that the buildings stand for Rome with its Colosseum, the Pantheon with its twin towers, a Roman aqueduct, and a square building which may be the Basilica of S. Giovanni in Laterno. The pastoral life belongs to Colin's past and he looks forward to his future "Virgilian" epic.

boasts that his work cannot be destroyed by the endless succession of years in the flight of ages. Spenser is the first, however, to claim that his poem will last through time because it applies to each year until the end of time. In effect, he claims that his poem has a plot in Aristotle's sense, an imitation not of what happened in a year in the 1570s but of what always happens in any year throughout time. As such, the poem serves the reader as a secular version of the church year.

Of the two calendars which measure man's life, the natural one—March to February—revives nature, and the religious one—January to December as traced by the church year—restores man's life. In the first, the sun renews his course; in the second, Christ, the true Son, renews the world. As E.K. notes, Christ's birth in December renews "the state of the decayed world, and return[s] the compasse of expired yeres to theyr former date and first commencement." In other words, instead of time repeating another cycle of the months, it returns to its first beginning, that is, to the golden age. As Colin's death fulfils the vision of man's life on the order of nature, the *Calender* with its sequence from January to December traces only the tragic vision of life. Yet in the canon of Spenser's poetry, it is followed almost immediately by Colin's triumphant re-emergence in the opening lines of *The Faerie Queene*:

> Lo I the man, whose Muse whilome did maske,
>
> As time her taught, in lowly Shepheards weeds,
>
> Am now enforst a far unfitter taske,
>
> For trumpets sterne to chaunge mine Oaten reeds.

Colin Clout is dead. Long live Colin Clout! Taught by time, he triumphs over time: his end becomes his beginning as he assumes his new identity as spokesman for England.

The Shepheardes Calender has served him as "the grene path way to lyfe." It may, too, for readers who are prepared to ask more from poetry than what Cuddie offers when he feeds youth's fancy: for readers who are prepared with the "old" Colin to be taught by time so that with the "new" Colin they may raise their minds "above the starrie skie."[23]

23. In writing this paper, I have tried not to remind myself that I have written an earlier article on the poem: "The argument of Spenser's *Shepheardes Calender*," *ELH*, 23 (1956), pp. 171-82. On turning back to it now, I find that I have nothing to retract. What I said then was limited in part by the need to answer the prevailing view that the "real meaning" of the *Calender* was "an attack on the Queen's proposed French marriage" and that its principle of unity was to be found "in the opinion of Harvey." Only twenty-three years later, such responses to the poem must strike readers as entirely unbelievable. If my present views strike readers in the same way twenty-three years from now, I suspect that the reason will be that we have not learned yet to respond directly to the poem's language rather than to its ideas.

John Lyly and
Pastoral Entertainment

ANNE LANCASHIRE

Of all Elizabethan dramatists John Lyly would seem, at least in quantitative terms, to be the most thoroughly pastoral. Of his eight known extant plays (attributions to him of other plays and entertainments are questionable) only two, *Campaspe* and *Mother Bombie*, have nothing whatsoever to do with the pastoral. Three of his plays—over one third of his output—are generally agreed, for reasons I'll deal with shortly, to be out-and-out pastorals: *Gallathea* (c.1585),[1] *Loves Metamorphosis* (c.1590: the only one of Lyly's plays to be called a pastoral on the title page of the first edition [1601]), and *Woman in the Moon* (c. 1593). One more, *Midas* (c. 1589), contains a couple of significantly pastoral episodes and motifs; another, *Sapho and Phao* (c.1584), begins in a pastoral vein and is throughout somewhat pastoral although most scholars have not thought so. Finally *Endimion* (1588) is pastoral in its origins in classical mythology; but since Lyly makes no use of its pastoralism in his version of the Endimion story, which deals with courtly matters and philosophical abstractions, I intend not to include Lyly's best-known play in this discussion. Even without *Endimion*, Lyly seems overwhelmingly a pastoral dramatist, with 37.5 per cent of his known plays fully pastoral and another 25 per cent partially so.

"The definition of pastoral," Peter Marinelli has written, "is no simple matter";[2] and W. W. Greg has maintained that pastoral cannot

---

1. This and subsequent play dates are taken from Alfred Harbage's *Annals of English Drama 975-1700*, rev. S. Schoenbaum (Philadelphia, 1964). Although there is controversy about the dating of a number of Lyly's plays, especially *Woman in the Moon* which some scholars place at the beginning and some at the end of Lyly's dramatic career, the *Annals* represents the scholarly consensus; and the order of the plays is not important in any case to my arguments in this paper.
2. Peter V. Marinelli, *Pastoral* (London, 1971), p. 5.

be defined.[3] I hasten, then, at this point, not to try to define pastoral in general but to set down an initial definition for the purposes of this paper. By pastoral, at this stage in the discussion I simply mean, very traditionally, a work the ostensible subject matter of which is rural life in Arcadia or its equivalent, involving shepherds and their like (shepherdesses, foresters, nymphs, fishermen), and the style of which is courtly—obviously sophisticated and contrived. Conventional motifs often found include the music competition, the wooing of a coy nymph by an amorous shepherd, the boar hunt, and the healing of a wound with herbs. The focus is on love; there is considerable description of the rural scene; and the classical gods usually figure prominently.

It is by this simple definition that *Gallathea, Loves Metamorphosis,* and *Woman in the Moon* are fully pastoral and *Midas* and *Sapho and Phao* are partially so. *Gallathea* is perhaps the most pastoral of Lyly's works in overall effect. The setting is throughout singly rural—a large oak tree, sacred to Neptune, which becomes a focus for the action; and the dialogue establishes a river and its banks, fields and flocks, and nearby woods. The play begins with lines echoing the opening of Virgil's *Eclogues* and giving a sensuous description of the rural landscape.

> The Sunne dooth beate vppon the playne fieldes, wherefore let vs sit downe *Gallathea,* vnder this faire Oake, by whose broade leaues beeing defended from the warme beames, we may enioy the fresh ayre, which softly breathes from Humber floodes. (I. i. 1-5)[4]

The main characters are shepherds and their daughters (appropriately named Tityrus, Gallathea, Melebeus and Phyllida), the subject matter is erotic love, and the gods Neptune, Diana, Venus and Cupid play a crucial role in events. The play ends with a promised rural marriage, reconciliation of the gods with man and with one another, and ostensible harmony all round. As in all of Lyly's plays, the style of dialogue and dramatic structure are alike contrived, balanced, pointedly artificial and ordered.

In *Loves Metamorphosis* we are again in a rural landscape, though this time one divided into several locations: a tree again, this time sacred

---

3. Walter W. Greg, *Pastoral Poetry and Pastoral Drama* (London, 1906), p. 417.
4. This and subsequent references to the texts of Lyly's plays are to R. Warwick Bond's *The Complete Works of John Lyly*, 3 vols. (Oxford, 1902; rpt. 1967). Play titles abbreviated in the notes are *Loves Metamorphosis* as *LM, Woman in the Moon* as *WM,* and *Sapho and Phao* as *S&P.*

to Ceres, the temple of Cupid, and the seashore (which includes a siren's rock).[5] Once again the dialogue establishes for us, though very occasionally and not in any detail, the forest and shore and nearby woods (e.g., IV. ii. 22, "Aye me, behold, a Syren haunts this shore!"). We begin with a focus on unrequited love (I. i) and with a rural holiday (I. ii). The main characters are typically pastoral: three amorous foresters and three disdainful nymphs, plus the forest ruler Erisichthon, his daughter Protea, and her lover Petulius. The gods Ceres and Cupid (and Neptune *in absentia*) participate in events, and Cupid and Neptune bring about an ending of love fulfilled. The style and structure are as in *Gallathea*.[6]

In *Woman in the Moon* we are in a classical Eden, Utopia, at the beginning of the world as created by Nature. Four shepherds beg Nature for a woman upon whom to beget children (I. i. 39-50); the resulting Pandora—so called because she combines the excellencies of the seven planets/gods (I. i. 107-108)—then becomes the centre of amorous contests and intrigues. Unlike *Gallathea* and *Loves Metamorphosis*, *Woman in the Moon* does not have a distinctly pastoral set, though its dialogue contains more rural description and references than does that of *Loves Metamorphosis* (e.g., I. i. 185-187, "Sweete Dame, if *Stesias* may content thine eye, / Commaund my Neate, my flock, and tender Kids, / Whereof great store do ouerspred our plaines"). The only large stage properties appear to be Nature's "shop" (I. i. 56.1), perhaps a seat for Pandora at the start (I. i. 177, "See where she sits") though more likely she sits on the ground (I. i. 178, "she sleepes"; I. i. 218, "O helpe to reare thy Mistresse from the ground"), and certainly a raised seat or throne throughout upon which the seven planets sit in turn to influence the action (e.g., II. i. 23, 176, III. i. 0.1, III. ii. 35). The structure, however, is even more formal and ordered than in *Gallathea* and *Loves Metamorphosis*: the seven planets process in turn to the seat above the main acting area where each one presides for a while over the action below. The dialogue, unique in Lyly's plays, is in blank verse. A number of typical pastoral motifs are included: for example, the wooing of the disinterested nymph, the boar hunt and the healing of a wound with

---

5. See Bond, III, p. 298, and Peter Saccio, *The Court Comedies of John Lyly* (Princeton, 1969), p. 19.
6. *Gallathea* of course has a comic subplot involving non-pastoral characters, *LM* does not; the similarities to which I refer are those of stylistic and structural balance and artificiality.

herbs.[7] The total effect is ceremonial, episodic, masque-like: a triumph of obvious dramatic craftsmanship.[8]

Midas contains two episodes which can be called pastoral: a scene (IV. ii) in which five shepherds discuss the state of the king and the realm,[9] and a music competition in a classical rural setting between the rural god Pan ("My Temple is in Arcadie," IV. i. 34) and Apollo, with nymphs and Midas for judges (IV. i).[10] A boar hunt also takes place. As well, the play begins with a description of Midas' state in terms of a prosperous rural estate.

> All thy grounds are vineyards, thy corne grapes, thy chambers sellers, thy houshold stuffe standing cuppes. . . . Wouldest thou haue the pipes of thy conducts to run wine, the vdders of thy beasts to drop nectar, or thy trees to bud ambrosia? (I. i. 5-10)

Finally, the scene locations of the play contrast, in thematic pastoral fashion, court and country: a palace courtyard or garden (I. i.-III. iii and V. ii) and a country grove (IV. i-V. i), with the final scene of resolution (V. iii) at Apollo's oracle at Delphi.[11]

Sapho and Phao is not usually thought of as pastoral,[12] but it begins with a lengthy speech by the ferryman (i.e., countryman) Phao in the traditional pastoral vein of court-country contrast.[13]

> Thou art a Ferriman, Phao, yet a free man, possessing for riches content, and for honors quiet. . . . As much doth it delight thee to rule thine oare in a calme streame, as it dooth Sapho to swaye the Scepter in her braue court. . . . Thine angle is ready, when thine oar is idle, and as sweet is the

---

7. Violet M. Jeffery, *John Lyly and the Italian Renaissance* (Paris, 1929), pp. 76-77.

8. Jeffery, pp. 73-74, has noted the masque-like nature of WM; and Michael Shapiro, *Children of the Revels* (New York, 1977) has commented (p. 145) that WM is more like a pageant than any other of Lyly's plays. See also Greg, p. 234.

9. G. K. Hunter, *John Lyly: The Humanist as Courtier* (London, 1962), following Greg (p. 225, n.1), calls this a proletarian, not pastoral, scene (p. 194).

10. Also IV. iii is a hunting scene, though involving non-pastoral subplot characters.

11. For the typical court-country contrast of the pastoral see, e.g.: Marinelli, p. 12; David Young, *The Heart's Forest: A Study of Shakespeare's Pastoral Plays* (New Haven and London, 1972), p. 3; Edward William Tayler, *Nature and Art in Renaissance Literature* (New York and London, 1964), p. 5; Hunter, *John Lyly*, p. 129. Hunter (p. 109) believes that in *Midas* the same scenic façade served for both the palace scenes and Delphi.

12. Hunter, however, allows it a "thin wash of rusticity" (*John Lyly*, p. 194). See also R. Mark Benbow, ed., Peele's *Araygnement of Paris*, in *The Dramatic Works of George Peele*, gen. ed. Charles Tyler Prouty (New Haven and London, 1970), p. 41, and Bond, II, p. 484.

13. This point is noted by, among others, Agnes Latham, ed., Shakespeare's *As You Like It* (London, 1975), p. lxiii.

fish which thou gettest in the ryuer, as the fowle which other buye in the market. Thou needst not feare poyson in thy glasse, nor treason in thy garde. The winde is thy greatest enemy, whose might is withstoode with pollicy. O sweete life, seldom found vnder a goldē couert, oftē vnder a thached cotage. (I. i. 1-16)

The set appears to be multiple (the ferry and Sybilla's cave, Vulcan's forge, Sapho's palace[14]) and is significantly, as in *Midas*, a mix of country and court. Acts I and II are set in the country, III and IV (all but one scene) at court, and V is mixed.[15] The dialogue at one point establishes an overall setting of fields near both country ferry and court. The multiple set would appear to be emblematic; geographically separate locations are to be considered as grouped together.

> SAPHO. Seeing I am onely come forth to take the ayre, I will crosse the Ferrie, and so the fieldes, then going in through the park, I thinke the walke wil be pleasant.
>
> TRACHI[NUS]. You will much delight in the flattering greene, which now beginneth to be in his glory. (II. ii. 13-17)[16]

The play ends, however, with Phao, unsuccessful in his love of Sapho, renouncing both court and country. The pastoral content of the opening has changed to the pastoral discontent of the close.

> I must nowe fall from loue to labour, and endeuour with mine oare to gette a fare, not with my penne to write a fancie. . . . A Ferrie, Phao, no the starres cannot call thee to a worser fortune. Rauing rather ouer the world, forsweare affections, entreate for death. . . . (V. iii. 9-14)

Sapho and Phao more than any other Lyly play deals explicitly with the standard court-country contrast which lies at the heart of the pastoral mode.

---

14. Saccio, *Court Comedies*, pp. 18-19 and 22-23, and Hunter, *John Lyly*, p. 109, see the areas as Sapho's palace and Sybilla's cave; the latter may double for Vulcan's forge or be separate from it. They believe the ferry location to be simply the free-stage area, as does W. J. Lawrence, *The Elizabethan Playhouse and Other Studies* (Stratford-upon-Avon, 1912), I, p. 240. It is more likely, however, that the ferry area was somehow represented on stage, in conjunction with the cave, since it provides a key contrast with Sapho's palace (as the opening and closing speeches of the play, as quoted above and below, make clear). *Cf.* the court-country set contrast in *Midas*.

15. Note that the order of *Midas* is reversed. *Midas* moves from court to country to court again (and Delphi); *S&P* moves from country to court back to the country again. Hunter (*John Lyly*, p. 167) thinks the setting of *S&P* "vague enough not to be noticed"; this is unlikely, given the physical locations required and their contrasting relationships.

16. This setting somewhat foreshadows the courtly parkland world of *Love's Labour's Lost*. Saccio notes (*Court Comedies*, p. 13) that evidence points to the use of natural greenery in pastorals at court.

Why the love affair between Lyly and the pastoral? There are several interrelated reasons which we can find immediately. One, the pastoral was fashionable at court in the 1580s (thanks in large part to Spenser's *Shepheardes Calender*), and Lyly was a court dramatist, writing to please the court and especially the Queen.[17] Two, the main subject matter of the "pure" pastoral is erotic love—and especially sexual psychology—which was also inevitably Lyly's subject matter in whatever genre he wrote. Three, the pastoral was a highly artificial and ordered mode of writing, compatible with the Euphuistic prose style developed to a fine art by Lyly and calling attention to its author's craftsmanship in the Queen's service, and suited as well to the ritualistic and artificial nature of the Elizabethan court entertainment in general and to the boy actors who performed Lyly's work. Four, by Lyly's day the pastoral was usually allegorical,[18] and thus was eminently suited to the complex examination of abstract ideas. Five, the pastoral, unlike comedy and tragedy, is a dramatic genre peculiarly dependent on place, and therefore potentially more static than other dramatic forms, which also suited Lyly's interest in the examination of ideas, often through debate, rather than in the development of dramatic character and action. Formal, stylized, highly crafted, allegorical, courtly, fashionable, intellectual, static: the pastoral was made for Lyly and his talents for it. No matter that the pastoral seemed to run counter to the active and varied nature of English theatre tradition, and so flourished under Queen Elizabeth mainly in the more static and emblematic pageants and other such shows of the period. Lyly's interests ran in the same direction—witness the scholars today who have even declined to call his dramas plays and have labelled all his stage productions, pastorals and non-pastorals alike, "masque dramas" or "court entertainments" as opposed to real dramas.[19]

So far, however, I have been dealing in superficialities. Granted that a number of Lyly's plays are conventionally pastoral in subject matter

17. See, e.g., M. C. Bradbrook, *The Growth and Structure of Elizabethan Comedy* (London, 1955; rev. 1973), pp. 61-62, and *The Rise of the Common Player* (London, 1962), pp. 218 and 247.
18. See Paul E. McLane, *Spenser's Shepheardes Calender: A Study in Elizabethan Allegory* (Notre Dame, 1961), pp. 4-7 (esp. 5), and W. L. Renwick, ed., Spenser's *The Shepherd's Calendar* (London, 1930), pp. 164-65.
19. See, e.g., Marie Axton, "The Tudor Mask and Elizabethan Court Drama," in Marie Axton and Raymond Williams, eds., *English Drama: Forms and Development* (Cambridge, 1977), p. 42, and Young, p. 16. Hereward T. Price, "Shakespeare and His Young Contemporaries," *PQ*, XLI (1962), pp. 37-57, goes so far as to say that "Lyly does not know what drama is" (p. 41). On the masque connection see also Bond, II, p. 249, and John Dover Wilson, *John Lyly* (1905; rpt. New York, 1970), p. 112.

and style: so what? Is there anything to be gained from a closer examination of these plays *as* pastorals? Recently it has not been thought useful to talk about Lyly's plays in conventional genre terms. Both G. K. Hunter and Peter Saccio, authors of highly influential works on Lyly, have suggested that other ways of approaching the plays work better in providing us with a deeper understanding of what Lyly is doing.[20] Hunter groups the dramas as, for example, plays unified around debate, and plays of "harmonious variety." Saccio divides them into situational dramas and plays which are more narrative.[21] And a number of scholars have suggested or implied that Lyly's pastoralism is only skin deep, merely decorative.[22] Lyly may be a complex dramatist, but is he necessarily in these three to five plays a pastorally complex one? Interestingly Saccio, who begins his book on Lyly by discarding as "inept and confusing" older play classifications such as "historical" and "pastoral," apparently ends by finding some significance in the pastoral classification after all,[23] but not for these three to five plays as a group, and I intend in any case to begin, not to end, with pastoralism and to take quite a different tack from Saccio's.

Let us now move beyond pastoral surfaces and into thematic concerns, though keeping the surfaces also very much in mind. Here I am treading on controversial ground; but when scholars look for value and complexity in Renaissance pastorals, of the sort that only the pastoral can provide, they seem to look above all at what we may call the pastoral golden vision, or ideal of human happiness. The visionary pastoral, through metaphoric use of its traditional subject matter, simultaneously looks back to a simple, rural and innocent human past (located historically in time—as in the pagan Golden Age or the Christian Eden—or located psychologically within the human individual—as in youth) and compares this ideal explicitly or implicitly with a complex, urban or courtly present, celebrating the ideal either nostalgically, as lost forever, or hopefully, as potentially realizable again, even if only temporarily, in the present or future. The positive visionary pastoral may show the ideal as realizable

20. Hunter, *John Lyly*, pp. 159-60; Saccio, *Court Comedies*, pp. 3-10.

21. Hunter, *John Lyly*, pp. 160 and 193; Saccio, *Court Comedies*, pp. 8-10.

22. Jeanette Marks, e.g., in *English Pastoral Drama* (London, 1908) says that *Midas*, *Gallathea*, and *WM* "are coloured by the pastoral" (p. 16) and that *LM* also has "[p]astoral elements" (p. 157). Greg calls *Gallathea*, *LM*, and *WM* plays with "pastoral tendency" (p. 225). Hunter (*John Lyly*) sees Lyly's pastoralism as a matter largely of *style* (p. 132) and, in *LM* and *WM*, of "convenience" (p. 135).

23. Saccio, *Court Comedies*, p. 3 (quotation) and pp. 216 and 221. The older classifications are used by, e.g., Bond, II, p. 249.

anew through love, politics, or religion, and on the private (individual) or public (social) level; but whatever the writer's approach, in this positive type of pastoral the golden vision creates for the reader/ audience a feeling of satisfaction and regeneration. A harmonious golden world has been revealed; an ideal of human happiness has been recaptured. Shakespeare in *As You Like It* is writing this type of positive, visionary pastoral, one looking back to the Golden Age, contrasting an evil courtly present with an innocent rural present, and culminating through rural simplicity and human love in a golden vision—not perfect but eminently satisfying—of personal and social harmony and order.

From this perspective let us look at *Gallathea, Loves Metamorphosis,* and *Woman in the Moon.* What might Lyly be trying to do thematically, in visionary terms, with his pastoral material? Usually scholars approach these plays expecting them, because of their Arcadian-type settings and emphasis on erotic love, to be visionary and positive pastorals focusing on past and future human happiness and regeneration. And hence the frequent critical disappointment in the plays as pastorals: for on examination one is immediately struck by the fact that, far from showing a golden world and satisfying most readers with a regenerative view of human life, all three dramas seem largely unsettling or ironic. A golden vision, either of the past or of the present and future, would seem to be entirely missing except in part in *Gallathea.* We can best see this briefly, before turning to each play in detail, through looking at the resolutions of the three plays, which are typical of their plays as a whole in working against any feeling of harmonious fulfilment. Although some attempts—most significantly by Saccio—have been made lately to explain positively the endings of the plays, let me first put the problems in their starkest form. *Gallathea* seems to end happily in spite of, not because of, its human characters, through a miraculous sex-change unexpectedly wrought by Venus and obviously manipulated by the playwright. *Loves Metamorphosis* ends with its three nymphs forced into love by the threat of monstrous metamorphoses at the hands of Cupid, and foretelling the future difficulties they will cause their lovers. *Woman in the Moon* ends with its heroine, Pandora, consigned by her own choice and by Nature to eternal fickleness and lunacy. We tend to feel vaguely dissatisfied at the conclusion of *Gallathea,* distinctly uneasy at the end of *Loves Metamorphosis,* and downright unhappy at the finale of *Woman in the Moon.* Lyly's other, non-pastoral dramatic resolutions are, paradoxically, more emotionally satisfying (though still not without problems too[24]): for example, the self-conquests of Alexander the Great in *Campaspe*, of Sapho in *Sapho and Phao*, and of Midas in the play of that title. Leaving aside the untypical *Mother Bombie*, which is Lyly's only venture into traditional Roman-type comedy, we see that at least part of the problem is related to the fact that Lyly's non-pastoral plays, reflecting authoritarian Elizabethan society, all contain, as G. K. Hunter has noted,[25] a single, royal, essentially human figure upon whom the action focuses and who can provide a final order, of a kind, at the play's end. The three pastoral plays, dealing with non-political rural societies, do not contain such a figure; their resolutions are imposed by gods as authority figures, or by Lyly as playwright. The human characters are in general powerless and do not develop towards any satisfying resolution;[26] and the gods, in that they are portrayed as proud, vengeful, lustful and so forth,[27] do not appear either to be regenerative forces, even though without the gods both *Gallathea* and *Loves Metamorphosis* would end unhappily. (*Woman in the Moon* ends unhappily even with the gods: in fact, because of them.) The worlds of Lyly's pastoral plays are disappointingly imperfect; their only golden visions seem to lie in the audience expectations at first raised, but never met, by their Arcadian-type subject matter. Certainly we do not have in Lyly's work the kind of visionary Arcadian pastoralism that we find in *As You Like It*.

There is one other way in which Lyly could be seen to be writing positive, visionary pastorals, and that is in relation to the traditional use by Lyly's day of the visionary pastoral to compliment a living monarch. Since Virgil, it had become customary for a pastoral author to laud a present ruler through suggesting similarities between the ruler's present or future state and that of the golden pastoral past. The monarch, for example, could be portrayed as a new Saturn (ruler of the Golden Age) or a new Astraea (Golden Age goddess of justice and truth).[28] Indeed, we might expect this customary political use of the pastoral to be yet one more reason for the genre's appeal to Lyly, since his court hopes depended upon pleasing the Queen. The golden

---

24. For example, David Lloyd Stevenson, *The Love-Game Comedy* (1946; rpt. New York, 1966) finds the happy endings of *Campaspe*, *S&P* and *Endimion* to be contrived as well (pp. 164-68, and see also p. 171).

25. *John Lyly*, p. 194.

26. A possible exception is Protea in *LM*; see below.

27. On the unpleasantness of Lyly's gods, especially in *WM*, see Michael Best, "Lyly's Static Drama," *RenD*, N. S. I (1968), p. 82.

28. On rulers as commonly praised through comparison to Saturn and to Astraea, see, e.g., Harry Levin, *The Myth of The Golden Age in the Renaissance* (Bloomington and London, 1969), p. 112.

vision of his plays, as of so many English pastorals of the period, would then lie in their praise of Elizabeth.[29] And in Lyly's non-pastorals Queen Elizabeth is complimented allegorically by being reflected, to varying extents, in the monarch figures shown: in *Campaspe*'s Alexander, *Sapho and Phao*'s Sapho, *Endimion*'s Cynthia, and *Midas'* ruler of Lesbos.[30] (Again I am leaving aside the untypical *Mother Bombie*.)

In Lyly's pastoral plays, however, where because of tradition we might most expect to see compliments to the Queen, such compliments turn out to be difficult or impossible to find. There are no earthly monarchs to figure the Queen; and attempts to find Elizabeth reflected in other figures such as the unlikable and helpless Pandora of *Woman in the Moon* obviously lead to problems. Is Lyly abandoning political compliment in the very plays where we might most expect to find it? Or is he attempting in his pastorals, through unexpectedly presenting unflattering parallels to Elizabeth, subtly to criticize — presumably in the tradition of licensed festal ridicule[31] — the very ruler upon whose favour his fortunes depend?

Examining *Gallathea*, *Loves Metamorphosis* and *Woman in the Moon* as pastorals, then, leads us at length to the question: Is Lyly perhaps using pastoral subject matter to write not visionary but ironic pastorals, or anti-pastorals, which deal, through contrast with the pastoral golden vision at first called to our minds by the pastoral surfaces of the plays, not with man's regeneration and happiness but with his inevitable degeneration and unhappiness, and which show the folly and limitations of man and ruler alike? This is possible, though certainly, at least in terms of monarchical folly and limitations, not what we would normally expect of a dramatist aspiring to royal

29. Levin comments (p. 114) on the obvious particular suitability of Elizabeth for the role of Astraea; and see Helen Cooper, *Pastoral: Mediaeval into Renaissance* (Ipswich, and Totawa, N.J., 1977), pp. 187, 193-207, and Elkin Calhoun Wilson, *England's Eliza* (Cambridge, Mass., 1939), chapter 4.

30. For scholars viewing these four plays as generally reflecting Queen Elizabeth in these figures, see, e.g.: Hunter, *John Lyly*, pp. 97 (on *Endimion* and *S&P*) and 160-93, and *Lyly and Peele* (London, 1968), pp. 32-33; David Bevington, *Tudor Drama and Politics* (Cambridge, Mass., 1968), pp. 171-84 and 187-89; G. Wilson Knight, *The Golden Labyrinth* (London, 1962), pp. 48-49. I do not wish to deal in this paper with theories of specific political allegories in these plays.

In *Endimion* Cynthia is both heavenly goddess and courtly ruler; and in *Midas* Lyly varies his complimentary technique by focusing on a foolish ruler (Midas) and hence defining largely by contrast (Hunter, *Lyly and Peele*, p. 33) his opposite, the excellent ruler of Lesbos (who is talked about but never appears).

31. See Shapiro, pp. 40-42. Axton has recently suggested (p. 42) that Lyly could criticize the Queen only because of the backing of "a powerful patron and a spirited court audience."

favour. As M. C. Bradbrook and Michael Shapiro have both recently pointed out, court plays of this period were above all gift offerings to the monarch;[32] and Elizabeth was used to fulsome compliments in the literary offerings made to her.[33] Let us look at each pastoral play in turn.

First, *Gallathea*, which comes closer to a golden vision than does either *Loves Metamorphosis* or *Woman in the Moon*. The main-plot action takes place in what is very much a fallen pastoral world, although there is at the play's opening a brief glimpse of a golden age which is located in history (literally) and probably also in youth (metaphorically). In times past, before men broke their vows, life was peaceful and god-centred (I. i. 13-28); but now the river and green fields are invaded every five years by a monster, the Agar, sent by Neptune to receive a virgin sacrifice from the inhabitants (I. i. 37-56). As the play's action unfolds we see present love to be misguided (two fathers cause only troubles by disguising their daughters as boys to save them from the virgin sacrifice—the appropriate father-daughter sexual psychology being metaphorically suggested), violent (the Agar has erotic associations), beastly (the gods, we are told, have become beasts to rape mortal women: see, e.g., I. i. 88-91), and blind (the two disguised girls fall in love with one another, each wilfully believing, against indications to the contrary, that the other is truly a boy). At the play's end, however, a harmonious resolution of sorts is achieved as Neptune gives up the virgin sacrifice and Venus changes the sex of one girl to allow physical consummation of love (the ultimate human happiness of the "pure" pastoral).

This resolution, however, is in a number of ways unsatisfactory. On a literal level it seems purely arbitrary: a way of solving a plot impasse.[34] On an allegorical level it seems false or ironic. If the gods in Lyly's work in part represent real divinity—powerful forces beyond man, as Saccio has argued[35]—then the vengeful, selfish and bickering gods of *Gallathea* serve as a rather bleak comment on the uncertainty of man's earthly lot at any time, and the play's happy ending seems

---

32. Bradbrook, *Player*, p. 218; Shapiro, p. 38. Bradbrook (pp. 231-32) believes that Lyly would not attack even the court audience, let alone the Queen, but would direct criticisms only against outsiders or the Queen's or his own patron's rivals or enemies.
33. Axton's view (p. 42) of Lyly's plays as partly critical of Elizabeth does not sufficiently take into account, I think, Lyly's dependence on the Queen's favour and the usual fulsome compliments to Elizabeth in drama and other literature of this period (see Bevington, pp. 168-70, and E. C. Wilson, *passim*).
34. See Jeffery, p. 84.
35. Saccio, *Court Comedies*, e.g., pp. 104-14.

one of luck,[36] not of regeneration. John Weld has recently argued that the gods' actions at the play's close represent a reconciliation between love and chastity possible only through divine (Christian) suspension of natural law;[37] but this to me seems most unlikely, given the gods as Lyly portrays them, with all their human failings such as pride and inconstancy. If the gods, on the other hand, represent at least in part forces within man (impulses towards power, virginity, sexual fulfilment and so forth) then the ending seems either deliberately ironic or inappropriate. First, no amount of wishful thinking can produce sex-change—and the ending may thus show how only in fiction can man's blind erotic impulses lead him to happiness. Or, if the ending is supposed, as Saccio has argued, to be an extreme metaphoric example of the harmonious coexistence of love and chastity (Venus and Diana as balanced: love plus enforced sexual non-consumation)[38] the final sex-change works against the metaphor in that it destroys the balance and turns the play into a demonstration of the ultimate success of insistent eroticism. Perhaps then we have after all the traditional pastoral celebration of erotic love?[39] But the play has emphasized throughout its heroines' self-deception in love, and the realistic subplot involving a Mariner, Alchemist and Astronomer has underlined human tendencies to self-deception and to satisfaction of appetite. Moreover, as Leah Scragg has pointed out, the play is full of transformations, both actual and discussed,[40] suggesting lack of stability and order. *Gallathea* seems from this perspective to be ironic pastoral—Lyly's attempt to show that, given human nature, no golden ideal can be achieved in this fallen world. After all, since the departure of the goddess Astraea from the earth (in pagan mythology), or since the fall of man (in Christian mythology), natural man has been appropriate subject matter not for idealistic but for ironic literary treatment. Still, in *Gallathea* we do look back to a golden age; we do see genuine erotic passion fulfilled happily, however unbelievably; the subplot characters are fresh portraits of Elizabethan innocents;[41] and the rural setting is

36. Saccio, more optimistic than I am about the play's ending, calls this destiny (*Court Comedies*, pp. 144-45). But the point still holds that it is something beyond the control of the human characters.
37. John Weld, *Meaning in Comedy* (Albany, 1975), p. 124.
38. Saccio, *Court Comedies*, pp. 146-47.
39. See, in part, Joel B. Altman, *The Tudor Play of Mind* (Berkeley, Los Angeles and London, 1978), pp. 215-16.
40. Leah Scragg, "Shakespeare, Lyly and Ovid: The Influence of 'Gallathea' on 'A Midsummer Night's Dream'," *ShS*, XXX (1977), pp. 128-32.
41. Anne Begor Lancashire, ed., Lyly's *Gallathea* and *Midas* (Lincoln, Nebraska, 1969), p. xxvi.

no classical dream but a sensuously described combination of conventional Arcadia with its gods and monsters and English Lincolnshire
with its fairies and frogs. We might call the play flickeringly golden.

Now for the problem of political compliment in *Gallathea*. Is the
goddess Diana (one of the three chief gods of the play) meant, as some
scholars have suggested,[42] to reflect and to compliment Queen
Elizabeth herself? Diana's determined virginity, her lectures on the
subject to her nymphs, and the fact that Elizabeth was often praised
in the figure of the virgin goddess Diana/Cynthia, all suggest that she
is; yet in *Gallathea* Neptune and Venus are more powerful than
Diana. If Diana is indeed in part a reflection of Elizabeth—as a
goddess over whom Venus and Neptune have no direct power but
who must come to terms with them and with their power over
ordinary mortals—the compliment is not inappropriate and yet not
of the extreme kind that Elizabeth was used to receiving. Is irony, and
an emphasis on the human limitations even of monarchs, operating
here as well? This is possible but, as I have already noted, would
seem at first glance unlikely, given Lyly's dependence on the Queen's
favour; yet it would suit the nature of the play as I have interpreted it
so far. Let us leave the question hanging, for the moment, and
turn to *Loves Metamorphosis*.

In the two plot strands of *Loves Metamorphosis* the scene is darker
than in *Gallathea*. The plot devoted to the three foresters and three
nymphs emphasizes the violence and vengefulness of unrequited
passion; when the foresters find their loves to be unreturned, they
arrange for Cupid to metamorphose the unco-operative nymphs into
a stone, a flower and a bird. Cupid, traditionally the force of eros
supreme, is the one great on-stage god in the play;[43] and the powerful
offstage Neptune figures largely as a seducer. The finale in which the
nymphs accept the foresters is no real victory for love; the nymphs
give in to love because threatened with a further metamorphosis
into monsters if they do not yield. This is doubtless psychological
allegory, the nymphs overcoming immature desires for virginity
through fear of being unnatural; but the overall effect is strongly

42. E.g., Bond, II, p. 256, and Albert Feuillerat, *John Lyly* (Cambridge, 1910), p. 138.
43. Saccio (*Court Comedies*, pp. 162-65) sees Cupid as (uncharacteristically) representing Neoplatonic love in *LM*; but Cupid's traditional metaphoric meaning of pure
sexual passion cannot, I think, be easily discarded, since it is entirely in keeping with
his supreme power in earthly matters shown (and emphasized as earthly) in the play.
E.g., Erisichthon has apparently served Cupid in his attack on the arborified nymph of
chastity, Fidelia: see V. i. 29-33.

negative or ironic. And the foresters are willing to accept much bitterness in love for the sake of erotic fulfilment.[44]

> Let them curse all day, so I may haue but one kisse at night. (V.iii. 19-20)

> Let me bleed euerie minute with the prickles of the Rose, so I may enjoy but one hower the sauour. (V.iv. 144-145)

In the other plot strand a forest ruler wreaks violence on a resolutely chaste nymph metamorphosed to a tree, and then sells his daughter for money to feed himself. (Overtones of rape and of prostitution are present.[45]) The daughter, Protea, has previously been seduced by Neptune; and a siren attempts to lure Protea's lover, Petulius. This plot ends happily only because Protea has earned, through her seduction, access to Neptune, who allows her to undergo voluntary metamorphoses to escape her buyers and to save Petulius from the siren's clutches. Paul Parnell has suggested that here we see the saving Power of unselfish love,[46] which rings true enough; but such love—which also is found nowhere else in the play—involves weakness (V. ii. 5) and deception. As Michael Best puts it, "the only dramatic movement in this part of the play is the discovery and acceptance of imperfection."[47] We might also keep in mind that to Elizabethans the god Proteus, from whom Protea takes her name, was an ambiguous figure; he could represent man's potentiality, adaptability and civilizing powers, or unwelcome mutability and the deceptiveness of appearances.[48] John Weld suggests that Cupid's intervention in the foresters-and-nymphs plot becomes metaphorically the Christian God's in His love for and pardon of erring man (hardly likely, I think, given Cupid's pride and threats), but even then admits that the play's ending seems one of "humorous despair" over human nature.[49] The play *is* a triumph of love, but seems heavily qualified: as Petulius puts it, "A straunge discourse, . . . by which I find the gods amorous, and Virgines immortall, goddesses full of crueltie, and men of vnhappinesse" (V.ii. 1-3).

---

44. See, e.g., Best, pp. 78-79, and Stevenson, p. 171.
45. See Paul E. Parnell, "Moral Allegory in Lyly's *Loves Metamorphosis*," *SP*, LII (1955), pp. 6-8, and Best, pp. 79-80.
46. Parnell, pp. 1-16.
47. Best, p. 80.
48. A. Bartlett Giamatti, "Proteus Unbound: Some Versions of the Sea God in the Renaissance," in *The Disciplines of Criticism*, ed. Peter Demetz, Thomas Greene, and Lowry Nelson, Jr. (New Haven and London, 1968), pp. 437-75.
49. Weld, pp. 132 and 131.

Unlike *Gallathea*, *Loves Metamorphosis* also shows us no ideal past, even in a brief glimpse, nor does it give us any sensuous description of the pastoral landscape. The setting established in such brief references as "let vs into the woods" (IV. ii. 100) is purely factual; and the set itself—multiple, in part focused on a building (Cupid's temple), and involving the early cutting down of its tree (I.ii.)—is not as traditionally pastoral as *Gallathea*'s. The play is also more emotionally remote from us than *Gallathea*, not only because of the increased coldness of sexual love and related lack of sensuous landscape description but also because of its entirely classical setting. No Lincolnshire here; no fairies or frogs. Scholars have apparently not found the play to be particularly appealing on any grounds other than formal ones. They comment on its superb structure and pattern but have little else to say about the work.[50] As for the play's possible compliments to the Queen and her court, the chaste goddess Ceres, whose nymphs are wooed by the foresters, may reflect Queen Elizabeth,[51] but her role is minor. Moreover, she is definitely subservient to Cupid—which seems an odd way for Lyly to compliment the Queen unless, again, an emphasis on imperfection and limitations is his aim.[52]

Woman in the Moon is the darkest pastoral of all, developed from the Greek myth of Pandora as a pagan Eve-figure responsible (implicitly through erotic love) for all the ills of the earth. David Bevington has called the play "a melancholy instance of an image tarnished and a vision lost."[53] The newly created world without a woman in it is unsatisfactory, as without a child-bearer the human race is doomed to

---

50. E.g., Hunter in *Lyly and Peele* calls *LM* "in many ways the *purest* of his [Lyly's] plays; the least human, but the most sharply defined in terms of pattern" (p. 32). In *John Lyly* he says that *LM* is not as classically pastoral as *Gallathea* for "nothing positive is made out of the [pastoral] background" (p. 135), though he also calls it "one of the best of Lyly's plays" (p. 206). Exceptions are Parnell and, in part, Bernard F. Huppé, "Allegory of Love in Lyly's Court Comedies," *ELH*, XIV (1947), pp. 107-111, and Saccio.

51. See, e.g., John Dover Wilson, p. 112, Bond, III., p. 297, and Parnell, p. 5.

52. Hunter, *John Lyly*, pp. 211-12, denies any Ceres-Elizabeth connection. G. Wilson Knight, "Lyly," *RES*, XV (1939), p. 156, suggests (like Feuillerat, p. 193) that Ceres stands allegorically for married chastity or fertility—which is most unlikely but which would certainly rule out any identification of Elizabeth with Ceres. Bevington (p. 185) suggests that the play was not performed at court (the title page of the first edition does not mention specific court performance); presumably then we would not need to look for compliments to Elizabeth in it; but surely it would have been odd for Lyly to have written the play without court performance in mind, whatever ultimately happened to the work. And after all, the title page does call the play a "courtly" pastoral. See also Saccio, *Court Comedies*, p. 11, n. 1.

53. Bevington, p. 185.

extinction; and Pandora is created by Nature purposely as a breeder (a somewhat cold if accurate way of depicting the biological basis of the erotic impulse). But the creation of Pandora in this classical Eden causes only trouble. She is entirely at the mercy of the seven planets/gods who, envious of her, take turns at influencing her for the bad. She wreaks havoc among the four shepherds, who compete for her; and when she does choose a mate (under the influence of the one benign planet, Sol), she shortly afterwards cuckolds him and deceives her lovers, and ultimately runs lunatic. The ideal of producing children is quickly forgotten; the dialogue becomes active and filled with disagreements; and the plot becomes steadily more involved and potentially disordered as the play proceeds. In the end Pandora is translated by Nature into the sphere of the moon, where she is to govern future women in fickleness and lunacy. Her cuckolded, vengeful mate is doomed to follow her as the man in the moon, and her lover-servant Gunophilus is metamorphosed into a bush with which her mate then threatens to scratch her if ever she turns to look at him. John Weld has perceptively called this the eternal comic triangle of the foolish lover, tortured husband and fantastical wife;[54] and, as in the original myth, Pandora's eroticism is entirely destructive.

No other plot line relieves the harshness of the action. The seven planets mount in turn to sit on a throne raised above the main acting area, as each one in turn influences Pandora; all is under Nature's rule; and the whole play becomes processional, abstract and cold. The love which is its subject matter is the inevitable sex drive which binds the shepherds to a helplessly vixenish siren who leads them to unhappiness, vengefulness and an ultimate renunciation of love. The gods nearly all work actively against human happiness. Scholars in general have felt the harshness of the play (though Weld in some desperation—"the only possible reaction is laughter"—calls its tone jocular), and some have attempted to see it as a political pastoral indirectly critizing Queen Elizabeth in the person of Pandora (a name which her admirers sometimes gave her[55]) at a time when Lyly was losing hopes of favour at the Queen's hands.[56] At the least the drama

---

54. Weld, p. 121.
55. In its meaning as given above, p. 24. See E. C. Wilson, pp. 142-43, n. 37.
56. E.g., Felix E. Schelling, *Elizabethan Playwrights* (1925; rpt. New York, 1965), p. 53. Stevenson (citing Feuillerat, p. 233) even feels that the audience would see Queen Elizabeth in Pandora whatever Lyly intended (p. 162). Best (p. 85) advances and then retracts the suggestion that Nature in WM is meant to reflect Elizabeth.

is usually regarded as a bitter satire against women in general.[57] As Hunter, Saccio, Bevington and others have pointed out, however, no matter how bitter Lyly might have felt about Elizabeth's treatment of him (he hoped long, and in vain, for significant favours from her), it would have been sheer madness for him to have criticized her in the character of Pandora.[58] However restive he might have become by about 1593 at Elizabeth's failure to advance him, he was still hoping for good fortune, as shown by his later petitions to the Queen.[59] Leaving aside as irrelevant here the matter of *Woman in the Moon's* auspices (the title page of the first edition does not mention an acting company, and some scholars have suggested that Lyly wrote the play for adult actors in the 1590s after the boys' companies had been suppressed[60]), we do know from the quarto title page that the play was performed before the Queen. We also know that Elizabeth never took personal criticisms lightly. A satiric attack on her, or even on women in general, in her own court, would at the very least have required its author to have given up at once all further hopes of court favour.

But what, then, are we to make of *Woman in the Moon?* As a pastoral it seems more than *Gallathea* and even *Loves Metamorphosis* to be anti-pastoral, showing the existence of no golden ideal even at the innocent beginnings of time,[61] and only human unhappiness to be possible through erotic fulfilment.[62] And as court entertainment it seems, if not to move into insult rather than compliment, at least to be not particularly suited to please the Queen and her ladies.[63]

57. E.g.: Bradbrook, *Growth*, p. 63; Marco Mincoff, "Shakespeare and Lyly," *ShS*, XIV (1961), p. 18; Jeffery, pp. 74-75 (who points out that the denunciation of women is a recurring motif in Italian eclogues and pastoral drama); Benbow, p. 50; Joseph W. Houppert, *John Lyly* (Boston, 1975), pp. 124-25; Price, p. 40. Some critics go only part way in this direction, not referring to satire but nevertheless talking about the play as a picture of womankind: see, e.g., Huppé, pp. 111-13, and also Hunter, *John Lyly*, p. 145, Weld, p. 121, and E. C. Wilson, pp. 142-43.
58. See especially Hunter, *John Lyly*, pp. 219-20, and also Bevington, p. 185. Bond also deals with the problem, II, pp. 256-57, n. 1.
59. See Hunter, *John Lyly*, pp. 85-88.
60. For adult auspices as probable, see, e.g., Hunter (*John Lyly*, pp. 82-83, and *Lyly and Peele*, pp. 35-36), Best (p. 81), Saccio (*Court Comedies*, p. 19), and Benbow (pp. 49-50); for boy company auspices, see Shapiro (p. 145). In fact the pageant-like nature of *WM* would have suited adult *or* child actors.
61. Note that Saturn was the traditional ruler of the Golden Age, which came to an end with his overthrow by Jupiter; but in *WM* even from the beginning Saturn is merely one of seven planets/gods taking a turn (albeit first) at influencing Pandora.
62. Best, p. 85, interprets the play as dealing with the inevitable imperfection of human love.
63. Bradbrook, however, interestingly suggests (*Player*, p. 232) that *WM* attacks a specific court lady, Ann Vavasour, disliked by the Queen.

It is of course highly likely that Lyly is more the precursor of the later private theatre dramatists such as Marston and at times Middleton than we have tended to think. Certainly one fruitful way of approaching his pastorals is to see them as emphasizing, through unexpected manipulation of pastoral conventions and audience expectations, human and monarchical limitations. For example, as Bradbrook has pointed out, generally in Lyly's work erotic love is treated as a kind of disease.[64] No pastoral celebration, here, of human sexuality. And, after all, Christianity denied any kind of ideal status to man—and especially to his sexuality—since the fall in Eden. The pastoral in Christian times is bound to be about human limitations (physical, mental, social); and Lyly's plays, although set in pagan times, were written and performed in Christian ones, for Christian audiences. Our fault is perhaps in expecting Lyly to be as non-Christian as his play settings. His Elizabethan audiences would have had no such expectation.[65]

It is also possible that, as dramatic craftsman supreme, Lyly is attempting to show in his pastorals that a golden world exists, and has always existed, only aesthetically, in artistic craftsmanship: in this case in the beautifully balanced phrasing, dialogue, moral allegorization and choreographed stage movements of his dramas. An important part of the golden world of the pastoral has always been very much the artistic style of its creator—an aesthetic beauty and order in part rising out of the subject matter and in part imposed upon it by the artist. The clash between nature and art—perhaps *the* major theme of the pastoral[66]—is resolved in the work of art itself: natural subject matter (real) presented through the writer's art (ideal) as an ultimately beautiful construct both artificial and natural. The ultimate image of this synthesis is the statue of Hermione at the end of the *Winter's Tale*.

It is perhaps significant that the most pastoral scene in *Midas* involves a competition of artists: the music contest between Pan and Apollo, in which Apollo's polished harmony proves Apollo's superiority to Pan, who cannot integrate his more rustic performance. (Pan's performance is all very well in its own way, but comparison

---

64. Bradbrook, *Growth*, p. 63.
65. Lyly's Christianity keeps slipping into his classical settings and plots: e.g., the "Church-dore" in *Gallathea*, V. iii. 171. A few recent analyses of Endimion have taken a Christian tack: e.g., Robert S. Knapp, "The Monarchy of Love in Lyly's *Endimion*," *MP*, LXXIII (1975-76), pp. 353-67, and Carolyn Ruth Swift Lenz, "The Allegory of Wisdom in Lyly's *Endimion*," *CompD*, X (1976-77), pp. 235-57; and see also Saccio, "The Oddity of Lyly's *Endimion*," in *The Elizabethan Theatre* V, ed. G. R. Hibbard (Toronto, 1975), p. 100.
66. See, e.g., Tayler, p. 5.

makes it odious.[67]) In *Woman in the Moon* the only benign influence exerted upon Pandora is that of Sol (god of creative artists), while the whole play is referred to in the Prologue as a poet's dream in Phoebus' holy bower (11. 17-18)—an artificial construct designed to please artistically. This artistic focus, however, seems an extreme narrowing of the visionary pastoral, though it is certainly one more aspect of Lyly's work that should not be overlooked.[68] And none of this, alone, is really what we would expect of a dramatist writing above all to please the Queen and her court.

And now, finally, we reach the main point that I would like to make. I want to argue that in at least one approach to Lyly's pastorals— through their staging as court entertainments—we can see the dramas functioning after all as traditionally visionary pastoral works and as fulsome compliments to the Queen. In the late sixteenth century in England, but before 1580, the dramatic pastoral seems to have occurred most notably, though episodically, in the royal entertainments presented to the Queen on her progresses through the noble estates of the English countryside.[69] In estate entertainments, as at the Earl of Leicester's Kenilworth Castle in 1575, the entire rural parkland of the estate itself became a pastoral stage—an "Arcadian world," as David Bergeron has put it[70]—upon which a variety of formal entertainments were performed outdoors, before the Queen, during the days of her stay; and at least some of these entertainments were also inevitably pastoral themselves. At the Queen's visit to Kenilworth, for example, an ivy-and-moss-covered Savage Man meets and praises the Queen as she returns from hunting, a burlesque rural marriage takes place, Sylvanus tells the Queen on her final hunt a tale of love involving Diana's nymph Zabeta, and nature mourns at the Queen's departure.[71] At Woodstock, later in the same summer,

67. Hunter (*John Lyly*, p. 181) suggests that Pan's music is "as good (in its own way) as that of Apollo," but Stephen S. Hilliard, "Lyly's *Midas* as an Allegory of Tyranny," *SEL*, XII (1972), pp. 243-58, rightly points out (pp. 245-46) the traditional folly of the choice of Pan's music over Apollo's. Saccio (*Court Comedies*, p. 196) also argues persuasively for Apollo's superiority.
68. Saccio (*Court Comedies*, p. 221) finds a "golden world" in the artistry of Lyly's pastorals.
69. Ashley H. Thorndike made this point as long ago as 1899, in "The Pastoral Element in the English Drama before 1605," *MLN*, XIV (1899), pp. 114-23, and posited the development of pastoral drama in England, as in Italy, from public pageants (p. 115). See also Young, pp. 13-15.
70. David M. Bergeron, *English Civic Pageantry 1558-1642* (Columbia, S.C., 1971), p. 30.
71. Ibid., pp. 30-35; John Nichols, *The Progresses and Public Processions of Queen Elizabeth*, 3 vols. (London, 1823), I, pp. 485-523.

Elizabeth is seated in an ivy-covered bower to listen to a tale by a hermit, and later music and song come from an oak tree.[72] In the most fully developed extant pastoral entertainment before the 1580s, in 1578 at Wanstead, Elizabeth is entertained in garden and grove with a competition between a shepherd and a forester for the love of the Lady of May; and the show includes a typically pastoral singing contest and debate.[73] We thus have in estate entertainments both an overall pastoral milieu and some specifically pastoral shows within that environment.

Not surprisingly, as compliments to Queen Elizabeth, these estate entertainments rely upon her as an ordering centre. They were written, as Bergeron has convincingly shown,[74] around the physical participation of the Queen herself and her court. The actors often speak directly to the Queen; she is herself physically involved in the action; and on at least one occasion, at Wanstead, she is called upon to deliver a judgment, within the show, affecting its outcome: decreeing whether shepherd or forester better deserves the May Lady. The monarch herself is the principal actor on the estate stage, and the shows depend upon her presence for their meaning and order. "The theme that binds all the pageants . . . together," writes Bergeron (though he is here speaking not just of pastoral entertainments), "is the celebration of Elizabeth's power, her spiritual, mystical, transforming power."[75] Elizabeth at Kenilworth is "a regenerating and liberating force"; "gods bring her gifts, wild men are tamed, the fearful are set free."[76] She supersedes the classical gods, who become obedient to her rule. Looking further ahead in time, into the 1590s (though here we are mainly—perhaps entirely—after the time of Lyly's pastoral plays): at Bisham (1592) the Queen tames a wild man, overcomes Pan more effectively than could Apollo, and rules Ceres;[77] at Sudeley (1592) she restores Daphne and brings a golden world to the Cotswold shepherds.[78] This is of course not only flattering to the Queen but is in line with orthodox Renaissance (and Christian) political theory. The monarch is God's agent on earth; the court is superior to the country. As Touchstone says of the country life in

72. Bergeron, pp. 35-36.
73. Ibid., pp. 36-37; Nichols, II, pp. 94-103.
74. Bergeron, pp. 9-64.
75. Ibid., p. 11.
76. Ibid., p. 35.
77. Bond, I, pp. 472-73, 475, 476-77.
78. Ibid., pp. 480-81.

As You Like It, "in respect it is in the fields, it pleaseth me well; but in respect it is not in the court, it is tedious" (III. ii. 17-19).[79]

In estate entertainments, then, the pastoral tends to be inclusive. Elizabeth herself as Queen and as audience becomes also the chief "stage" presence: the focus of the work and the final arbiter of the action. All problems are solved, all disorders harmonized, through the presence of the "goddess" Eliza, Queen of classical shepherds and of Christian England, in a new golden age.[80]

> Live here, good Queene, live here; you are amongst your friends;...
> Dame Ceres and Dame Flora both will with you still indure.
> Diana would be glad to meet you in the chase;
> Silvanus and the Forest Gods would follow you apace.
> Yea, Pan would pipe his part such daunces as he can:
> Or els Apollo musicke make, and Mars would be your man.[81]

"Throughout these progress entertainments . . . one constant feature dominates: the rather complete apotheosis of Elizabeth. . . . Mythological gods and goddesses surrender their claims on deity in her presence, the one who seemingly embodies all virtue."[82]

Here we are also in part in the tradition of the Tudor court masque,[83] an occasional show in which the monarch traditionally participated, if not simply through physical presence then also through dancing; and Henry VIII (though not Elizabeth) even acted a variety of masque roles: what Marie Axton has described as the playing of multiple roles which expressed his complex power.[84] Now, what happens when the outdoor pastoral entertainment moves indoors, as a combination of entertainment, masque and stage play?

George Peele's pastoral *Arraignment of Paris* (c.1581) shows what can happen, for this play or court entertainment depends for its meaning, like the estate pastorals, on the watching Queen Elizabeth, who resolves the plot difficulties at its end simply by her presence in the hall. The golden ball which the shepherd Paris must give to the fairest of three pagan goddesses, Venus, Juno and Pallas, is awarded in Peele's play to the watching Elizabeth, who combines in her one person the various excellencies of all three goddesses and more. "This

79. The quotation is from the text of *As You Like It* in *The Riverside Shakespeare*, textual ed., G. Blakemore Evans (Boston, 1974).
80. For Elizabeth as the ruler of a new golden age, see Cooper, pp. 204-205, and n. 29, above.
81. Nichols, I, p. 522; at Kenilworth.
82. Bergeron, p. 63.
83. Greg, p. 370, comments on the early connection of pastoral with masque.
84. Axton, pp. 25-26.

Paragon, this onely this is shee, / In whom do meete so manie giftes in one, / On whom our countrie gods so often gaze."[85] Elizabeth thus silently participates in the action of the play—and in multiple personae, as the various goddesses combined. Without Elizabeth the play could not reach a happy conclusion, but would point inevitably, as in the original myth, only towards the abduction of Helen and the destruction of Troy. With Elizabeth, seen in the tradition of the ruler of a second Troy (ll. 1150-54), the action moves into harmony and peace. A second, preserved Troy has replaced the first (which was destroyed as a result of Paris' award of the prize to Venus); the imperfect world of classical history and mythology has been replaced by the new and golden Elizabethan age. The comic resolution of Peele's play, both because of Elizabeth's presence and because this kind of resolution of the story of Paris' judgment was a "commonplace of Renaissance flattery" in pageants and in poems,[86] is doubtless implicit throughout the action, although only at the very end of the drama do the actors physically and explicitly turn to Elizabeth. The court audience, watching not only the play but also the Queen-watching-the-play, would *see* long before it *heard about* the importance of her physical presence to the unfolding action. With Elizabeth the play moves from past to present, from an insecure pagan world to a stable Christian one, from an old flawed ideal to a new dispensation.[87] The pastoral *Arraignment* is thus simultaneously stage play and court entertainment, and in its formal stage movements and use of a special actor-audience relationship also resembles masque.[88] David Bevington sees it as belonging to what he calls a new genre: the flattering courtly play of the 1580s, in which compliments to Elizabeth are "the nucleus of dramatic meaning." "Elizabeth becomes the controller of human destiny, superior to the Olympian gods and goddesses, the leader of a new society explicitly contrasted with the foibles of men in ancient legend or romance."[89]

I suggest that a fruitful way of looking at Lyly's court pastorals is as entertainments implicitly involving the Queen as much as Peele's play explicitly involves her. And here we must consider how Lyly's plays were staged at court in the 1580s and early 1590s. There is some controversy over details, but it is generally agreed today that, at court,

---

85. Benbow's edn., ll. 1166-68.
86. Benbow, p. 20.
87. See, e.g., Bevington, pp. 170-71.
88. See, e.g., Stephen Orgel, *The Jonsonian Masque* (Cambridge, Mass., 1967), pp. 6-7, and Benbow, pp. 46-47.
89. Bevington, p. 168.

entertainments such as Peele's *Arraignment* and Lyly's plays would have been performed in a large hall temporarily fitted out for acting, with a playing area (raised or not) probably at one end, though possibly sometimes in the centre of the hall or in multiple locations around the room.[90] The Queen might be seated in/on the playing area or in front of it; either way, she would occupy a raised chair or throne and be as much a part of the total spectacle as the entertainment being performed for her.[91] As Hunter writes, "The Queen . . . was not only the principal spectator, but almost the principal performer ('the observed of all observers')."[92] And Stephen Orgel concludes, "At these performances what the rest of the spectators watched was not a play but the queen at a play, and their response would have been not simply to the drama, but to the relationship between the drama and its primary audience, the royal spectator."[93] Note that the physical positioning of the Queen above the rest of the court also places her in a special relationship with the actors. If they are on a raised stage, her raised throne in front of it associates her with them as much as with the seated court beside and behind her. If they are not on a raised stage, she, God-like, presides from above over court and play alike. Or if she is in/on the playing area itself, again she presides over both court and actors, in closer association this time with the play world than with the court world. Inevitably through staging she becomes a notable part of the play, regardless of whether the dramatic dialogue makes this explicit; and yet she is also differentiated from the actors, as a rival focus to them. When thematically the Queen is brought explicitly into court entertainment, as in the *Arraignment*, the dialogue and staging effect support one another; in Peele's work she is seen as like the pagan goddesses being depicted before her, but as greater than they, a presiding supreme deity over all; and as a combination of Venus, Juno, Pallas and Diana she brings a new golden age into being. G. K. Hunter points out that this kind of representation is not simply flattery of the Queen but didacticism: "the myth represents what ought to be";[94] the dramatic game, including the total spectacle, gets at the eternal truth beneath mutable accidentals. The play both as

90. See Hunter, *John Lyly*, pp. 105-106, and Shapiro, pp. 33-34. The Tudor masque usually took place in the centre of the hall and sometimes with no raised stage but simply with various properties distributed about the floor (Orgel, *Jonsonian Masque*, p. 9).
91. See Hunter, *John Lyly*, pp. 105-107.
92. Hunter, *Lyly and Peele*, p. 23.
93. Stephen Orgel, *The Illusion of Power: Political Theater in the English Renaissance* (Berkeley, Los Angeles and London, 1975), p. 9; see also pp. 14-16.
94. *John Lyly*, pp. 141-42.

heard and as seen represents the Renaissance visionary ideal of political rule.

With this in mind, let us turn again to Lyly's pastorals. Lyly's plays, it is true, were written for performance not only before the Queen but also before a paying audience, as nominal "rehearsals" for court performance, in the intimate private theatres of the Blackfriars and St. Paul's. Still, Lyly's main purpose in playwriting would have been to please the Queen; that way, only, lay court advancement and possible wealth. Court performance would have been the *raison d'être* of Lyly's work.[95] The challenge for Lyly would have been to write plays involving the Queen and yet, unlike the *Arraignment*, existing independently of her as well—realizable without her, but fully complete only in her presence.

Let us see what the presence of the Queen as silent performer does to our interpretation of *Gallathea, Loves Metamorphosis,* and *Woman in the Moon.* Of these three plays only *Gallathea* directly addresses the Queen in an extant prologue; but from the prologues and epilogues which have come down with the texts of some of Lyly's other plays (*Campaspe, Sapho and Phao, Endimion*) we may deduce that customarily, for court performance, a special prologue and epilogue were written which usually addressed the sovereign directly and made her explicitly at the opening and close of the play a part of its dramatic world. Each play would begin clearly with an overview, as it were, of the Queen watching a play, would move partially away from this into close-ups of the specific dramatic action, and would then move back into an overview at the close. But throughout the action the watching Queen could never be forgotten.

Woman in the Moon, the most masque-like of Lyly's plays, is the most interesting to examine as a staged court pastoral. Here Lyly takes care to show a central woman who is not a monarch. The Prologue tells us (1. 6) that in Utopia only Nature is queen; we are in a pagan Eden where political rule is unknown, and at her creation Pandora is wholly subservient to Nature. Next she becomes a helpless victim of planetary influences. The dialogue emphasizes her earthliness: she is a "merror of the earth" (I. i. 60), an "earthly starre" (I. i. 134), and lies on the ground (I. i. 218); she acts against royal ceremony and order (I. i. 177-226), and when Jupiter wishes to tempt her, he does so with promises of sovereignty. She wrongly demands the rites of majesty from her servant Gunophilus and from the shepherds when she is

95. Shapiro logically argues that court plays at this period would be above all offerings to the Queen and only secondarily for private theatre profit: see pp. 15-16, 32-33, 38.

under the malign influence of Jupiter; and she lacks a throne (II. i. 46). She fights (II. i. 195-200), takes a husband, commits adultery, is associated with the destructive Helen of Troy (III. ii. 66-67 and IV. i. 134-36), and at the play's end is to stay with the moon, who is characterized as the "lowest of the erring starres" (V. i. 2) and is not, either, an Elizabeth figure. (The traditional association of Elizabeth with the moon was with Diana/Cynthia in her virgin-goddess aspect, and with the eternal renewal of the moon's youth through time.) The play seems generally critical of sexuality, and unrelated (except in its philosophical anti-eroticism, which presumably would have pleased Elizabeth) to the court.

In court staging, however, *Woman in the Moon* for all its bitterness surprisingly can become a visionary golden pastoral. The stage presentation of the play demands, significantly, a raised throne for the planets who ascend in turn to exert their influence over Pandora. This raised throne could be on an upper acting area but is more likely at centre-stage rear: Jupiter on his seat at one point must hand a sceptre to Pandora on earth (II. i. 44). A trap door is also required, through which the tricked husband goes down into a cave, *ad inferos* (III. ii. 241): and here we have a pagan version of the three-level heaven-earth-hell stage of some medieval mystery plays. But in court performance there is another enthroned divinity as part of the total dramatic scene. Either beside the throne of the gods or opposite it, on the stage or facing it, is the canopied chair of state of Elizabeth; and thus she becomes equated not with Pandora (an anti-ceremonial figure under Saturn; a personification of the disruptiveness of erotic love; a pretender, under Jupiter, to sovereignty—cf. Lucifer aspiring to God's throne in medieval creation drama) but with the influential planets/ pagan deities. Moreover, as a constant *one* to their episodic sequence of seven, she becomes, as the play proceeds, a stable alternative to their variety, a point of constancy in an inconstant world.[96] Elizabeth, the staging implies, is superior not only to Pandora but also to the classical deities.[97] Lyly is using balance and contrast in total staging, just as he uses them in dialogue, character, and scene within the play, to make a thematic point.[98] The technique also harks back to the opposing Heaven and Hell mansion stages of medieval dramatic tradition.

The world of *Woman in the Moon* is that of a pagan Eden, and Lyly concentrates on showing us its flaws. No prelapsarian golden age here,

96. Much mutability is a mark of the Iron, not Golden, Age.
97. Elizabeth was commonly represented in this way in the literature of the period. See Cooper, pp. 205-206, and Bergeron, p. 63.

but an imperfect and disordered pagan world from the start, under Nature's sovereignty alone; and since this is the world of fallible human nature, no happy resolution of the action is possible within the play itself. But the order and stability represented by the Queen's presence in the total dramatic scene suggests throughout a golden age in the Christian present, when (virgin) Queen and dramatist together combine to create order out of chaos.[99] *Woman in the Moon* becomes implicitly the supreme pastoral compliment to Elizabeth, who does not merely preside over a new golden age but like the artist creates the golden ideal where before there was none: politically, morally and, as the inspirer of artists, artistically. She is the (Christian) courtly equivalent of the Christian redeemer—regeneration personified. A performance of *Woman in the Moon* without Elizabeth present would indeed be merely a rehearsal, incomplete. The play becomes fully realized (and thus like masque is occasional) only in court performance.[100]

Let us turn now from *Woman in the Moon* briefly to *Gallathea*. Like *Woman in the Moon* with its dramatic focus on the throne of the gods versus the throne of Queen Elizabeth, *Gallathea* with its single set piece of a large oak tree sacred to the play's supreme god, Neptune, creates in total court staging two foci: tree (pagan countryside) and throne (Elizabethan court). Here, within the total spectacle only, is the typical court-country contrast of the pastoral—and again Lyly emphasizes the imperfections of the pagan rural world, so as to contrast it implicitly with the courtly and Christian order represented by Elizabeth. This world is postlapsarian, not golden. *Gallathea* is a play of transformations, of mutability, and ends like the *Arraignment* with a focus on separate gods on stage and in power over mortal affairs, and with Venus and Diana still in conflicting positions.[101] As tradi-

---

98. Saccio (*Court Comedies*, pp. 22-25) has already pointed out the importance of the patterning of physical properties (of place) on the Lylian stage; I am extending his point to include one more property/location—Queen Elizabeth's throne. In this volume (p. 153) Eugene Waith suggests a similar use of the throne in masque staging in France at this period.
99. For Elizabeth as the cause of pastoral poetry, see Cooper, p. 207, and also Terry Comito, "The Lady in a Landscape and the Poetics of Elizabethan Pastoral," *UTQ*, XLI (1971-72), pp. 200-218. Harold E. Toliver, *Pastoral: Forms and Attitudes* (London and Berkeley, 1971) notes (p. 24) that in Italian pastoral masques often the Golden Age is restored by a prince allegorically situated at the centre of the pageantry.
100. The relationship of play alone to play-plus-court is significantly like that of antimasque to masque proper (with royalty and nobility also traditionally taking part in the formal and ordered masque proper).
101. Scragg, pp. 131-32. G. K. Hunter (*John Lyly*, p. 144) has pointed out that "the sixteenth century was bequeathed a whole tradition where gods and goddesses were set in postures of opposition over moral problems."

tionally Elizabeth was portrayed as surpassing and combining the various excellencies of the separate pagan deities, in *Gallathea* implicitly as in the *Arraignment* explicitly we may see her as expressing in her single physical presence, enthroned in the order of her court, a combination and harmonizing of virtues which creates a present golden world compared to the imperfect pagan past of the play. In the pagan world of Neptune, Diana, Venus and Cupid, either man's folly places him at the mercy of capricious and selfish deities, so that his happiness becomes a matter of chance, or his folly brings him to the point where only in fiction can human happiness be achieved. The single, unchanging, synthesizing figure of Elizabeth before her court is a silent reminder of the order of the golden Elizabethan state. She becomes a new Tree of Life, perfecting the old.[102]

Finally, *Loves Metamorphosis*. Here the set is more complex; it involves at least two and probably three definite locations: Cupid's temple, Ceres' tree (cut down in I. ii), and the seashore. Here the physically disunified and flawed pastoral world (emblematized, for example, in the felled tree) is implicitly contrasted with the unified and visually perfect court world before which it is presented. Cupid, the siren, Ceres, the absent Neptune: each is either destructive to men or insufficient for their lasting happiness; but their powers for good are combined and surpassed in the watching Elizabeth, supreme Christian ruler of a new court of love.

In modern examination of the staging of Lyly's three pastorals thus lies the key to one possible interpretative response to the works: a response dependent on seeing the plays in historical time, as pastoral entertainments centred on Queen Elizabeth. Without the Queen's presence the plays as pastorals are ironic or incomplete; they show on all levels a flawed, not golden, world, full of erring mortals and capricious gods and without internal capacity for regeneration. This is the real world of fallible, erotically enslaved humanity, for which regenerative pastoralism cannot exist. Enter Elizabeth, enthroned in state as a focal point for the entertainment, and the audience itself with the Queen as its centre becomes, as a political entity, the ordered, golden ideal: court over country, art over nature, masque

---

102. The oak, associated in *Gallathea* with Neptune, the play's chief deity, was well known as a royal tree (Saccio, *Court Comedies*, p. 116); and in the Entertainment at Cowdray, 1591 (Bond, I, p. 425), Queen Elizabeth is described (in direct address) as an oak. On the emblematic use of landscape scenery in English pageantry in general, see David M. Bergeron, "Symbolic Landscape in English Civic Pageantry," *RenQ*, XXII (1969), pp. 32-37; and on the iconographic and stage tradition of the tree, see Werner Habicht, "Tree Properties and Tree Scenes in Elizabethan Theater," *RenD*, N. S. IV (1971), pp. 69-92.

over antimasque, Christianity over paganism, civilization over barbarism.[103] (Compare Shakespeare's pastorals, in which the court is also ultimately superior to the country, although in Shakespeare the country world does have its own regenerative power.) Significantly, Lyly's two partial pastorals, *Midas* and *Sapho and Phao*, also ultimately reject the pastoral world as insufficient—above all because it is inferior to the court. In *Midas* rustic Pan is defeated by courtly Apollo (the sun god, patron of the arts, and metaphoric equivalent of earthly monarchs); and Midas, who has allied himself with Pan and rules in an iron age of war, wealth and ambition,[104] must learn to model himself instead on the courtly ruler of Lesbos (a reflection of the watching Queen).[105] In *Sapho and Phao* the rustic Phao comes to see the superiority of the court, where "are times in perfection" (I. ii. 16), over the country; but his non-courtly origin condemns him (unlike Endimion) to eternal separation from the courtly ideal.[106]

Lyly's dramatic pastorals thus are golden not in internal subject matter but in total artistic treatment of that subject matter—an artistry not simply of dramatic style and structure but also of inclusive staging which moves us from art to life and which shows in court performance the golden age of the returned Astraea, Elizabeth, as in every way superior to the pagan Eden of *Woman in the Moon*, the postlapsarian world of *Gallathea*, and the vengeful eros-dominated world of *Loves Metamorphosis*. Interestingly, the pastoral which comes closest in its internal subject matter to Elizabethan life, *Gallathea*, is also the most harmonious of Lyly's three full pastorals; the one furthest from Elizabethan life, *Woman in the Moon*, is internally the darkest. Arcadia is realized only through and at the court of Elizabeth.

From the perspective of court performance, then, Lyly's pastorals are traditionally golden: in supreme compliment to the Queen presenting a golden present in contrast to a flawed past. But Lyly could both have his cake and eat it too. In private theatre performance, without the court context, the pastorals would become ironic; and

103. We have lately become used to the idea of Elizabethan staging as often emblematic, but have not yet become accustomed to dealing with the total audience-inclusive effect of civic and courtly entertainments.

104. See Henry Kamen, "Golden age, iron age: a conflict of concepts in the Renaissance," *JMRS*, IV (1974), pp. 144-52.

105. See also Lancashire, Lyly's *Gallathea* and *Midas*, p. xix, on the song to Apollo at the play's end as probably sung to Elizabeth.

106. On the late sixteenth-century elevation of court above country, in masque, see Orgel, *Illusion*, pp. 49-50. Before 1616 the typical masque using pastoral began, like *S&P*, with the wildness of nature and ended with sophistication and complex order.

Elsewhere in this volume (p. 174) James Yoch discusses the imperfections of the pagan gods and the country world as presented in Italian pastoral masques of the period.

even at court, cynics in the audience could think about the flawed personal realities beneath the golden public façade of Elizabeth's political world. (This is where specific political allegory in the plays fits in.) Indeed, the plays' artistic ordering of the subject matter of flawed humanity also might be taken as an image of the political Elizabethan ordering of a personally flawed court world. But the limitations, or flaws, *are* personal; the ideal is public, political, abstract. The effect is Platonic: ideal form and imperfect specific realizations. Lyly presents to us a world both pastoral and courtly, and an age simultaneously of iron and of gold.

In Lyly's pastoral plays court and country are two separate locations which become fused in the final court performance which turns irony to celebration.[107] The technique is dependent upon the boys' companies which acted Lyly's plays being troupes existing above all for the Queen's service. And thus the technique could be used only in the 1580s, for after the suppression of the boys' troupes throughout the 1590s, in the early seventeenth century the reactivated boys' companies became essentially identical to adult companies in performance conditions. They had become divorced from ultimate court performance as their *raison d'être*.[108] And their plays, no longer conditioned by final court performance, became purely satiric—a triumph of human limitations, as subject matter, over golden ideals. Astraea returned to heaven; the day of the Elizabethan court drama had passed.

107. Public-theatre pastorals tend to combine court and country within the play itself.
108. See Bradbrook, *Player*, pp. 213, 234-40.

The Monster in Shakespeare's Landscape

JAMES BLACK

My theme is Shakespeare's teratologies: a teratology having been recognized since the seventeenth century as a discourse or narrative concerning prodigies, or a marvellous tale; and since the nineteenth century as the study of monstrosities or abnormal formations. Monsters and prodigies are conveniently defined by Ambrose Parey, whose *Works* were translated into English in 1634:

> Wee call Monsters, what things soever are brought forth contrary to the common decree and order of natu₁e. So wee terme that infant monstrous, which is borne with one arme alone, or with two heads. But we define Prodigies, those things which happen contrary to the whole course of nature, that is, altogether differing and dissenting from nature: as, if a woman should bee delivered of a Snake, or a Dogge.[1]

Shakespeare's first tetralogy of histories is a teratology because they present Richard of Gloucester, both misshapen monster and prodigy who made the midwife wonder and the women cry (*3 Henry VI*, V. vii. 68-83), and Caliban makes a teratology of *The Tempest*. But because I want to discuss more disquietingly possible monsters than are to be found in those plays (or among the aberrations and chimeras in Ovid) I am going to use the theme of monsters to link, perhaps prodigiously, two plays not often closely associated with one another, *A Midsummer Night's Dream* and *King Lear*.

In both the *Dream* and *Lear* there is a swift rush to the open air and to a world which is upside-down. Each opening movement has the abruptness—indeed, in the *Dream* some parallel details—of the

---

1. Ambroise Paré, *The Workes of Ambrose Parey*, trans. T. Johnson (London; 1649), p. 648.

beginning of *The Faerie Queene* and other Spenserian adventures. For instance, in Book One of *The Faerie Queene* Redcrosse and Una come, after only six introductory and scene-setting stanzas, into the Wood of Error where they promptly are entangled and set on a course of trials. So in the first two scenes of the *Dream* the lovers and the mechanicals turn their faces to the Wood near Athens, while in the first scene of *Lear* the King, forgetting himself, makes inevitable his thrusting-out into a landscape which on his map may be "champaigns rich'd, . . . plenteous rivers and wide-skirted meads"[2] but in reality is a world of unaccommodation. Wandering in the wood, Lysander expresses the plight of Redcrosse, Una and Lear as well as that of the *Dream's* lovers when he admits, "To speak truth—I have forgot our way" (*Dream*, II. ii. 41-2).

In a Spenserian telling, a monster of some kind usually lurks in the heart of the wood. Shakespeare conceals the boar there in *Venus and Adonis*—and of course that white boar Richard III roots about in his political thicket. As Venus desperately searches for Adonis she is in a maze, the world reeling about her:

> A thousand spleens bear her a thousand ways;
> She treads the path that she untreads again;
> Her more than haste is mated with delays,
> Like the proceedings of a drunken brain. (ll.907-10)

So in the first wood scene of the *Dream* things turn until they are upside-down. Oberon's and Titania's quarrel has made

> The seasons alter; hoary-headed frosts
> Fall in the fresh lap of the crimson rose,
> And on old Hiems' thin and icy crown
> An odorous chaplet of sweet summer buds
> Is as in mockery set. The spring, the summer,
> The childing autumn, angry winter change
> Their wonted liveries, and the mazed world
> By their increase now knows not which is which.
> And this same progeny of evils
> Comes from our debate, from our dissension.
> We are their parents and original. (II. i. 107-17)

Parents and progeny of evils: more than the practical jokes of Puck

---

2. The New Arden, *King Lear*, ed. Kenneth Muir (London, 1963), I. i. 64-65. All subsequent references to *King Lear* cite this edition. *Midsummer Night's Dream* citations are to the New Penguin edition, ed. Stanley Wells (Harmondsworth, 1967).

are figured here; it seems that in a world of comic turnabout we already look forward to *King Lear*.

But, of course, parents and progeny are a strong preoccupation of Shakespeare's from the marriage sonnets to the betrothal masque of *The Tempest*. We might notice that in the hearty salesmanship of those sonnets a kind of genetic theory is being propounded—that the parents' beauty (or lack of it) gets pretty well exactly reproduced:

> Let those whom Nature hath not made for store,
> Harsh, featureless, and rude, barrenly perish:
> Look, whom she best endow'd she gave the more;
> Which bounteous gift thou shouldst in bounty cherish
>
> (Sonnet 11);

"Thou art thy mother's glass" (Sonnet 3); "[Nature] carv'd thee for her seal, and meant thereby/Thou shouldst print more, not let that copy die" (Sonnet 11). The "printing" or "stamping" seems on balance to be done mainly by the male parent. Henry V says that his father "was thinking of civil wars when he got me; therefore was I created with a stubborn visage, with an aspect of iron" (*Henry V*, V. ii. 242-44); despite the fact that Caliban has received some of his distressing physical features from his mother Sycorax, he's cheerfully convinced that had he been allowed his way with Miranda he would have peopled all the isle with reproductions of himself, and Prospero appears to share this conviction. Perdita, of course, has the wonderful and (to Leontes) the unsettling quality of looking when an infant exactly like her father (*Winter's Tale* II. iii. 95-108) and when a girl like her mother (V. i. 223-28), but usually Shakespeare suggests that women take on impressions rather than give them. In *Measure for Measure* Claudio is in trouble with the law for "[Coining] Heaven's image,/In stamps that are forbid", (II. iv. 45-46) and Isabella concedes to Angelo that women are frail "and credulous to false prints" (II. iv. 128-30).

From the beginning of the *Dream* this printing or coining idea receives heavy emphasis. Egeus complains that Lysander has with tokens, trifles and verses "stolen the impression of [Hermia's] fantasy" (I. i. 30-32). Theseus picks up the theme:

> What say you, Hermia? Be advised, fair maid:
> To you your father should be as a god;
> One that composed your beauties—yea, and one
> To whom you are but as a form in wax
> By him imprinted, and within his power
> To leave the figure or disfigure it. (I. i. 46-51)

53

And also early in the play there is that curious and charming account of a pregnant female taking an impression from what she sees. Titania is refusing Oberon the changeling boy:

> His mother was a votaress of my order,
> And in the spiced Indian air by night
> Full often hath she gossiped by my side,
> And sat with me on Neptune's yellow sands
> Marking th'embarked traders on the flood,
> When we have laughed to see the sails conceive
> And grow big-bellied with the wanton wind;
> Which she with pretty and with swimming gait
> Following—her womb then rich with my young squire—
> Would imitate, and sail upon the land
> To fetch me trifles, and return again
> As from a voyage, rich with merchandise. (II. i. 123-34)

There is nothing particularly ominous about this reported bit of play-acting: the lady is seeing and doing. Seeing, though, is of course crucial in the processes of the *Dream*. The love-juice-infected eye dotes on what it spies and creates beauty where there is ugliness, attachment in place of aversion. Love "looks not with the eyes, but with the mind" says Helena (I. i. 234); but Bottom asserts that "reason and love keep little company together nowadays" (III. i. 136-37) and the fact that he is in the arms of the bewitched Titania when he says so gives his point validity. Fancy *is* bred in the eye, and Shylock's bitter words could hold for the *Dream*:

> Affection,
> Mistress of passion, sways it to the mood
> Of what it likes or loathes. (*Merchant of Venice*, IV. i. 50-52)

Shylock knows, of course, about "breeding in the eye": we remember his extended account of how Jacob was supposed to have influenced the generating of Laban's flocks by controlling what the breeding ewes saw. Jacob set up peeled wands before the ewes, "Who then conceiving, did in eaning time/Fall parti-coloured lambs", (I. iii. 82-83). None of the many critics who have wrestled with the meaning of the Jacob and Laban anecdote in *The Merchant of Venice* has noticed that it makes at least a neat counterweight to the casket test set up by Portia's late father, giving the play instances of both prenatal and postmortem influencing. It is of course this prenatal "stamping" idea in Shakespeare which I leave with you as we return to the Wood near Athens.

As "the story changes"—to use Helena's phrase—the wood is presented not only as a place where Titania can sleep

> Quite overcanopied with luscious woodbine
> With sweet muskroses and with eglantine. . . .
> Lulled in these flowers with dances and delight
> (II. i. 251-54)

but also as a landscape potentially "full of hateful fantasies" (II. i. 258) inspired in the characters' minds. These opposing possibilities or characteristics of the wood collide when, precisely as the fairy lullaby ends—"Never harm/Nor spell nor charm/Come our lovely lady nigh"—and Titania sleeps, Oberon pronounces his spell:

> What thou seest when thou dost wake,
> Do it for thy true love take; . . .
> Be it ounce or cat or bear,
> Pard or boar with bristled hair
> In thy eye that shall appear
> When thou wakest, it is thy dear.
> Wake when some vile thing is near! (II. ii. 33-40)

Hateful fantasies also are close to the thoughts of the human lovers as they stumble wearily through the darkness: for instance, in Helena's "fancy-sick" despair about her own attractiveness:

> I am as ugly as a bear;
> For beasts that meet me run away for fear.
> Therefore no marvel that Demetrius
> Do as a monster fly my presence thus. (II. ii. 100-103)

And in Hermia's nightmare:

> Help me, Lysander, help me! Do thy best
> To pluck this crawling serpent from my breast! . . .
> Methought a serpent ate my heart away,
> And you sat smiling at his cruel prey. (II. ii. 151-6)

The mechanicals carry on this theme with their comic nervousness about frightening the ladies who are to see their play: whether the ladies can abide Pyramus killing himself, and whether they will be afraid of the lion. Bottom asserts that a lion among ladies is a most dreadful thing, and solves the problem of this fearful wildfowl by devising a contradiction, a comic monster or prodigy who will be played by Snug the joiner with half his face seen through the lion's neck (III. i. 27-33). Just as Oberon and Titania are parents and original of a progeny of evils, Bottom cheerfully creates a number of what he calls "defects" (he means "effects"), specifying that Snug must speak "thus, or to the same defect," that Starveling must "disfigure . . . the person" of Moonshine (III. i. 34, 54-55). A short time after, Bottom himself is translated to a monster, a combination of opposites, man and beast, while his fellows are chased about the wood by apparitions: "Sometime a horse I'll be, sometime a hound, / A hog, a headless bear, sometime a fire" (III. i. 102-103).

So now, in the deepest part of the wood, near the cradle of the fairy queen, there is a monster. He is of course an embodiment of all the comic contradictions that up to now have been present in his speech: his words—"I'll speak in a monstrous little voice"; "I will roar you as gently as any sucking dove" (I. ii. 47, 77)—are matched by discordant flesh. And he embodies as well other movements in the play of heterogenous elements yoked by violence together: Egeus would wrench Hermia into wedlock with Demetrius, while tragedy and mirth, tedium and brevity, are yoked in that monstrosity of a play, "Pyramus and Thisbe." Most prodigious of all—that is, most contrary to the course of nature—Titania is in love with the translated mechanical.

There is no need to speculate on whatever erotic fantasies may seem to be inherent in the joining together of fairy queen and monster, or to contemplate, with Jan Kott, the full extent of "the dark sphere of sex"[3] which he sees Titania entering. It is clear that the course of this love hardly can run smooth, and Bottom's ass-head might well correspond in some way to "the jaws of darkness" which Hermia and Lysander feared (I. i. 132-49)—there is no darkness but ignorance, as Feste shrewdly remarks,[4] and Bottom when translated can be profoundly ignorant. Kott finds the scenes "between Titania and the ass . . . at the same time real and unreal, fascinating and repulsive,"[5] but the comic aspects of the situation deflect many potential anxieties. The centaur-figure (a creature part human and part ass is an onocentaur) which Bottom has become *could* be considered as glancing at deep yearnings to be as beautiful as a human and as virile as a beast. But we cannot get around the comic fact that poor Bottom's luck is to have the centaur elements in reverse: he is as beautiful as a beast and at best merely as virile as a human. (I think Shakespeare comes back to this kind of joke with Caliban. Caliban is terribly confident about his virility, and one critic sees him as "a New World

3. *Shakespeare Our Contemporary* (London, 1967), p. 183, and see pp. 179-84.
4. *Twelfth Night*, IV. ii. 46-47.
5. *Shakespeare Our Comtemporary*, p. 183.

Minotaur," a "bestial product of woman's lust to be possessed."[6]
But fleshly as he may be or profess to be, Caliban also is part fish,
and fish, lenten fare—notwithstanding Jonathan Swift's joke about
their being a prolific diet—are in the sexual context made fun of in
Shakespeare: witness Falstaff's contempt for the virility of young men
who make fish meals.[7]) The scenes of Titania's wooing *are* of course
representative of wish-fulfilment: we may recall Romeo's "I dreamt
my lady came and found me dead . . . And breath'd such life with
kisses on my lips/That I reviv'd and was an emperor" (*Romeo and
Juliet* V. i. 6-9). In Bottom's case the wishes are comically granted.
We remember his regret when "Pyramus and Thisbe" was being cast:
assigned the part of a lover, he was pleased, but his chief humour, he
said, was for a tyrant (stubborn and contrary as an ass, if Pyramus
had been a tyrant's part no doubt he would have wished to play a
lover). Lover and tyrant he now can be as paramour and consort of
the fairy queen—"Hail mortal!" is the accolade from her retinue
(III. i. 170-73). If ever Bottom had a part or parts to tear a cat in, now
is the time. But as Titania's lover he is lethargic, as her consort, proletarian. This lethargy is characteristic of the translated Bottom.
Monstrous as he is in appearance, he is far from representing what
Willard Farnham sees as being typical of the medieval (and, I would
add, the Spenserian) grotesque, a "theme of violent struggle engaged
in by human beings and by animals or monsters, within and against an
entanglement in the form of vegetation."[8] His looks are beastly but
his experience and his reaction to that experience are gentle.
Awakened and restored, he knows he has had a rare vision, a dream
past the wit of man to say what dream it was, and his most strenuous
struggle in the play is to recapture the gleam of that vision (IV. i. 199-
216). Like Hamlet, who wrestles with the riddle of whether the Ghost
was a spirit of health or goblin damned and who decides that he will
have the players act out the story of his father's murder before his
uncle, Bottom acutely elects to turn his own puzzling experience into
art, to "get Peter Quince to write a ballad of this dream . . .; and I will
sing it in the latter end of a play before the Duke." The ballad of
Bottom's dream is not sung at the end of "Pyramus and Thisbe," but

6. Leslie Fielder, *The Stranger in Shakespeare* (New York, 1972), p. 233.
7. "We are told by a grave Author, an eminent French Physician, that *Fish being a prolifick Dyet*, there are more Children born in *Roman Catholick Countries* about Nine Months after *Lent* than at any other Season" (*A Modest Proposal*, in Ricardo Quintana, ed., *Gulliver's Travels and Other Writings* (New York, 1958), pp. 490-91. For Falstaff's remark, see *Henry IV*, Part Two, IV. iii. 97-101. *Cf.* also Mercutio's "O flesh, flesh, how art thou fishified!" (*Romeo and Juliet*, II. iv. 39-40).
8. *The Shakespearean Grotesque: Its Genesis and Transformations* (Oxford, 1971), p. 11.

something of the matter of Bottom's translation is embodied in the incantation delivered as the *Dream's* epilogue.

When the scene moves back to Athens the only "monster" there is Snug got up as the lion: he speaks the lines which Bottom suggested for him and presumably the stage direction "Snug *as Lion*" indicates that he is lion-bodied and joiner-headed. There is no indication that the ladies are frightened of him, and all the forest fears seem to be caught up and mocked in the play of Pyramus and Thisbe. The concord of discord is found. However, Oberon, Puck and company bring back with them not just the story of the night and some sense of the night's fierce vexations—"Now the hungry lion roars/And the wolf behowls the moon"—but also the promise of a carefully directed blessing against a particular terror which, however comically, the night has shown:

> To the best bride bed will we,
> Which by us shall blessèd be;
> And the issue there create
> Ever shall be fortunate.
> So shall all the couples three
> Ever true in loving be,
> And the blots of nature's hand
> Shall not in their issue stand.
> Never mole, harelip, nor scar,
> Nor mark prodigious, such as are
> Despised in nativity,
> Shall upon their children be. (V. i. 392-404)

The blots of nature's hand and marks prodigious are not small matters. The blessing or benign spell is on the house of Theseus and, we may fancy, upon the house in which this marriage comedy may have been designed to be given in private performance. Stanley Wells says that "the belief that the wedding blessing of the last Act had some extra-dramatic significance encourages a loose assumption that it is superfluous, and has been used to justify its omission in performance."[9] Far from being extra-dramatic, the blessing answers to what has been seen in the play—and I would stress "seen." For comic, rude and thick-skinned as he may be, Bottom's experience gathers to itself all the important themes of this play, and "Bottom's Dream" rivals the actual title as a designation for what we have witnessed (the events after all may be very midsummer madness but they could take

9. Introduction to the New Penguin *Midsummer Night's Dream*, pp. 12-13.

place on the last night of April and on May Day,[10] so that "A Mid-summer Night's Dream" is not quite accurate). Above all, Bottom in his translated form is the most powerful image in the *Dream*, whether the play is being seen, read or recalled. This discord—and it is a visual discord as well as a great visual joke—is no more to be removed from the audience's consciousness with a simple "Robin, take off this head" than it is from Bottom's own consciousness. It lingers in the verbal mismatchings of Bottom's attempt ("eye . . . hath not heard, . . . ear . . . hath not seen") to recollect the vision; and I believe that it clearly is recalled and invoked against in the epilogue's "blots of nature's hand" and "mark prodigious." In all, Bottom translated leaves such a powerful *impression* that it seems only prudent for a play-wright who apparently had at least thought about the idea of prenatal influencing to put in a saving clause in the form of a blessing against monstrous births—especially if the play *was* commissioned for a wedding.

In the fierce vexation of *King Lear* there are no visible prodigies such as Bottom. *Lear's* remarkable, compressed opening scene—a scene which is about love, impetuosity, giving in marriage, banish-ment and blindness—begins and ends with suggestions of sexual passion past and to come: recollected in Gloucester's boasts about the good sport at Edmund's making and forecast in Goneril's con-cluding line. Ironically, this cool rationalist who with her sister has just worked on Lear's fatal tendency to strike while the iron is hot tells Regan "We must do something, and i' th' heat" (I. i. 308). She means primarily that they must take the earliest opportunity of exploiting the "unruly waywardness that [Lear's] infirm and choleric years bring with them" (I. i. 298-99). It is this "heat," in the sense of choler, which has just given them a kingdom. But there seems in Goneril's words to be a sly Shakespearean play on the phrase "in heat,"[11] and the scene which began with Gloucester, that Cupid and "walking fire" as he later is called (III. iv. 117), bragging about his endeavours in getting Edmund, turns quietly and prophetically to its close in this agreement between the sisters who for all their rationality in politics will each lust after that Edmund and die for his sake. Between these first and last moments of the opening scene of *King Lear* there are a striking number of allusions to generation: "breeding" (1.9), "conceive you" (1.12), "grew round-womb'd . . . her cradle" (1.15), "the issue" (1.17), "his making" (1.23), "begot me, bred me"

10. See IV. i. 103 and Wells' note.
11. *Cf. Measure*, V. i. 477 ("in the heat of blood"). and *Love's Labour's Lost*, V. i. 810 ("in heat of blood").

(1.96), "his generation" (1.117), "our potency" (1.172). And just at the moment when Lear angrily offers Cordelia, dowerless, in marriage to Burgundy or France—to whomever will have her as she is, "New-adopted to our hate,/Dower'd with our curse and stranger'd with our oath"—there comes in the first talk of the monstrous. It is strange, says France, that she "should in this trice of time commit a thing so monstrous," and

> Sure, her offence
> Must be of such unnatural degree
> That monsters it. . . . . (I. i. 216-20)

Bradley labels Goneril and Regan "monsters" and says that Goneril is "the most hideous human being (if she is one) that Shakespeare ever drew."[12] His inverted commas around the word "monsters" and his parenthetical "if she is one" are interestingly tentative and tend to cancel one another out: if Goneril isn't a human being then she is a prodigy, a monster, without inverted commas. Edmund, of course, affirms his social grievance as cheerfully and logically as Richard III presents his deformity. Richard's logic is that as he cannot prove a lover he is determined to be a villain: in a manner of speaking, not being Adonis he'll be the boar. Edmund is "proper" in physical shape— as Richard can only, after his success with Anne, fancy himself to be. So Edmund can be, and is, both lover and villain: it is only a short step to Bottom's terms lover and tyrant. Though, as Spurgeon says, "the idea of unnatural horrors, of human beings preying on themselves 'like monsters of the deep,' or like wolves and tigers tearing one another's flesh, is . . . constantly before us in King Lear,"[13] Goneril, Regan and Edmund all look beautiful and undeformed, angels on the outward side. The marks prodigious are all within, yet the blots of nature's hand clearly exist in these issue.

It is a blot of nature's hand, a moral monster, that Lear calls down on Goneril when she first defies him:

> If she must teem,
> Create her child of spleen, that it may live
> And be a thwart disnatur'd torment to her!
> Let is stamp wrinkles in her brow of youth,
> With cadent tears fret channels in her cheeks,
> Turn all her mother's pains and benefits
> To laughter and contempt, that she may feel
> How sharper than a serpent's tooth it is
> To have a thankless child! (I. iv. 290-98)

12. *Shakespearian Tragedy* (London, 1960), pp. 248-49.
13. *Shakespeare's Imagery and What It Tells Us* (Boston 1958), p. 341.

Lear has defined his own plight, and his plight will puzzle him for a long time, as he seeks "the cause": "Let them anatomize Regan, see what breeds about her heart. Is there any cause in nature that make these hard hearts?" (III. vi. 78-79). Kent, too, puzzles over the mystery of why Cordelia is as she is and Goneril and Regan as they are:

> It is the stars,
> The stars above us govern our conditions;
> Else one self mate and make could not beget
> Such different issues.   (IV. iii. 33-36)

Though Gloucester's situation appears to parallel Lear's, Gloucester will not go to nearly the same lengths as Lear in puzzling out a cause. When he hears from Edmund of Edgar's supposed treacherous violence and sees Edmund's wounded arm he reaches for some word to describe this unnatural son, and the word is "strange": "O strange and fast'ned villain" (II. i. 77); and at once he tries to externalize the menace: "I never got him" (II. i. 78). From this point until the time of his enlightenment (just as he is being blinded) he speaks of Edgar in the past tense and with a sense of outrage and self-pity:

> I had a son,
> Now outlaw'd from my blood; he sought my life,
> But lately, very late; I lov'd him, friend,
> No father his son dearer; true to tell thee,
> The grief hath craz'd my wits. (III. iv. 170-44)

It may be because Gloucester never really gets close to taking any sort of blame for what is happening to him that Shakespeare has Edgar pronounce that strange and terrible speech to Edmund which begins so gently, "Let's exchange charity . . . . My name is Edgar, and thy father's son," and goes on to speak not of charity but of a terrible justice:

> The gods are just, and of our pleasant vices
> Make instruments to plague us;
> The dark and vicious place where thee he got
> Cost him his eyes.   (V. iii. 166-173)

Lear has some early moments when, like Gloucester, he would deny that the terrors which confront him are of his own creation. "Are you our daughter?" he asks Goneril (I. iv. 227), and says, "By the marks of sovereignty, knowledge, and reason, I should be false persuaded I had daughters" (I. iv. 240-42). Driven to seek comfort from Regan, he tells her that if she should not be glad to see him "I would divorce me from thy mother's tomb,/Sepulchring an adultress" (II. iv. 132-

33). But moving beyond these parallels with Gloucester's "I never got him," and moving also beyond simple, outraged invective are Lear's attempts to name what his daughters are becoming. As if peering through a thickening fog to distinguish frightening shapes, he tries to find similitudes for Goneril. At first, he does not straightforwardly call her a monster:

> Ingratitude, thou marble-hearted fiend,
> More hideous, when thous show'st thee in a child,
> Than the sea-monster.   (I. iv. 268-70)

In his next lines she is a "detested kite," her guilt infinitely greater than Cordelia's "most small fault" which showed itself "How ugly"; she is "this [one senses in the four-foot line a groping for a term] creature" (1.286), and at the end of the act he personifies her as "Monster Ingratitude" (I. v. 40). In the second act he again curses Goneril, this time using words which Shakespeare later would put into the mouth of Caliban:

> Strike her young bones,
> You taking airs, with lameness! . . .
> . . . Infect her beauty,
> You fen-suck'd fogs, drawn by the pow'rful sun,
> To fall and blister her!   (II. iv. 164-9)[14]

These fearsome invectives on the yet-unborn ("Young bones") and the just-born as well as on Goneril as a mother have suggestions, in "fen-suck'd" and "drawn," of a close and parasitic relationship between parent and child. Lear in the first scene invited Cordelia to "draw" her portion of his wealth and in the third act the "cub-drawn bear" cowers from the storm—in the states both of opulence and deprivation parents are drained. But these parasites cannot simply be shaken off or denied: when Goneril joins Lear and Regan in Act Two, Lear attempts the words—"my child"—that he will not speak again until he says them to Cordelia after his madness is cured: "I prithee, daughter, do not make me mad:/I will not trouble thee, my child: farewell (II.iv. 220-21). Wonderingly he says, "But yet thou art my flesh, my blood, my daughter," and then seizes on what seems to him at this time the only possible explanation of the mystery, that she is his only as a disease may be said to be his:

> Or rather a disease that's in my flesh,
> Which I must needs call mine: thou art a boil,
> A plague-sore, or embossed carbuncle,
> In my corrupted blood.   (II. iv. 224-27)

14. Cf. The Tempest, II. ii. 1-3.

The external landscape of this play is strongly rendered through Lear's catalogues of his gifts of territory, Edgar's description of the poor pelting villages, sheep-cotes and mills through which he will wander as a bedlam, and the evocation of the storm on the heath— bleak winds sorely ruffling while for many miles about there's scarce a bush. But it should be noticed that Lear, who formerly knew only his territories, now is learning and scanning as it were his own land-scape: pinching himself when he wonders if he is dreaming when Goneril first crosses him (I. iv. 237); beating at his head, the gate that let his folly in and his dear judgment out (I. iv. 280-81), fearing his rising heart (II. iv. 56-57, 121) and feeling it assailed by "Sharptooth'd unkindness, like a vulture" (II. iv. 136). *King Lear* is of course the most "physical" of all Shakespeare's plays, with its dominant and "floating" image—as Spurgeon says[15]—of a human body in anguished movement. Edmund boasts of his dimensions, shape and composi-tion, and Edgar strips himself on-stage, metamorphosing from clothed, propertied, titled, and sane man to "this horrible object," the poor bare forked animal who will spring at Lear from the hovel. And of course Lear is stripped, systematically by numbers, of his hundred-knight prerogative until he is invested with nothing. In a way this undressing assists him to better examine himself and to pursue the mystery of "the cause."

When Lear and the Fool are in the storm, the King cries out in anger against the generative secrets of the body, calling on the thunder to "Crack Nature's moulds, all germens spill at once/That makes ungrateful man!" (III. ii. 6-9). He shouts too that the storm itself and the battles it wages above him and against him are "high-engender'd"—everything in nature gets its conception or birth some-where, and in these moments everything that has ever been conceived and born, whether elements, daughters or ingrateful man in general, is against him. The Fool chimes in with his song about the penances of sexuality—about the cod-piece that *will* house before the head has any—and when Kent enters to ask "Who's there?" the Fool's reply is "Here's grace and a cod-piece; that's a wise man and a Fool" (III. ii. 39-41). He leaves it to Kent to decide, if he cares to, which is which, but Lear is the one whose "cod-piece has housed" and who now most spectacularly as a result has no house to put his head in. And it seems appropriate that the King now speaks a kind of apology for his bodily needs: "The art of our necessities is strange/And can make vile things precious" (III. ii. 70-71). These words refer directly to the hovel

15. Spurgeon, *Shakespeare's Imagery*, p. 339.

straw which is offered as a bed, but coming as soon as they do after the cod-piece references there is an additional sense of ruefulness about physicality, especially if we know the passage in Florio's Montaigne from which Shakespeare could have derived the thought:

> Nature hath like a kinde mother observed this, that such actions as shee for our necessities hath enjoyned unto us, should also be voluptuous unto us.[16]

Lear's body, his own flesh and blood, has out of necessity done and now is doing strange things to itself, the mouth tearing the hand. Still, as one who can yet think of himself as a man more sinned against than sinning, Lear has a desire to punish home ("home" is a significant word).

When Edgar appears *he* is seen by Lear as punishing home, hurting himself for having given life to daughters who then discarded him: "Judicious punishment! 'twas this flesh begot/Those pelican daughters" (III. iv. 74-5). And as Edgar discourses on his supposed fleshly sins, how he "in woman out-paramour'd the Turk", and Lear identifies himself with him and tries to undress, in comes the walking fire Gloucester, whom Edgar characterizes as the fiend who has given so many birth defects, some of which are the marks prodigious against which Oberon's charm was pronounced:

> This is the foul Flibbertigibbet: he begins at curfew, and walks till the first cock; he gives the web and the pin, squinies the eye, and makes the hare-lip. (III. iv. 118-21)

Then Edgar goes on to sing of Swithin meeting the night-mare.

Gloucester still is full of self-pity: "Our flesh and blood, my lord, is grown so vile,/That it doth hate what gets it" (III. iv. 149-50). But Lear is by now long past this comparatively simple sense of grievance. He has turned to Edgar as to a professional wise man, one acquainted with the secrets of nature, and asks him the kind of question which the Fool had earlier posed to the King, "What is the cause of thunder?" (III. iv. 158). Edgar has no answers for Lear, and soon he will have terrible questions of his own when he sees his blinded father.

The mythical monster Flibbertigibbet may be said to give the web and the pin (cataract) and to squiny the eye, but the real-life terrors who are Regan and Cornwall blind Gloucester in earnest. The servant who sees this atrocity and the killing of his fellow by Regan can only grope, as Lear has been groping, for some reason or cause:

---

16. See Kenneth Muir's note on III. ii. 70 in the New Arden *King Lear*.

> If she live long,
> And in the end meet the old course of death,
> Women will all turn monsters. (III. vii. 99-101)

It is the "turn" or "change" from natural courses which makes Goneril and Regan frightening. Goneril startles Albany by revealing herself as a "changed and self-covered thing" bemonstered in feature (IV. ii. 62-3), and by a form of sinister alteration she proposes to "change arms at home, and give the distaff/Into [her] husband's hands (IV. ii. 17-18). (In his discourse on monsters and prodigies Parey has a chapter "Of the Changeing of Sex."[17]) When he expresses his helpless despair at seeing his blind father, Edgar uses a phrase with a curiously modern ring: "World, world, O world!/But that thy strange mutations make us hate thee,/Life would not yield to age" (IV. i. 10-12). By such strange mutations humanity, in Albany's prediction, could prey on itself "Like monsters of the deep" (IV. ii. 48-49).

At "Dover" there are two imagined monsters. The first is that fiend of despair which makes Gloucester want to take his own life. After saving him, Edgar, who knows his father very well, produces a verbal description of this creature who never was, to convince Gloucester that the foul fiend has been defied and left behind on the cliff-top from which Gloucester supposedly has fallen. The speech functions like Oberon's blessing, warding off the monster (we remember that Edgar's mock-study as Tom was "How to prevent the fiend, and to kill vermin:" here at Dover he takes a monster from Gloucester's back, and he kills Oswald). The superstitious and blind father is perfectly satisfied that the prodigy which Edgar describes is the kind of creature which would have led him to the cliff, an apparition whose eyes "Were two full moons; he had a thousand noses,/Horns whelk'd and wav'd like the enridged sea" (IV. vi. 69-71).

But just as Gloucester's reaction to his experience is everywhere simplistic compared with Lear's, so the fiend which Gloucester can accept and blame ("he led me to that place") for his suicidal desires is a puppet in comparison with the chimera which lives in and poisons the landscape of Lear's mind when Lear enters a few moments later. The "landscape of Lear's mind" seems an appropriate term, for Lear now is nothing but a discordant mind, "as mad as the vex'd sea," dressed in flowers and weeds and with an imagination crowded with counterfeiters, soldiers, memories of the rain that came to wet him

17. Paré, *The Workes*, Bk. 25, Ch. 5.

65

and the wind that made him chatter, authorities, thieves, beggars, adulterers, beadles and prostitutes. The landscape in which Lear now thinks himself to be living is far from being those opulent meadows, forests and rivers which he gave away in the first scene. Rather it corresponds to the bleak and heartless stretch of nature and society toward which Edgar turned on disguising himself as Poor Tom, those "Poor pelting villages, sheep-cotes, and mills." And in this inner landscape is the second monster of this scene and the great monster of the play. Hating all life and the source from which life is born, Lear sees "yond simp'ring dame,/Whose face between her forks presages snow" (IV. iv. 121). Woman as well as man is a forked animal—and with riotous appetite: "Down from the waist they are Centaurs/Though women all above."

Lear has become a teratologist, a student of monsters; this monstrous vision or night-mare of his is Shakespeare's other centaur—Bottom was the first. And this other centaur-vision truly occupies—to use again the words which Jan Kott misapplies to the Bottom-Titania relationship—"the dark sphere of sex." Bottom's dream puzzlingly but cheerfully "had no bottom"; Lear's vision, terrifyingly, has no bottom either: "there's hell, there's darkness,/There is the sulphurous pit" (IV. vi. 129-30). As a centaur Bottom was comic and harmless, a joke on the human desire to be lover and tyrant. Lear's horrifying centaur also is an especially curious monster, for centaurs usually are depicted as having male, not female torsos (though Ovid mentions a female centaur in Book XII of The Metamorphoses).[18] There is something deeply grotesque, a very strange mutation indeed, in this image of women excessively desirous of sexual satisfaction and, as centaurs, infinitely capable of giving or receiving it. The truth is that in this moment of Lear's deepest disgust with human nature it is male as well as female nature against which he inveighs: the centaur after all represents mankind divided against itself, torn between good and evil.[19] Lear's daughters, "got 'tween the lawful sheets," are his flesh, his blood. Their lust never would have been possible without his lust, and Lear knows and says that his hand, like theirs, smells of mortality. Lear's very first line in this scene was "No, they cannot touch me for coining" (IV. vi. 83): we already have

18. *Shakespeare's Ovid*, ed. W. H. D. Rouse (London 1961), p. 246: Book XII, ll. 443-56.
19. *Cf.* Robert B. Heilman, *This Great Stage: Image and Structure in "King Lear"* (Seattle, 1963), pp. 234-35. For the centaur as vengeful and a symbol of vengefulness, see *Metamorphoses* Book XII and George Ferguson, *Signs and Symbols in Christian Art* (New York, 1961), p. 14.

seen how mothers are said to be stamped and children to be "coined." If Lear's coinages are centaurs, so also may the coiner be, king or no king. For even though he protests "I'll not love" when he sees Gloucester and accuses and absolves him of the sin of adultery (of which the centaur was a symbol), Lear is vengeful, and vengefulness also was associated with centaurs. Father of two horrific children, himself given to violent evocations of the terrors of the earth, Lear has all this while been searching or smelling out a mystery posed in Montaigne's essay "Of the Resemblance betweene Children and Fathers":

> What monster is it that this teare or drop of seed, whereof we are ingendred brings with it; and in it the impressions, not only of the corporall forme, but even of the very thoughts and inclinations of our fathers?[20]

The Lear experience, then, is not that monsters are, as Parey has it, things "brought forth *contrary* [my italics] to the common decree and order of Nature," but that they are, as Montaigne more than hints, all too possible in the ordinary course of generation. Ripeness is all, and Lear himself is on his way to the conclusion which Prospero will draw from the contemplation of *his* monster: "This thing of darkness I/ Acknowledge mine" (*The Tempest*, V. i. 275-76).

But part of the mystery of generation is that good as well as evil may be engendered. Towards the end of his great storm of rage, vengefulness and futility, Lear comes back again to those references to birth which have echoed throughout the play. This time, however, it is birth not so much in sin or misshapenness as in deep and understanding sadness: "Thou must be patient, we came crying hither," and "When we are born, we cry that we are come/To this great stage of fools" (IV. vi. 180, 184-85). Edgar, who recognizes that Lear speaks reason in madness, seems to pick up this theme of the wise and experienced new-born as well as the curious male-female confusion in Lear's reference to the centaur, for a few minutes after he tells Gloucester that he is a most poor man "who, by the art of known and feeling sorrows,/Am pregnant to good pity" (IV. vi. 223-4).

So, like Child Rowland coming to the dark tower in Edgar's rhyme, Lear, the teratologist, has traced his monster children through a dark landscape to their source or first cause—himself. But human beings can be "pregnant to" good things as well as monsters. The Gentleman who comes to rescue Lear for Cordelia addresses the King ambiguously —"Sir, Your most dear daughter"—and thus to Lear could well be a

---

20. *Montaigne's Essays*, tr. John Florio (London and New York, 1965), III. p. 496.

67

glib agent of Goneril's or Regan's. Consequently Lear dodges the rescuers, but the Gentleman closes off this movement of the play on a note of reassurance and sets the tone for the scene of reconciliation with Cordelia:

> Thou hast one daughter,
> Who redeems nature from the general curse
> Which twain have brought her to. (IV.vi. 206-8)

Cordelia's redemption of nature is moral and spiritual: in the general curse which falls upon so many of the principals, including the monsters themselves, in the last movement of the play she cannot save Lear nor can he save her. Perhaps it is not a consolation that before they both die Lear has had a chance to call Cordelia what he called the monstrous Goneril—"my child." We can say that at the last he knows his part in his children and knows the differences between them. Such knowledge gives considerable weight to Lear's claim, in the final act, that he is ready to take upon himself an equivalent of Bottom's "rare vision." "The mystery of things" into which his experiences entitle him to look includes the mystery of generation itself.

The Savage Man in Spenser Shakespeare and Renaissance English Drama

G. M. PINCISS

A reader of English Renaissance pastoral will quickly discover that the savage man is among the most frequently met inhabitants of that literary convention, almost as often encountered amid those artificial trees as the shepherds and aristocrats one expects to find in that special forest.[1] In large measure, the savage man's usefulness to poets and playwrights explains his popularity, for he can function both as an entertainer and as a philosophic symbol. To arrive at a better appreciation of this creature, of his scope and function in a pastoral setting, we shall draw examples from *The Faerie Queene*, from Shakespearean drama, and from the popular stage. In this way, too, we shall be able to contrast how a similar figure was used by writers of subtlety and genius as well as by those whose gifts were more modest.

First, however, our discussion quite properly should begin by considering the savage man's genealogy. As we might expect, the savage man could trace his ancestry back both to classical mythology

1. Among many recent studies of the pastoral, I have found the following especially valuable: John Arthos, *On the Poetry of Spenser and the Forms of Romance* (London, 1956); Donald Cheney, *Spenser's Image of Nature: Wild Man and Shepherd in the Faerie Queene* (New Haven, 1966); Rosalie Colie, *Shakespeare's Living Art* (Princeton, 1974); Patrick Cullen, *Spenser, Marvell, and Renaissance Pastoral* (Cambridge, Mass., 1970); Water R. Davis, *Sidney's Arcadia* (New Haven, 1965); Howard Felperin, *Shakespearean Romance* (Princeton, 1972); R. G. Hunter, *Shakespeare and the Comedy of Forgiveness* (New York, 1965); Frank Kermode, ed. *The Tempest* (Cambridge, Mass., 1954); Maynard Mack, *King Lear in Our Time* (Berkeley, 1965); Edward William Tayler, *Nature and Art in Renaissance Literature* (New York 1964); Humphrey Tonkin, *Spenser's Courteous Pastoral* (Oxford, 1972); David Young, *The Heart's Forest* (New Haven, 1972), and *Something of Great Constancy: The Art of 'A Midsummer Night's Dream'* (New Haven, 1966).

and to European folklore.[2] From classical mythology, for example, the Renaissance learned of Romulus, who was reared by a she-wolf; of Hercules, the friend of man, who dressed in a lion's skin and carried a club; and of satyrs, fauns, and sileni, who existed in a golden age and a state of innocence. These were positive examples of kindly and beneficent creatures living happily in accord with nature. They represented the "soft" view of primitivism formulated by Hesiod, described by Ovid's golden age, and championed by Locke, Rousseau and, most recently, Levi-Strauss.

The opposing point of view held that primitive existence was truly bestial and that society, through collective effort and human reason, was the only means of improving the quality of life. The savage man's constant struggle for survival, his unrestrained response to physical desires, his brutal existence in a world of fallen nature explained his violent, lascivious, unpredictable, and even cannibalistic behaviour. And, naturally, the same examples served: Romulus murdered his brother; Hercules went mad; and satyrs and fauns, creatures of prodigious sexual capacity, worshipped Bacchus in frenzy. This line of reasoning represents the "hard" view of primitivism, argued since the Renaissance by Machiavelli, Hobbes, Vico and Freud.

In addition to his ambivalent classical ancestry, the Renaissance savage man derived a part of his lineage from an equally ambivalent medieval folklore. By the early Middle Ages natives of Italy, France and Switzerland could be terrorized by rumours of a forest-dwelling wild folk living in a state of nature.[3] These savages were associated with demons of the earth as well as with ghosts of the underworld and were thought of as enemies of living things and of man himself. Another strain, encountered with only slightly less fear, was associated with the elves and fairies of country lore, impish, not always kindly, and connected with vegetation and fertility. However, by the High Middle Ages, European attitudes had shifted. The frustration caused by a rigid, elaborate and artificial code of courtly manners precluding spontaneity of expression and denying natural conduct led men to long to escape the repressions of society, to live unrestrained in nature. Accordingly, the wild man then became a model for human conduct, a creature free, happy and loving.

This range of possible attitudes goes some way to explaining why Spenser can present a savage nation of fauns and satyrs in such a

2. Hayden White, "The Forms of Wildness: Archaeology of an Idea," in *The Wild Man Within*, ed. Edward Dudley and Maximillian Novak (Pittsburgh, 1972).
3. Richard Bernheimer, *Wild Men in the Middle Ages* (Cambridge, Mass., 1952).

variety of guises.[4] In Book I of *The Faerie Queene*, for example, we meet a "salvage nation" who live at ease in nature. They are capable of recognizing the holiness of Una and protecting her, even if they cannot correctly comprehend her notion of the true faith. But unlike them, their relations in Book III are not herbivorous; a goat-herding tribe, this lot is most remarkable for its unrestrained sexuality. With bagpipes, dances and garlands they celebrate the acquisition of the strumpet Hellenore as their "Maylady"—which is what they call her. Finally, in Book VI, the unfortunate Serena is captured by another bagpipe-playing "salvage nation," one that does not practise trade, "drive/ The painefull plough, or cattell for to breed/ . . . But on the labours of poore men to feed." And, it turns out, they feed on poor men themselves, for, once they have seen Serena, "of her dainty flesh they did devise/To make a common feast." Depending on the needs of the allegory and the choice of genealogy, savages can be found to fit every description.

In this matter of description we may be, at first, somewhat surprised at the identification of the savage man with creatures that are at least half beast. But the wild man as a gentle or beneficent creature of the forest was not very different after all from those inhabitants of woods and streams, the satyrs, fauns, nymphs and sileni of classical mythology. Bernheimer in his study of the wild man in the Middle Ages notes that by the twelfth century "the wild man himself is given the traits of a satyr": hairiness, strength, virility, semi-nakedness and aphasia.[5] Moreover, as Hayden White has pointed out, the positive revaluation of the image of the wild man as a benign creature occurred simultaneously with the "recovery of classical culture, the revival of humanist values, and the improvisation of a new conception of nature more classical than Judeo-Christian in inspiration."[6] By the early Renaissance all human and even semi-human creatures of the forest were simply thought of as savage or wild men, whatever their origin.

We shall have to exercise some selectivity to bring our subject into manageable dimensions. Accordingly, we shall concentrate our analysis on three distinct types of savage men: first, we shall take up examples of the least human and most bestial; next, we shall look at a more recognizably human species, the child reared in and often by the animal world who retains domination over it; last, we shall consider that most modern and often youthful of paradigms, the

4. For a comprehensive discussion see Herbert Foltinek, "Die Wilden Männer in Edmund Spenser's *Faerie Queene*," *Die Neueren Sprachen*, 10 (1961), pp. 443-512.
5. P. 99.
6. Pp. 22-23.

social drop-out, one who becomes a savage when he rejects society for a period of isolation and introspection. Having retreated to a state of nature, he, like other varieties of savage men, may be found with his hair uncut and unkempt, his clothing disintegrated, his manners forgotten, and his power of speech lost.

As an introduction to the first type, the most bestial, we might well spend a moment on Bremo, who appears in the anonymous play *Mucedorus;* Bremo is quite possibly the most popular and long-lived of his species on the public stage, one no doubt familiar to Spenser, Shakespeare and their audience. Bremo displays all the signs of his class:

> With restless rage I wander through these woods;
> No creature here but feareth Bremo's force;
> Man, woman, child, beast, and bird,
> And everything that doth approach my sight
> Are forced to fall if Bremo once do frown. (vii)[7]

But having captured the Princess Amadine, he finds that his own fierceness is mollified by a new emotion; he discovers that "her beauty hath bewitched my force/ Or else within me altered nature's course." Where he had first thought to "feed on flesh" and "glut" his "greedy guts with lukewarm blood," he is now overcome with love. This new sensation causes him to recite what passes for the best lyric poetry in the play—"pastoral" in style.

> The satyrs and the wood-nymphs shall attend on thee
> And lull thee asleep with music's sound,
> And in the morning when thou dost awake,
> The lark shall sing good morrow to my queen,
> And, whilst he sings, I'll kiss my Amadine. (xv)

That Amadine can retain her chastity must be proof of the strength of her influence over Bremo and the degree of his love for her. And the power of her love is further tried when she persuades Bremo to spare Mucedorus. Mucedorus explains to Bremo that his life style is barbaric and uncivilized, that a "goodly golden age" occurred when men led by reason "grew to perfect amity," forsaking the woods and living in cities and towns. Nevertheless, Mucedorus agrees to serve as Bremo's servant while "the monster . . . doth murder all he meets;/ He spareth none, and none doth him escape." In short order, how-

---

7. *Mucedorus*, ed. by Russell A. Fraser and Norman Rabkin, *Drama of the English Renaissance,* (New York, 1976), I. p. 476.

ever, Mucedorous tricks Bremo into giving him a club and with that "strikes him down dead."

Some elements in the characterization of Bremo we shall meet again. Fierceness and bluster, susceptibility to love and an unexpected gift for lyricism, credulity and guilelessness. Despite what must have been a threatening appearance on stage—his "huff, snuff, ruff" speeches are delightfully cruel—Bremo is very much a child, wilful, innocent, and subject to extreme rage. There is in any case nothing of the sinful or wicked about him. He functions in this plot purely as an exciting but temporary obstacle to the happy ending.

The equivalent creature for Spenser, however, has lost whatever charm he may have had. Although he displays the usual characteristics of his kind—he is strong, speechless, armed with an oak tree, covered in hair, and dressed with a wreath of green ivy—there is nothing attractive in his person.

> It was to weet a wilde and salvage man,
> Yet was no man, but onely like in shape
> And eke in stature higher by a span,
> All overgrowne with haire, that could awhape
> An hardy hart, and his wide mouth did gape
> With huge great teeth, like to a tusked Bore
> For he liv'd all on ravin and on rape
> Of men and beasts; and fed on fleshly gore,
> The signe whereof yet stain'd his bloudy lips afore. (IV. vii)

His resemblance to humanity is hard to find: his head bears a pouch-like nether lip, a "huge great nose . . . empurpled all with bloud," and "wide, long eares. . . More great than th' eares of Elephants." As the distraught Amoret learns, this creature makes a specialty of women: "For on the spoile of women he doth live," and "with his shamefull lust doth first deflowre,/ And afterwards themselves doth cruelly devoure."

In his efforts to come to Amoret's aid, Timias is unsuccessful, for her captor uses the terrified maiden as a shield. Inadvertently wounding her, Timias, with his modesty and natural grace, is insufficiently powerful to overcome Spenser's monster of "greedie lust." But ultimately that savage proves no match against Belphoebe and the force of her virginity. Her arrow pierces his throat and his "sinfull sowle/ Having his carrion corse quite sencelesse left,/ Was fled to hell."

Since sexual potency is a common attribute of the species, this "wilde and salvage man" can easily function as the embodiment of

uncontrolled sexuality.[8] And the emphasis here on evil and wickedness, sin and damnation, makes explicit the moral point of the allegory:
modesty and grace together with a woman's natural impulse to pre-
serve her virginity save her from lust. But she is hurt by her own
defender, for her shame at feeling or almost yielding to sexual tempta-
tions wounds this modesty and grace.[9]

In this brief episode the general outline of the allegorical significance
is straightforward enough; the symbolic encounters and emblematic
figures are simply the raw material for the poet.

We shall return to this episode later and follow Timias's history.
But for the moment let us leave him in true Spenserian fashion
consoling the tearful Amoret and continue our discussion with
Shakespeare's treatment of his Bremo-like savage, Caliban. Although
this creature in *The Tempest* is in many ways strikingly different from
all other varieties, that he shares some of Bremo's characteristics is
hardly surprising. In a revival of *Mucedorous*, Bremo, after all, had
appeared before King James in a performance acted by Shakespeare's
company at about the time *The Tempest* was itself being composed for
royal presentation.

Caliban is described in the First Folio list of characters as "salvage
and deformed." We shall recognize his ancestry most readily with the
help of Edmund Malone's note on his costuming: Caliban's dress
"which doubtless was originally prescribed by the poet himself and
has been continued, I believe, since his time, is a large bear skin, or
the skin of some other animal; and he is usually represented with long
shaggy hair."[10] That he is compared by Trinculo and Stephano to a fish
or associated with fishiness must attest rather to his strangeness and to
his smell than to his derivation. Like Bremo, Caliban is both threatening and comic, and like him also he has learned speech. In addition, he,
too, is capable of a lyric outburst:

8. See James Nohanberg, *The Analogy of the Faerie Queene* (Princeton, 1976), p. 265n,
for an analysis of this creature's appearance. My colleague Calvin Edwards has pointed
out to me that Spenser's association of the figure of lust with "a tusked Bore" refers,
perhaps, to the interpretation of the boar as destructive lust in some of the allegorized
readings of Ovid's story of Venus and Adnois.
9. John Erskine Hankins, *Source and Meaning in Spenser's Allegory: A Study of The
Faerie Queene* (Oxford, 1971), pp. 160-61. For another reading, see William Nelson,
The Poetry of Edmund Spenser (New York, 1963), pp. 253-54.
10. *The Tempest*, ed. Frank Kermode, p. 63. As Rosalie Colie has noted, "The satyr-
figure, half-animal, half-human, sometimes represents disorder and danger in the
pastoral world and at other times exhibits heightened pathos. The ambiguity of this
type is very important in aspects of Caliban's presentation." *Shakespeare's Living Art*,
p. 285, footnote 4.

> the isle is full of noises,
> Sounds and sweet airs, that give delight, and hurt not.
> Sometimes a thousand twangling instruments
> Will hum about mine ears; and sometimes voices,
> That, if I then had wak'd after long sleep,
> Will make me sleep again; and then, in dreaming,
> The clouds methought would open, and show riches
> Ready to drop upon me; that, when I wak'd,
> I cried to dream again. (III. ii.)

How Bremo acquired language is not explained, but Caliban had the advantage of Miranda's instruction. As she reminds him, [I]

> Took pains to make thee speak, taught thee each hour
> One thing or other: when thou didst not, savage,
> Know thine own meaning, but wouldst gabble like
> A thing most brutish, I endow'd thy purposes
> With words that made them known. (I. ii.)

Perhaps among her lessons she also converted Caliban from cannibalism; as we have seen, it was a practice common among his ilk and one, as his name suggests, that had not always been alien to him. Finally, in his lusting for Miranda and in his near success at peopling the isle with little Calibans, he fulfills that last of the major qualities of the wild man.

But Caliban, "savage and deformed," has more subtle responses and emotions than his predecessors. In part, his origins themselves are more complicated. He is not simply a wild, two-legged creature, but the offspring "got by the devil himself" upon a witch. And combined with his supernatural parentage, his heredity also includes a historical element, for Shakespeare has made his savage a native inhabitant of the New World. Caliban might be found both among the cannibals and in the Caribbean.[11]

Shakespeare's imaginative powers and psychological insight coupled with some actual travellers' accounts of experiences in the New World enabled him to design a savage of far greater sophistication and complexity. For example, Caliban, denied the pleasure of Miranda's bed and forced to serve Prospero's will, expresses a very human bitterness over lost love: "When thou cam'st first,/ Thou strok'st me, and made much of me . . . and then I lov'd thee,/ And show'd thee all

11. Kermode, p. xxxviii ff. See also Charles Frey, "The Tempest and the New World," Shakespeare Quarterly, Vol, 30, No. 1 (Winter, 1979), pp. 29-41; and John E. Hankins, "Caliban and the Natural Man," PMLA, 62 (1947), pp. 793-801.

the qualities o' th' isle." That he is capable of such affection is unusual; that he is capable of improvement through instruction indicates an intelligence quotient far above that of the purely literary or mythological breed of savage men.

Since his behaviour is uncontrolled, purely *id* directed, and since he has never attained an understanding of any moral code, he is truly beyond good and evil. His intention of murdering Prospero is restrained by fear not of damnation but of detection and punishment. Moreover, he has the sense not to be distracted from his purpose with "trash", like Stephano and Trinculo.

But, in fact, Caliban's attempt would fail even if it were to succeed; he would merely replace one master with another. His efforts to attain freedom are misdirected. The lesson that Ferdinand expresses, that fulfilment of the will comes through submission of the will, that freedom is found through restraint, is a paradox too subtle for Caliban— at least before the very ending of the play. In this last speech, Caliban acknowledges his foolishness and announces: "I'll be wise hereafter, And seek for grace" (V. i.).

In this introduction to the Arden edition, Frank Kermode points out that "Caliban is the ground of the play."[12] And, indeed, to every character and thread of the action he provides a point of contrast. He is a servant who wants his freedom; Ariel is another. But Caliban is composed of the low and heavy elements, earth and water, while Ariel is all fire and air. Caliban is deformed and lustful, one who cannot be made to bear logs without the threat of punishment; Prince Ferdinand, on the other hand, is one of the handsomest of his kind, who accepts his log-bearing as the imposition of "poor matters" for "rich ends." Ferdinand's desires can never "melt . . . honour into lust." Between the two we are presented with the opposition of self-restraint with lawlessness, of self-control with wilful behaviour. And, since Caliban is motivated by lawlessness and lust, he has proved largely unresponsive to Prospero's efforts:

> Thou most lying slave,
> Whom stripes may move, not kindness! I have us'd thee,
> Filth as thou art, with human care; and lodg'd thee
> In mine own cell, till thou didst seek to violate
> The honour of my child. (I. ii.)

Even the very words Caliban has learned are turned to curses in his

12. P. xxv.

mouth. He seems the product of forces forever in opposition to those higher powers, civilizing and refining, of Prospero's art.

In the action of the play, Caliban's resentment at his treatment by Prospero and Miranda leads him to encourage Stephano and Trinculo to aid in the murder of Prospero and set themselves up as lords of the island. Caliban's efforts parallel the temptation of Antonio, who encourages Sebastian to murder his brother and make himself the King of Milan. Antonio, after all, knows this practice well, for he has succeeded in supplanting Prospero, his own brother, as Duke of Naples.

Yet here we begin to realize that what had seemed clear-cut distinctions between the civilized and the savage no longer hold. In fact, the more closely we examine the play, the more deceptive is its simplicity. Caliban is, after all, a part of all of us, even the most rarified examples. Prospero himself admits: "this thing of darkness I acknowledge mine." And we must balance Prospero's discouragement with Caliban—"He is one on whom my nurture would never stick," "He is one on whom my pains are all lost, quite lost"—with Caliban's own closing comment that he will "seek for grace." Even to acknowledge its desirability suggests that Caliban is a savage capable of humanity, a possibility expressed by Gonzalo, that old man who makes a practice of being right in essence while being wrong in detail:

> If in Naples
> I should report this now, would they believe me?
> For I should say, I saw such islanders,—
> For, certes, these are people of the island,—
> Who, though they are of monstrous shape, yet, note,
> Their manners are more gentle, kind, than of
> Our human generation you shall find
> Many, nay, almost any. (III. iii.)

Moreover, Caliban has the wit to repent as well as the sense to seek improvement. Sebastian and Antonio, men who commit evil in full knowledge of their wickedness, never sue for forgiveness or promise reformation. And this points to the ultimate paradox of The Tempest: that the savage in his uncivilized amorality may indeed be potentially more human than some of civilization's most aristocratic products; that in the final analysis, Caliban may prove Antonio, the European, the more savage creature. Breeding may be an insufficient basis on which to predicate conduct. As Miranda wisely observes, "Good wombs have borne bad sons."

The Tempest is indeed a play rich and strange. Even Montaigne in

G.M. Pinciss

his delightful essay "Of the Cannibals," which Shakespeare probably enjoyed, did not push cultural relativism this far. The potential for growth and development we discover in Caliban must come as something of a surprise, even though the turn of events is entirely appropriate in a play about forgiveness, redemption and reformation. Still, we hardly expect to find Caliban portrayed in a way that suggests his superiority to European aristocracy. One of the principal tenets of the pastoral convention, after all, was the inherent virtue of class and breeding. Even when their experiences have been confined to sheep and pastures, the truly noble will reveal themselves. Pastorella and Perdita are two exemplary figures of this kind, and the hero of *As You Like It*, denied the education and society appropriate for one of his blood, nevertheless remains "full of noble device." Caliban serves to raise one's doubts about all this.

Moreover, Shakespeare was well aware that another type of wild man, a more noble savage, in fact, could make just the point that good breeding predisposed one to virtue. And this brings us to our second category.

In this case, too, there were earlier models in literature. As Bremo in *Mucedorus* represents for us the savage savage, Orson in *Valentine and Orson* exemplifies the gentle or noble variety. The medieval romance of *Valentine and Orson* had been turned into a popular play at least by the time Sidney wrote the *Apology for Poetry*; and, like *Mucedorus*, *Valentine and Orson* was acted over a long period by the Queen's Men.[13] Unfortunately, no text of their play has been found, although it was entered in the Stationers' Register both in 1595 and again in 1600. Nor is the version extant for which Henslowe paid Munday and Hathaway five pounds in 1598.[14] We will have to rely on what we can reconstruct about the essential points of the fable from sixteenth-century prose versions.[15] But these efforts will prove rewarding because the title characters will serve us well as prototypes of our second category.

The story of Valentine and Orson begins with the banishment of the innocent and chaste Queen Bellissant, wife of Alexander, Emperor of Constantinople, and sister of King Pepin of France. Wrongly convinced of her infidelity, Alexander exiles his pregnant wife, who

13. Sidney's reference will be found in the *Apology for Poetry*, ed. Geoffrey Shepherd (London, 1965), p. 135. The title page and Stationers' Register information are cited by E. K. Chambers, *The Elizabethan Stage*, IV (Oxford, 1951), pp. 403-404.
14. *Henslowe's Diary*, ed. R. A. Foakes and R. T. Rickert (Cambridge, 1961), p. 93.
15. The most detailed study of the story will be found in Arthur Dickson, *Valentine and Orson, A Study in Late Medieval Romance* (New York, 1919).

78

delivers twin boys while traveling in a forest outside Orleans. One infant is stolen by a bear, who rears him with her cubs; the other is discovered by King Pepin's men and brought up at court. Years later, the young courtier Valentine undertakes to prove his valour by overpowering a fierce savage man who ravages the forest near Orleans. The struggle between these two powerful and equally matched combatants ends when the wild man surrenders not to Valentine's superior strength but to his gentle words and to what one version calls the "force of nature." The bear-son responds intuitively to feelings, values and patterns of behaviour that are beyond the capacities of the purely bestial. He submits to Valentine and accompanies him to court. Gradually acculturated, Orson protects Valentine in their many adventures. At last, through the aid of tokens and the oracular pronouncements of a brazen head, their true relationship is disclosed. Orson is granted the power of speech—under instruction from the brazen head a thread under his tongue is cut—their mother is found and exonerated, and the tale ends with the reunion and reconciliation of the family and the marriages of the brothers to Christian princesses.

A child of royal, or at least, of noble blood who has been raised exclusively by and among animals is not an uncommon inhabitant of a pastoral setting. Such a creature, of course, exhibits some of the attributes of the savage man we have discussed earlier: speechlessness, great strength, near nudity, domination over the animal kingdom. But since this particular type is of aristocratic lineage, he is endowed with an innate sensitivity, compassion and gentility that one does not find among animals.

In Book VI of *The Faerie Queene*, Spenser presents another innately noble savage.[16] Attracted by the cries of Serena and Sir Calepine, this "Salvage Man" defends them against the attack of Sir Turpine, whom he puts to flight. Spenser's creation is fearless and invulnerable, though without needful vestments or language. Yet he is skilled in the medicines of the forest, capable of pity, gentleness, "deepe compassion," and even a kind of reason. Living only on the nourishment of wild fruit, he "neither plough'd nor sowed,/ Ne fed on flesh, ne ever of wyld beast/ Did taste the bloud, obaying natures first beheast." His sympathy for the wounded lady as well as his regard for her safety and respect for her chastity indicate that

---

16. For background, see Roy Harvey Pearce, "Primitivistic Ideas in the 'Faerie Queene'," *JEGP*, 44 (1945), pp. 139-51. A most rewarding discussion of the themes raised here will be found in Tonkin, p. 58ff; and Cheney, especially p. 209ff.

> though he were still in this desert wood,
> Mongst salvage beasts, both rudely borne and bred,
> Ne ever saw faire guize, ne learned good,
> Yet shewd some token of his gentle blood,
> By gentle usage of that wretched Dame.
> For certes he was borne of noble blood,
> How ever by hard hap he hether came;
> As ye may know, when time shall be to tell the same. (VI. v.)

Although Spenser unfortunately never completed the story of the Salvage Man, a self-contained incident that the poet combines with the Salvage Man's history offers an indirect comment on it. This short episode involves Sir Calepine's rescuing an infant from the mouth of a bear and bestowing the baby on the childless Lady Matilde. As Sir Calepine points out, in this infant, whatever his real parentage, the adopting parents

> may enchace
> What ever formes ye list thereto apply,
> Being now soft and fit them to embrace
> Whether ye list him traine in chevalry,
> Or noursle up in lore of learn'd Philosophy. (VI. iv.)

In Spenser's notion of child development, heredity is important but environment plays a major role as well:

> certes it hath oftentimes bene seene,
> That of the like, whose linage was unknowne,
> More brave and noble knights have raysed beene,
> Then those, which have bene dandled in the lap. (IV. iv.)

The two stories taken together reflect on one another. The refined and civilized qualities of the Salvage Man are due entirely to his lineage. His growth as a creature of the forest has not prevented the development of humane feelings. As his birthright, he has retained the characteristics of his noble origins. Yet *The Faerie Queene* presents many examples of knights like Sir Turpine who conduct themselves most ignobly, or who for a time mistake the paths of chivalry. Spenser implies that gentle breeding is in itself neither a guarantee nor a *sine qua non* of virtuous and courtly behaviour, even if it is a customary concomitant.[17]

Much the same point is made by Shakespeare in his portrayal of

17. "Spenser is not enough of an optimist to espouse the view that the aristocracy possesses out-and-out moral superiority" (Tonkin, p. 162).

similar characters in *Cymbeline*.[18] The two brothers in this play are probably the closest parallels in Shakespeare's works to the friendship and rivalry in brotherly love dramatized in *Valentine and Orson*, and Orson's improbable wet nurse and rearing find an approximation in the histories of Cymbeline's sons, Guiderius and Arviragus.

When two and three years old, these princes were kidnapped by the banished general Belarius, who has since acted as their father for some twenty years. Although they have been raised as foresters in a Welsh cave, nevertheless their character has been determined by their blood:

> though train'd up thus meanly,
> I' th' cave wherein they bow, their thoughts do hit
> The roofs of palaces, and Nature prompts them
> In simple and low things to prince it, much
> Beyond the tricks of others. (III. iii.)

Their generosity and loving kindness to the disguised and fainting Imogen, their courage and valour in battle, their sympathy and tenderness in the funeral dirge are all manifestations of the gifts of Nature. And just to ensure that we do not miss the point, we are constantly reminded of it by the moralizing of Belarius:

> 'Tis wonder
> That an invisible instinct should frame them
> To royalty unlearn'd, honour untaught,
> Civility not seen from other, valour
> That wildly grows in them, but yields a crop
> As if it had been sow'd. (IV. ii.)

As we might suspect, however, Shakespeare is hardly content to render simply another version of a romance involving near-twins, banishments, slanders, adventures, coincidences and reconciliations.[19] The nominal hero of the play, Posthumus, is still another son of noble parentage reared parentless. Orphaned at birth, he has been brought up at court like Valentine. There he acquires "all the learnings that his time/ Could make him the receiver of, which he took,/ As we do air, fast as 'twas minister'd" (I. i.). Good seeds, it seems, will grow in any soil; Posthumus without family at court, or Cymbeline's

18. All references are to the New Arden, edited by James Nosworthy (London, 1969).
19. For an analysis of Shakespeare's debt to the romance tradition, see E. C. Pettet, *Shakespeare and the Romance Tradition* (London, 1949). Rosalie Colie discusses the pastoral aspects of *Cymbeline* and its treatment of the nature-nurture opposition, p. 242ff.

sons roughing it in the hills of Wales are examples of men with innate virtue.

Cymbeline's step-son Cloten, on the other hand, has nothing to commend him. A fool and a braggart, a gambler on bowls and cards, one who "Cannot take two from twenty, for his heart,/ And leave eighteen," is, nevertheless, the child of "a woman that/ Bears all down with her brain" (II. i.). The wickedness and scheming of the Queen are reflected in Cloten's plan to revenge himself on Imogen by raping her and killing Posthumus. Cloten is clearly the equal of his mother in his cruel and malicious intentions, but he lacks her cleverness and intelligence. As Imogen is more sensible than her father, so Cloten is less capable than his mother. And in the conflict between step-brothers—a version of the combat between Valentine and Orson—we can rightly anticipate that Guiderius will not reform Cloten but eliminate him.

In *Cymbeline*, Shakespeare takes up the variations one can play on melodies sounded more simply by the *Valentine and Orson* story. There, we will recall, the resolution was accomplished through the aid of a brazen head; in Shakespeare's version the final turning point of the action occurs in Posthumus' dream, a dream in which Jupiter on his eagle answers the pleas of Posthumus' family. This dream sequence shows Shakespeare focusing on the fundamental philosophical question at the heart of the issue: the balance of the gifts of Fortune with the gifts of Nature. In Posthumus, according to his father, "Great nature, like his ancestry,/ Moulded the stuff so fair,/ That he deserved the praise o' th' world" (V. iv.). Yet this worthy hero is made to suffer an inappropriate fortune: he has never received "The graces for his merits due."

Jupiter's answer, illogical but consistent with the hero's career, explains that worthiness and fortune are not in accord: "Whom best I love I cross; to make my gift,/ The more delay'd, delighted" (v. iv.). The misfortunes of his life, according to Jupiter, ultimately will leave Posthumus "happier much by his affliction made." Sorrow will be the cause of joy, misfortune of happiness, and what is long awaited will be all the more pleasurable. Unlike *Valentine and Orson*, in which adventure is the sum and substance, *Cymbeline* provides a rationale for the disparate events of the romance, which is proved to be a mode capable of handling more than simply high adventure. Shakespeare's achievement here is considerable. In its treatment of the materials of romance, in its use of the conventions of the pastoral, and in its skillful combination of diverse thematic and intellectual elements, *Cymbeline* is a play more complicated, more sophisticated, and more philosophical than any pastoral tragicomedy that had preceded it.

Our third category of salvage man is the most human, the most subtle, complex and popular. This species is composed of those who reject civilized life, take up residence alone, and gradually reverse the process of acculturation that Orson had undergone. Their reasons for fleeing the society of men may vary, but most frequently they are either ordered into exile or banishment—usually as a result of slander—or they suffer from the betrayal of love or friendship.

Traditional Renaissance sources provided examples of this civilized man turned savage. The sudden madness that afflicts a proud king like Nebuchadnezzar who "was driven from men, and did eat grass as oxen, and his body was wet with the dew of heaven, till his hairs were grown like eagles' feathers, and his nails like birds' claws" (Daniel IV. 25) is an Old Testament instance of the power of the deity. And Ariosto in the *Orlando Furioso* describes a hero who demonstrates the power of frustrated love. Distressed to find that Angelica has been untrue, Orlando "Did on the sudden all his sense enrage/ With hate, with fury, with revenge, and rage" (23)—to quote from Sir John Harington's translation (1591).[20] After a frenzy of destruction, Orlando collapses into a catatonic state for three days to emerge "with rage and not with reason waked,/ He rents his clothes and runs about stark naked," tearing up trees and terrorizing herdsmen and shepherds. When Astolfo finds Orlando some fifteen cantos later, we learn "such a change/ There was in all his shape from top to toe/ He rather seemed a beast more than a man in show" (39).

Perhaps this also describes how Orlando was performed in the theatre, for the stage direction in Greene's *Orlando Furioso* simply announces: "Enter Orlando attired like a mad-man" (III. i.). [21] In any case, the presentation was a popular one. The play seems to have been in the repertory of the Queen's Men, the Lord Admiral's, and Lord Strange's, who acted it at the Rose 1591/2. Quarto editions appeared in 1594 and again in 1599.

The popularity of Greene's drama is based on the broadest kind of appeal. In Greene's treatment the hero suffers no tragic loss of heroic dimension, the action presents no pathetic contrast between a former glory and the hero's present condition, and the poetry suggests none of the rich and subtle irony of Ariosto's attitude toward love.

20. Edited by Rudolf Gottfried (Bloomington, 1963).
21. Edited by W. W. Greg (Oxford, 1907).

> But thrice hath Cynthia changde her hiew
> Since thou infected with a lunasie,
> Hast gadded up and downe these lands & groves
> Performing strange and ruthfull stratagemes,
> All for the loue of faire Angelica,
> Whome thou with Medor didst suppose plaide false,
> But Sacrepant had grauen these rundelaies,
> To sting thee with infecting jealousie. (1317-1324)

In Greene one finds merely spectacle, bombast and slapstick.

In the hands of finer writers, however, madness over love and life, cruel and savage, tormenting and denigrating, is a subject that receives more sensitive and powerful treatment. To turn for a last time to *The Faerie Queene*, we notice that Spenser, in relating the tale of Amoret, moves quickly from presenting one type of savage man to another. After the hideous beast of greedie lust has been killed by Belphoebe, she finds Timias offering solace to the terrified and swooning Amoret:

> From her faire eyes wiping the deawy wet,
> Which softly stild, and kissing them atweene,
> And handling soft the hurts, which she did get.
> For of that Carle she sorely bruz'd had beene,
> Als of his own rash hand one wound was to be seene. (IV.vii.)

Observing Timias's actions "with sodaine glauncing eye," Belphoebe, scarcely controlling her urge to punish them both, turns on Timias: "Is this the faith, she said, and said no more,/ But turned her face, and fled away for evermore." Although it can eliminate lust, virginity is nonetheless subject to jealousy. Belphoebe refuses to hear Timias's explanation. Punished by "her sharpe reproofe," tormented by the "dread of her displeasures," and, finally, left without "hope of grace," Timias retreats to the depths of the forest: "Unto those woods he turned backe againe,/ Full of sad anguish, and in heavy case," where the "shade/ And sad melancholy" can match his mood. There he builds a cabin in a "gloomy glade," throws away his weapons, shuns society, redesigns his clothing,

> And his faire lockes, that wont with ointment sweet
> To be embaulm'd, and sweat out dainty dew,
> He let to grown and griesly to concrew,
> Uncomb'd, uncurl'd, and carelessly unshed,
> That in short time his face they overgrew,
> And over all his shoulders did dispred,
> That who he whilome was, uneath was to be red. (IV. vii.)

Living in isolation and despondency, he is forgotten by his fellow men and so tranformed that even Arthur does not recognize his former squire. Language, too, is lost through grief: to Arthur's words, Timias

> aunswered no whit,
> But stood still mute, as if he had beene dum,
> Ne sign of sence did shew, ne common wit,
> As one with grief and anguishe overcum
> And unto every thing did aunswere mum.

Unable to rouse him to intelligible response, Arthur leaves the "strange wight"—"Till time for him should remedy provide,/ And him restore to former grace againe." But the prince has some notion that the "rude brutishnesse" of this forest creature conceals a "gentle swaine," for he has engraved every tree with "the name . . . Which likly was his liefest love to be,/ For whom he now so sorely was bestad" (IV. vii.).

And, in fact, the state of living in the forest or of being out of one's mind has a linguistic basis: according to Bernheimer, wildness and insanity were almost interchangeable terms.[22] Furthermore, a factual basis underlies this confusion: the harmless insane were allowed to wander freely, and they could be taken for wild men.

In describing Timias's anguish, Spenser seems concerned to demonstrate how severely one may suffer in love and how wisdom may be gained in suffering. Later, when he is once again accepted into Belphoebe's favour, Timias seems to comprehend the full joys of his non-physical love for her. He has learned finally to delight in what is the proper relationship between them and he is no longer troubled by those emotions that had seemed so impossible to control when he had first met her and "her matchlesse beautie him dismayd" (III. v.).[23]

Shakespeare finds this somewhat depressed and misanthropic figure interesting enough to give us several versions. In *Pericles*, for example, the hero displays the characteristics of the wild man. Believing both his wife and daughter dead, Pericles "swears/ Never to wash his face, nor cut his hairs" (IV. iv.).[24] And when his ship reaches Mytilene we are told "for this three months [he] hath not spoken/ To any one, nor taken sustenance/ But to prorogue his grief" (V. i.).

22. P. 12.
23. According to Tonkin, Timias's restoration into Belphoebe's favour has hints of religious meaning since the word "grace" may indicate "the qualities of deity present in the beloved" (p. 229). In their reunion, Timias "of her grace did stand againe assured,/ To happie blisse." (VI. v.)
24. Edited by F. D. Hoeniger (London, 1963).

We can learn, perhaps, even more of the savage appearance of this hero from the description in George Wilkins' *Painfull Adventures of Pericles Prince of Tyre* (1608), a narrative that combines aspects of Shakespeare's sources with knowledge of a stage version, quite possibly Shakespeare's own.[25] According to Wilkins, Pericles in his grief appeared "attired from the ordinary habite of other men, as with a long over-growne beard, diffused hayre, undecent nayles on his fingers, and himselfe lying uppon his cowch groveling on his face." When a visitor called his name, "hee arose up sodainely with a fierce countenaunce: but seeing him to be a stranger, verie comely and honourably attyred, hee shruncke himself downe uppon his pillow, and held his peace." When Marina comes to console him, she finds a man even more violent than his counterpart in Shakespeare, for Wilkins explains that "in this rash distemperature" Pericles does not merely push the young woman away but strikes her so powerfully on the face that she falls into a swoon, bleeding.

Shakespeare's Pericles, having found incest, fraud and jealousy among men, having felt the loss of all he held dear, and having seen nature seemingly indifferent both to human justice and human misery, becomes something less than human in his catatonia. Perhaps we are being made the witness of his profound suffering in order that we can wonder and delight in his change of fortune. In his reunion with Marina, sorrow and happiness seem to meet; opposing and intense emotions are juxtaposed so that we can watch the merging " 'Twixt two extremes of passion, joy and grief," as Edgar describes his reconciliation with his own father. But unlike the deaths in *King Lear*, the destinies of parents in this play are more fortunate, even though the gods remain as ambiguous. Pericles tells Marina:

O, I am mock'd,
And thou by some incensed god sent hither
To make the world to laugh at me. (V. i.)

Shakespeare has traced the course of Pericles' pain so that we might relish the "great sea of joys" that now overwhelms him with its sweetness and makes "past miseries sport." This commixture of contradictory emotions, the merging of irreconcilable opposites in the

25. Hoeniger and Thomas Edwards, "An Approach to the Problem of *Pericles*," *Shakespeare Survey* V (1952), pp. 25-49, believe the novel was affected by Shakespeare's dramatization. Kenneth Muir in *Shakespeare as Collaborator* (New York, 1960) and Gerard Barker, "Themes and Variations in Shakespeare's *Pericles*," *English Studies*, XLIV (1963), pp. 401-444, argue that Wilkins became a source for Shakespeare's play. I have used Geoffrey Bullough, *Narrative and Dramatic Sources* VI (New York, 1966), p. 541 for my citations from Wilkins.

story itself, expresses something fundamental to the meaning of the play and basic to its presentation. Shakespeare has used the conventions of the savage man here to dramatize how sorrow may lead a strong man to reject his own humanity, how a hero may imitate the beast in his desire to escape the shocks that flesh is heir to. But such efforts can never succeed fully, for what is inhuman is not only incapable of man's anguish but also ignorant of his bliss. The intensity of his final happiness is the measure of Pericles' former sorrows, just as the recovery of his daughter marks the rebirth of her father to his true humanity: "Thou that beget'st him that did thee beget." And when he cries out ecstatically, "Give me my robes; I am wild in my beholding," his desire to change garments marks his return to normalcy, for this "wildness" is the elation and excitement of a rational mind.

The references to *King Lear* in the discussion of *Pericles* point up how closely related this tragedy is to the romances that followed it; indeed, to paraphrase Goneril, the observation that so many have made of this hath not been little. Moreover, we can hardly fail to notice that Edgar embodies many of the characteristics we have identified as belonging to the savage man. For these reasons and because Shakespeare's purpose here seems different from anything we have met elsewhere, we shall close with a few words on this play.

In a work that asks what essential differences separate the human and the animal world, we should not be surprised to find Edgar portrayed as a type of savage man. He tells us himself that in his disguise as Poor Tom he will mortify his flesh, "elf" all his hair in knots, grime his face with filth, and take "the basest and most poorest shape/ That ever penury, in contempt of man,/ Brought near to beast." Since the appearance of the Bedlam beggar has an historical reality, we must allow a degree of realism to his words. Nevertheless, what Edgar dramatizes in his appearance is a vision of "man/ Brought near to beast." And that is an appropriate sight in a play full of animal imagery and crowded with comparisons of man to animal: daughters are "dog-hearted"; bears are tied by the neck, men by the legs; women are as lascivious as the fitchew and the soilèd horse; on a night when "The lion and the belly-pinched wolf/ Keep their fur dry," King Lear unbonneted runs on to the stormy heath.

With the sight of Poor Tom, naked and shivering, Lear truly understands that "unaccommodated man is no more but such a poor, bare, forked animal." He had only moments before come to the realization that man stripped of those comforts that reinforce his human identity is simply another creature without distinction or importance. Now, in his encounter with Poor Tom, Lear reaches a new awareness. Reducing human existence to its essentials debases it, "Man's life is cheap as beast's." If man is more than or inherently different from the animal, the distinctions must rest not with physical or material qualities, but with rational and spiritual values, with notions of duty, ceremonious affection, kindness, pity, fortitude, and forgiveness.

Moreover, as Poor Tom, Edgar subsumes all the evils that flesh is capable of: the cruelty and lust of Goneril and Regan, the calculated self-interest of Edmund, the self-serving immorality of Oswald.

> A serving man, proud in heart and mind. . . . [One that] swore as many oaths as I spake words, and broke them in the sweet face of heaven; one that slept in the contriving of lust . . . false of heart, light of ear, bloody of hand; hog in sloth, fox in stealth, wolf in greediness, dog in madness, lion in prey. III. iv.).

And in the same way Edgar shares in the lives of the good characters, knowing like the Fool, Kent and Cordelia what it is to be "whipp'd from tithing to tithing, and stocked, punish'd, and imprison'd." In the words of one of Beckett's tramps, "He's all humanity."

In enacting the role of Poor Tom, Edgar embodies the lowest pitch of human existence—Gloucester recalls that the sight of the beggar made him think a man a worm. But through Edgar's various impersonations we watch him re-establish order and hierarchy among humanity. Starting with the bare, forked animal, "the thing itself," Edgar becomes by turns peasant, soldier, knight incognito, and perhaps even king.[26] He stands for the great range of human potential in behaviour and class at the same time that he reminds us of the "narrow distance between noblemen and beggar, accommodated man and the forked animal." Through his variety of disguises he portrays not only man's closeness to the beast but also his distance from the animal. And in emphasizing man's common humanity, Edgar is perhaps the most powerful, poignant and comprehensive presentation of the savage man in literature.

Embodiments of the savage man seem to pervade Renaissance writing and their frequent appearances are easily explained. The popularity of these creatures both for the immediacy of their impact on an audience and for the range of their expressiveness as symbols explains their appeal to writers: to sum up, their antics could delight and terrify, and their behaviour could demonstrate that life in a state of nature is possibly inferior or possibly superior to civilized life.

26. Bernard McElroy, *Shakespeare's Mature Tragedies* (Princeton, 1973), p. 159.

Furthermore, the savage man's removal from society allowed him to display the effects of heredity and environment on individual development. Finally, the wild man represented an important link in that chain which, by degrees, connects everything in creation.And while he provides the bridge between the human and the animal, he also clarifies the distinctions between man and beast.

That this literary creation can do so much so well explains its durability, for the wild man has managed to keep his hold on the imagination of civilized men despite the encroachments of science and technology on life beyond the suburbs. Writers as diverse as Swift and Rousseau, philosophers as opposed as Hobbes and Locke, have appreciated the symbolic value of this creature. If Bremo, or Orson, or Orlando are not familiar names today, modern readers may recognize their offspring more readily in Mowgli, or Tarzan, or King Kong.

Shakespeare's Pastoral Metamorphoses

J. M. NOSWORTHY

Let me begin by confessing that when, many years ago, I encountered H. W. Garrod's denunciation of A *Shropshire Lad* as "false pastoralism," assurance yielded to a confusion that I have never been able to resolve. Garrod's norms of comparison were Spenser, Mantuan and Pope, and, if the artificial conventions which they promote are true pastoralism while Housman's manifest realism, notwithstanding its conscious distortion of reality, is a fake, I was left wondering how far true is false and false is true. I find, now that I turn to the pastoralism of a Warwickshire lad, that incertainties are very far from crowning themselves assured but draw comfort from the possibly self-deluding conviction that Shakespeare's notion of pastoralism, if not as confused as my own, was, at least, highly idiosyncratic. One must, I suppose, accept that pastoralism begins with sheep, which have a tendency to stray, and that it involves shepherds and shepherdesses, who also tend to stray in a different sense. To claim that Shakespeare also strayed may smack of heresy, but it is clear that, when he addressed himself to pastoral themes, his uncontainable imagination led him into territory wholly unknown to his more conventional predecessors.

Shakespeare's poetic and dramatic thinking drew liberally upon the matter of pastoralism but without ever granting that matter the prominence which it enjoys in the plays of, say, Guarini, Lyly or Fletcher. In general it is true to say that pastoral images or allusions are always liable to break through, and sometimes in distinctly unusual contexts. There is, for instance, the debauched pastoralism of Iago's "Even now, now, very now, an old black ram/ Is tupping your white ewe," a figure which leads Brabantio, who takes the words literally, to protest: "This is Venice;/ My house is not a grange."

Or again, in another of Shakespeare's least Arcadian plays, there is Volumnia's simile: "Forth he goes,/ Like to a harvest-man, that's task't to mow/ Or all, or lose his hire," which momentarily transforms the blood-stained swordsman into a sunburn'd sickleman. It has long been recognized that when Hamlet exclaims, "Could you on this fair mountain leave to feed,/ And batten on this moor?" he is likening his mother to a ewe, and it is pertinent to remark that what is a "fair mountain" in one language is "Belmont" in another, so that Portia's residence should, in theory if not in fact, be good for several flocks of sheep. Be that as it may, The Merchant of Venice, though it can scarcely be accounted a pastoral comedy, does have an under-layer of pastoralism formed out of what may have been unconscious associations. The necessary mercantile noun "argosy" would have brought to mind the story of the Argonauts and the Golden Fleece, to which the play once or twice alludes, and it is but a short step from Phrixus's ram to what Sidney calls Aesop's "pretty tales of wolves and sheep" which furnish imagery and allusion relevant to the Shylock-Antonio conflict. There is also the matter of Laban's sheep.

The view that Shakespeare was fascinated with pastoralism receives corroboration of a rather unusual kind from Polonius, when he informs Hamlet that the players have come to Elsinore:

> The best actors in the world, either for tragedy, comedy, history, pastoral, pastoral-comical, historical-pastoral, tragical-historical, tragical-comical-historical-pastoral, scene individable, or poem unlimited.

Our first impression may be that this is just another instance of Polonius mouthing his musty superfluities, but we should not lose sight of the fact that, at this point in the play, Shakespeare is using his characters as mouthpieces for his own comments on the fortunes of the Lord Chamberlain's company—the tragedians of the city which should be Copenhagen but which we know to be London. There is also the attractive suggestion, made by Neil Porter, the Shakespearian actor, that Polonius is, in fact, reading the words from a play-bill, and this, if correct, would eliminate any possibility of Polonian elaboration. It is basically the seeming absurdity and extravagance of "tragical-comical-historical-pastoral" that leads us to assume that the passage is in character. Yet for proof that the category is a perfectly valid one we have only to turn to Peele's David and Bethsabe. Tragical—it includes what the title page calles "the Tragedie of Absalon"; comical—it tells of the love and marriage of David and Bathsheba; historical—see the Second Book of Samuel, chapters 11-19; pastoral

—"Thus saith the Lord of hosts, I took thee from the sheepcote, from following the sheep, to be ruler over my people," and Peele's imagery does, after all, draw rather heavily upon The Song of Solomon. If it be urged that more particulars must justify my knowledge, I would simply observe that a greater and more influential genius than Peele took London by storm with a historical tragi-comedy dealing with the exploits of a Scythian shepherd.

If this, the most elaborate of Polonius's dramatic kinds makes sense, the odds are that the remainder do likewise and I do not think that we have to rack our brains or search our memories too strenuously to recognise that they do. Hence, the speech, in spite of the speaker, emerges as a thoroughly businesslike formulation of the various kinds of drama that had held the stage throughout the last twenty years of the sixteenth century. It is, as anyone who has talked or written about Shakespeare must concede, a great deal more useful than the tripartite ordering of the 1623 Folio and considerably more penetrating than the list given in the Induction to Marston's What You Will, which, with its inclusion of the "nocturnal," merely supplements the painfully obvious with the tantalizingly obscure. The fact that the word "pastoral" figures in no less than four of the eight categories mentioned by Polonius has a twofold significance. It reveals Shakespeare's awareness of the extent to which the poetic revolution precipitated by Spenser had been absorbed into professional drama; and it discloses, in a way familiar to students of Freud, a certain preoccupation with pastoralism attaching either to Polonius or his creator. And since Polonius, unlike his son and daughter, is singularly devoid of pastoral graces, we must, I think, accept that the preoccupation was Shakespeare's own.

Yet, in the Shakespeare canon as a whole, this preoccupation manifests itself principally in the kind of incidentals that I have already mentioned and there are, by my reckoning, only five plays which fit readily into the category of pastoral or, more strictly, pastoral-comical:—Love's Labour's Lost, A Midsummer Night's Dream, As You Like It, The Winter's Tale and The Tempest. Some would, perhaps, wish to add The Merry Wives of Windsor and Cymbeline, but neither play seems to me to carry a sufficiency of the requisite material and I would suggest that, if the list had to be extended, the strongest candidates would be Macbeth, where pastoralism dances to the Devil's tune, and Timon of Athens, which drifts into a kind of sour pastoralism irreconcilable with the demands of tragedy. But that way madness lies.

Since the theme of this conference was chosen to commemorate the quatercentenary of the publication of The Shepheardes Calender, it is fitting that I should begin with the year 1579. Lyly's *Euphues* had just begun to exert its formidable, some would say baneful, influence and the year saw the publication of Gosson's *The Schoole of Abuse* which, though intrinsically worthless, was to have important consequences. Directly or indirectly these works, current in 1579, relate to the three great pastoral innovators: Spenser, who proceeded towards pastoral epic in his own majestic way; Lyly, who was soon to find an outlet for his very considerable gifts in pastoral comedies which, however limited their scope, achieve near-perfection in their kind; and Philip Sidney. It is true that Sidney's major contributions came later and that, even then, they were not exactly hurried into print, but Leicester had staged *The Lady of the May* at Wanstead in 1578 and its author's personal reputation was, in any case, sufficient to ensure that anything that engaged his interest would instantly become the fashion. It is inconceivable that Shakespeare was unaware of these developments or that he was unresponsive to them. He had now reached that age when, for many writers, literary aspirations begin to harden into commitment and the serious endeavours of the dedicated spirit get under way. There has been much speculation about Shakespeare's so-called hidden years but it is, I think, a probability tantamount to certainty that they witnessed the composition of a substantial number of pastoral and Petrarchan verses which he later suppressed—though *A Lover's Complaint* and Sonnet 145 may have been the two that got away. I am tempted to risk the further conjecture that it was in or about 1579 that he bought or borrowed a copy of that year's other significant publication, North's *Plutarch*. It is hard to imagine anything less pastoral than this particular monument of English prose but it could well have had a sobering effect on a young and impressionable mind intoxicated with the new wine of pastoralism. What is certain, I think, is that Plutarch and pastoral became somehow linked in Shakespeare's mind.

When, fifteen years later, Shakespeare turned to pastoral comedy, he did so in the knowledge, begotten of experience, that he was playing a fascinating but dangerous game. It is the measure of Spenser's genius that his pastoralism was, and still is, enjoyable. As anyone who has struggled through the *Eclogues* of Alexander Barclay will know, there is no essential difference between them and the eclogues that make up *The Shepheardes Calender*, save that the latter work contains the new miracle ingredient, poetry. The Elizabethan age produced few Spensers but many Barclays, and the merits of two or three dozen anthology pieces should not blind us to the fact that sixteenth-century literary pastoralism, pursued through volumes, proves to be as sterile, repetitive and downright boring as its companion vogue of Petrarchanism.

That, I think, would have been Shakespeare's own verdict and there are certainly no grounds for supposing that, once he had committed himself to the writing of plays, he ever seriously applied himself to the writing of pastoral poetry. *Venus and Adonis* is a valediction. The sense in which it was the first heir of his invention may be obscure, but that in which it was the last is not.

As a practising dramatist whose gaze remained firmly fixed on the needs of the public theatre even when he was devising plays which, in the first instance, were for private performance, Shakespeare would undoubtedly have been acutely aware that the pastoral convention and the two-hour traffic of the stage make strange bedfellows, and the efforts of his immediate predecessors would have revealed to him, as they do to us, the limitations of pastoral drama. He would have seen that Lyly's delicate art, so sensitively adapted to the tastes of a court audience and the restricted skills of the child-actors, was not for all markets—the mind boggles at the thought of *Midas* or *Endymion* at the Globe—and that Marlowe, once he had made dramatic capital out of the pastoralism imposed by the sources of *Tamburlaine*, banished it as something wholly incompatible with his dramatic purposes. He would have observed how, by contrast, Peele's dedication to pastoralism betrayed him into turning what should have been powerful dramatic situations to favour and to prettiness. Greene's ramshackle structures would have alerted him to the dangers of unintegrated pastoralism and he could well have drawn a moral from the fact that it was the most fatuous of Elizabethan dramatists, Anthony Munday, commended by Meres, as "our best plotter" but held by Ben Jonson to be better qualified for a dumb-show, whose pastoral endeavours earned him the soubriquet, "The Shepherd Tony." If, as the available evidence suggests, *The Two Angry Women of Abingdon* was on the boards some ten years prior to its publication in 1599,[1] it could have persuaded Shakespeare that pastoral comedy is none the worse for an infusion of earthy realism and a diminution of obsolescent conventions. All in all there was much for Shakespeare to learn from his predecessors, but the primary lesson was, I think, that, if pastoral comedy was to be his object, it would have to be achieved through methods of his own devising.

In contrast to most of his predecessors, Shakespeare started with one major handicap—his abundant sense of humour. This is a quality lacking in Spenser and Sidney, both of whom were touched with

---

1. An allusion in Richard Harvey's *Plaine Percivall* seems to establish 1589 as the forward limit of composition. See H. C. Hart, *3 Henry VI* (First Arden), p. xlii.

puritanism and directed their art towards moral earnestness, while, as for Lyly, granting that he was, as his contemporaries claimed, eloquent and witty, we are still left wondering whether anyone with a shred of genuine humour in his make-up could ever have written *Euphues* in the first place. Nor, as far as my experience goes, do any of the university wits qualify as humorists. Now when a sense of humour comes into the contact with pastoral convention, the result can be surprising. Devotees of Firbank will recall how, in *Valmouth*, the carefully contrived pastoral atmosphere is shattered by a single word when David Tooke, the "crazy Corydon," fails to turn up for his clandestine meeting with Lady Parvula and she consoles herself with the words: "What keeps him ever? Some horrid cow? I can't bear to think of the man I love under some cow's chidderkins." Chidderkins, the elected and predestined word, should, in theory, annihilate without trace but the fragments are, in fact, speedily reassembled. The process can, I think, best be likened to that by which children deflate balloons simply for the pleasure of blowing them up again. Shakespeare, too, yielded to this irresistible impulse to kill the thing he loved, only to recreate it, as we see, time and again, in *As You Like It*. Touchstone's "cow's dugs" are, I think, inferior to Firbank's "chidderkins" but elsewhere Shakespeare's absolute mastery stands revealed in "the copulation of cattle," the "country copulatives," "these couples" that "are coming to the ark" and the "pair of very strange beasts which in all tongues are call'd fools."

If the formula had to make provision for a humorous disposition, it had also to resolve the problem of diversifying the substance of classical and Renaissance pastoralism in a manner compatible with the needs of a five-act play intended for the widest possible audience. Aesop's "pretty tales of wolves and sheep" might, as Sidney claims, "include the whole considerations of wrong doing and patience," but in drama they can scarcely rise above the level of secondary analogues, while the Arcadian exploits of shepherds and herdsmen, however diverting, represent an extreme simplification of life which could hardly have commended itself to a mind that ranged over the infinite complexities of human experience. As for the moral most frequently derived from the pastoral, that the virtuous pleasures of country life stand in violent contrast to the corrupting influences of town life, that "Society is all but rude/ To this delicious solitude," this was something that contemporary poets could, and all too frequently did, proclaim, but a dramatist could not normally take it as the *terminus ad quem* of comedy. Such sentiments might be voiced as occasion served by the banished Duke or by Imogen or Perdita, but the final scene invariably finds them returning unprotestingly to court. It is only the penitents, like Duke Frederick, or the eccentrics, like Jaques, who voluntarily retire to the wilderness. Since it was to the city and the court that Shakespeare owed his fame and fortune, we know what his personal attitude ought to have been.

I suggest that, in consequence of these personal and professional considerations, Shakespeare, for the five plays that I have mentioned, worked out a formula whose subtleties defy close analysis but whose main components are susceptible of definition. The received pastoral conventions are extended to cover a wide range of normal country activities, so that, for instance, there are hunting scenes in four of the plays. Lyrics, songs and dances are accommodated with a profusion seldom found elsewhere and provision is made for pageant, inner-play or masque. The dramatist's pastoralism, being essentially classical in conception, draws freely upon Greek and Roman legend and mythology, with the ancient gods and heroes making a distinctive, though not always immediately perceptible contribution, and this goes hand in hand with the principle of metamorphosis. One familiar characteristic of those gods was their propensity for changing either themselves or others into unexpected shapes, so that "Jupiter / Became a bull and bellow'd," while

> Apollo hunted Daphne so,
> Only that she might laurel grow:
> And Pan did after Syrinx speed
> Not as a nymph, but for a reed.

It seems that, when the mating urge came upon them, they proceeded less often after the downright way of human creation than by metamorphic deception. Ovid's *Metamorphoses* is, of course, a comprehensive guide to all their transformations and Shakespeare's obligations to it are manifold, though if, as I shall argue, metamorphism is one of the most important ingredients of the pastoral formula, its origins were by no means exclusively Ovidian. It should, however, be remarked that Ovid ultimately turns from mythology to the history of Rome and the deification of Julius Caesar. The final metamorphosis thus impinges on the subject matter of one of Shakespeare's tragedies and establishes a link with the lives of noble Greeks and Romans in general. It is not, therefore, altogether surprising that North's *Plutarch* contributes to at least two of the pastoral comedies or that the gods and demigods should assume a special prominence which, though not exclusive to the five plays under reveiw, is neverthelss as exception to Shakespeare's normal practice.

That, for the Elizabethans, metamorphism was little, if at all, less attractive than pastoralism itself is attested by the mere titles of various publications relating to the metamorphoses of Love and Scilla, maids and gipsies and, of course, water-closets and also by numerous writings, usually inspired by Ovid, which cover a wide variety of transformations. Shakespeare was ready to follow prevailing fashion, to use whatever lay to hand, but to do so in a way that vindicates Keat's contention that he lived a life of allegory and that his works are a comment on it. It was also a life of metamorphosis in the sense that all drama is an act of transformation. Edward Alleyne, leaving, as Nashe might have put it, the trade of innkeeper, whereto he was born, projected himself into the person of Tamburlaine, then Barabbas, then Guise, then Faustus, while Richard Burbage, though to the manner born, was no less a Proteus for shapes. This, I fear, is to state the painfully obvious and I must apologize for continuing to do so by remarking that the process went a good deal further when it transformed little scrubbed boys into love-lorn maidens, queens, courtesans and pelican daughters, and further still when it turned Rosalind back into Ganymede, not, I think, to cover up the inadequacies of a boy-actor, but to make capital out of a metamorphosis already present in the narrative source. Another practical metamorphosis occurred when the dramatist decreed and his audience willingly accepted that the modest amenities of the wooden O represented the fields of France, the Forest of Arden, Elsinore, Illyria or the sea-coast of Bohemia, and it must be emphasized that such illusions were entirely the work of the playwright. Stage properties, such as those listed in Henslowe's inventory, were not used to establish a scene—the Elizabethans were curiously restricted in their response to natural landscape—but to implement an action. If one or two trees were dotted about the stage it was because they were convenient things for hiding behind or for hanging sonnets on or for letting "every soldier hew him down a bough."

Though all these things are, as I have said, transparently obvious, they are material to the comprehensive pattern of metamorphism which informs Shakespeare's pastoral plays and also material to my own needs, which are to squeeze as many meanings as possible out of the word "metamorphosis." If I now mention another familiar transformation effected through the spoken word, that of day turning to night or night to day, it is because this leads into the double time device, usually associated with *Othello*, thence to the double age scheme discernible in *Hamlet, King Lear* and *Macbeth*, and finally to the antithesis of double dimension which attaches to the heroes of the

Roman plays. But these contrivances, which are double in the tragedies and so represent, even when repeated, a single kind of metamorphosis, are made multiple in the pastoral plays and sustain a wide variety of transformations that are, especially in A *Midsummer Night's Dream*, virtually beyond computation or definition.

The more orthodox forms of metamorphosis—the physical, which turns prince into frog, and the psychological, which debases good men and reforms bad ones—I shall mention in connection with the individual plays. Shakespeare's obligations to Ovid are too evident for detection, but it should be remarked that the *Metamorphoses* is not pre-eminently a pastoral poem and that its divinely ordained transformations are rarely, if at all, used by the dramatist as primary material. And for the Elizabethans, who owed their mythology to the Renaissance and, one susupects, their superstition to the Reformation, the changes wrought by the gods could be just as easily achieved by sorcerers. Hence there was a conflation for which the prime exemplar was *The Metamorphosis of Lucius Apuleius*, better known as *The Golden Ass*. This more familiar title—something of a misnomer since the ass is never described as being golden—appears to have been pre-Augustinian and presumably testifies to the book's long-standing popularity, and that its appeal remained undiminished in Shakespeare's time can be inferred from the fact that William Adlington's translation, published in 1566, had been reprinted at least four times by 1600. This fascinating chronicle, which, in combining the activities of the old gods with the mysterious rites of Isis and Osiris, affords a rough analogue to the Renaissance-Reformation interaction, incorporates the classical and the romantic, the pastoral and the picaresque, the sinister and the comic, the gentle and the brutal. So I might say in passing, does *The Winter's Tale*, but for the moment I am content to hazard the conjecture that *The Golden Ass* formed part of Shakespeare's boyhood reading and that it was often in his thoughts. One critic has recently traced its influence upon the Bradleian tragedies, and though the examples that he cites are not individually compelling they are cumulatively persuasive.[2]

It now remains to relate Shakespeare's pastoral plays to the principle of metamorphosis and, where necessary, to their other ingredients, and this I wish to do in the light of one or two propositions. The first concerns adumbration and is merely a reaffirmation of the familiar view that, in Shakespeare's final plays, there is notable

2. J. J. R. Tobin, "Apuleius and the Bradleian Tragedies," *Shakespeare Survey* 31, pp. 33-34.

reversion to his early practices. This is an aspect of his mind and art that has not yet been fully examined, but Professor G. R. Hibbard's recent essay, "Adumbrations of *The Tempest* in *A Midsummer Night's Dream*,"[3] deals suggestively with the relationship between those two plays. That being so, I am relieved of the need to say very much about *The Tempest*, whose affinities with the other pastoral comedies, or at least with my interpretation of them, will, in any case, be readily apparent. The second proposition is that Shakespeare sometimes paired off his writings so that one piece complemented its immediate predecessor—a practice which may have owed something to Plutarch's comparisons. *Venus and Adonis* and *The Rape of Lucrece* exploit radically different aspects of Ovid's art, the one in sunlight and the other in darkness. The same distinction, extended to fields by day and woods by night, applies to the two comedies that follow the narrative poems, and Shakespeare, rather unusually relying on plots of his own devising, shews in the one that, though the path of true love never did run smooth, all ends in fulfilment, and in the other that, when it runs a little too smoothly, the end is frustration. *Henry the Fifth* and *Julius Caesar* may sound strange bedfellows, but Harry of Monmouth is very much a metamorphosis of Alexander of Macedon and the collocation is warranted by Plutarch. The dereliction and torrid sexuality of *Antony and Cleopatra* yield to the incorruptibility and frigid chastity of *Coriolanus*; and finally we have *The Winter's Tale* and *The Tempest*, with their community of themes presented, in the one, with a wild disregard for time and place and, in other, within the strict limits of classical unity. The fact that, of these eight plays, four are pastoral and the other four, directly or indirectly, Plutarchan may be pure coincidence. I am, nevertheless, fortified in the belief that Plutarch and pastoralism somehow cohered in Shakespeare's mind.

My third, more tentative, proposition, is that the titles that Shakespeare gave to his pastoral comedies are less casual then they may at first appear, and this leads directly to a consideration of *Love's Labour's Lost*, a play which, though undeniably pastoral, may seem already to have demolished all that I have said about its author's ingredients, particularly to those who regard it as a satirical allegory. As my own interpretation has been published elsewhere,[4] it may suffice here to state how my conclusions were reached. Like many others, I had long been baffled as to how and why the words of Mercury are harsh after

---

3. *Shakespeare Survey* 31, pp. 77-83.
4. "The Importance of Being Marcade," *Shakespeare Survey* 32, pp. 105-114.

the songs of Apollo until, some years ago, I came across five instances of the name "Markady" in Robert Wilson's comedy, *The Cobbler's Prophecy*, where it occurs as the cobbler's misnomer for the god Mercury. This seemed to throw a new light on Monsieur Marcade, a Messenger, who, in less than thirty words, makes such an enormous impact and who combines two of Mercury's major functions—those of messenger and psychopomp. The words of Marcade are indeed harsh and effect a drastic reversal in a play which has thitherto been largely subject to the rule of Apollo, the lord of sunshine, the inspirer of songs and sonnets, the patron of academes, the preceptor of moderation and self-knowledge and, ultimately, the bringer of sudden death. Armado's dictum suggests that there has been a conflict between Mercury and Apollo, but this must be ruled out since the two gods were close friends and frequent allies. The underlying conflict is between them on the one hand and, on the other, Cupid, who is mentioned time and again, and not surprisingly since so many of his arrows have struck home with a vengeance. Hence, I suggest that "Love" in the play's title is a personification rather than an abstraction, and that his labours are lost when Mercury is metamorphosed into Marcade. For the rest, Berowne's constant alternations between denunciation and vulnerability may not, in themselves, be metamorphic, but they induce a Protean use of language which constantly allows him to combine affectation and homeliness in a single sentence. At the end it is decreed that he and his companions shall be transformed into something utterly alien to their true natures, and the decree adumbrates the theme of probation which figures so conspicuously in the late romances. Ferdinand of Navarre must justify himself by becoming a hermit. I wonder whether it is pure coincidence that, sixteen years later, another Ferdinand has to prove his worth by carrying logs.

Of *A Midsummer Night's Dream* Coleridge observed: "I am convinced that Shakespeare availed himself of the title of this play in his own mind, and worked upon it as dream throughout"—a judgment from which we can scarcely dissent since the whole fabric of this pastoral nocturnal is one of anomaly, distortion, confusion, contradiction, hallucination and metamorphosis with the plot alone achieving consistency. Critics have complained that the four-day action promised at the start is, in fact, accomplished in two, while others have carped about the rites of May being observed on June 24, and Shakespeare has, as usual, been convicted of carelessness. Yet those days apparently occur at a time when the moon is invisible but when, according to Peter Quince's almanac, it is nearly at the full, when "Phoebe doth behold/ Her silver visage in the wat'ry glass," when Titania is "ill met by moonlight" and when "the wolf behowls the moon." Two days or four, it matters little since this is, by any reckoning, all too short a date for the preparation of a play by a bunch of rude mechanicals who are distinctly less literate than most of the pageant-mongers of *Love's Labour's Lost*. And that play, said to be "some ten words long," actually lasts about twenty minutes yet fills up the three hours from suppertime to midnight. When we add to this that these unmistakably Elizabethan artisans are performing in ancient Greece before Theseus, Demetrius and Lysander, all of whom belong to different centuries, we realize that time in A *Midsummer Night's Dream* is very multiple indeed, and the same holds for dimension. Oberon, the king of elves, is married to Titania, whose name proclaims her descent from the race of giants, yet she is simultaneously so small that the cowslips are her pensioners and Moth, Cobweb, Peaseblossom and Mustardseed her attendants but so big that she can be Theseus's quondam mistress, can foster an Indian boy of, presumably, normal height and can eventually become enamoured of an ass. Oberon's own infidelities have been with a bouncing Amazon of manifestly more than elfin proportions and Puck's mutations are as variable in size as they are in shape. Such variations are not, perhaps, unusual with fairies, but they also apply to some of the humans, Leaving aside the translation of Bottom, we have the curious case of Helena and Hermia. They so much resemble each other as to be likened to "two lovely berries moulded on one stem," yet, within minutes, one has become a "tall personage," a "painted maypole," and the other a puppet, "so dwarfish and so low," a minimus, a bead, an acorn, who "was a vixen when she went to school"—a charge which cannot be reconciled with Helena's earlier account of their idyllic schoolgirl friendship.

Such diversification of time, shape and dimension is incident to most dreams, but, as we all know, dream patterns can be profoundly disturbing as well as gratifying. It may be that, enthralled by the sheer magic of the play, we tend to overlook its several nightmare elements. Hermia's dream of the crawling serpent is memorably unnerving but it is slight in comparison with Helena's prolonged and intense anguish. Titania's liaison with an ass may be richly comical but it is grounded on bestiality, which, notwithstanding Shakespeare's poetry, Mendelssohn's music and the compassionate attitudes of the permissive society, was and is a very ugly practice. And there is that appalling weather in Act II, scene i, which, despite all that I have read about the summer of 1594 and all that I have known about those of 1978 and 1979, seems to me to register nightmare rather than reality.

It is generally acknowledged that the play has no single comprehensive source. It seems that Shakespeare simply allowed his imagination to run riot over a wide range of reading, theatre-going, folklore and, perhaps, personal relationships, drawing upon them for episodes, character traits and allusions and allowing them to develop with the illogicality of a dream into an ultimately coherent synthesis. As the identification of all its hooked atoms must await the emergence of a second John Livingstone Lowes, all that I can do here is to offer some random comments on matters relevant to my general ideas about Shakespeare's pastoralism.

Puck, I suspect, owes more to oral than to literary tradition and it is with some trepidation that I hazard the suggestion that, if he owes anything to a book or play, that obligation is to the parasitic serving-man, Hodge, in *The Two Angry Women of Abingdon*. In that pleasant comedy, with its quarrels, its runaway lovers, its irate parents, and its mistaking of identities in the woods by night, all of which resemble *A Midsummer Night's Dream* with the magic left out, it is the elusive Hodge who, through his love of mischief and his capacity for minicry, is the primary agent of confusion. It is he who goads his companions into preparing for a fight which they are too exhausted to engage in, with the result that, to borrow Shakespeare's famous direction, "they sleep all the act." If, as I suggest, Shakespeare, without any supernatural soliciting, transformed Hodge into hobgoblin, it would not have been beyond him to convert four attendant eunuchs into four attendant fairies and a fair matron into the Fairy Queen herself. I turn then to *The Tenth Book of Lucius Apuleius:*

> . . . there were foure Eunuches that lay on a bed of downe on the ground with Boulsters accordingly for us to lye on, the Coverlet was of cloth of Gold, and the pillows soft and tender, whereon the delicate Matron had accustomed to lay her head. Then the Eunuches not minding to delay any longer the pleasure of their Mistresse closed the doores of the Chamber and departed away: within the Chamber were lamps that gave a cleare light all the place over: Then she put off all her Garments to her naked skinne, and taking the Lampe that stood next to her, began to annoint all her body with balme, and mine likewise, but especially my nose, which done, she kissed me, not as they accustome to doe at the stewes, or in brothell houses, or in the Curtiant Schooles for gaine of money, but purely, sincerely, and with great affection, casting out these and like loving words:

Thou art he whom I love, thou art he whom I onely desire, without thee I cannot live, and other like preamble of talke as women can use well enough, when as they mind to shew or declare their burning passions and great affection of love: Then she tooke me by the halter and caste me downe upon the bed, which was nothing strange unto me, considering that she was so beautifull a Matron and I so wel boldened out with wine, and perfumed with balme, whereby I was readily prepared for the purpose: But nothing grieved me so much as to think, how I should with my huge and great legs imbrace so faire a Matron, or how I should touch her fine, dainty, and silken skinne, with my hard hoofes, or how it was possible to kisse her soft, pretty and ruddy lips, with my monstrous mouth and stony teeth, or how she, who was young and tender, could be able to receive me.

This episode, which is strangely omitted in Professor Geoffrey Bullough's monumental survey, affords a sufficient source for the whole Bottom-Titania relationship, though, for several obvious reasons, Shakespeare does not go as far as Apuleius. But it is a near miss and one that reminds me of the American schoolboy's remark a propos of *The Idylls of the King*: "There is some pretty hot necking in Lord Tennyson, only they never quite make it."

> Sleep thou, and I will wind thee in my arms . . .
> So doth the woodbine the sweet honeysuckle
> Gently entwist; the female ivy so
> Enrings the barky fingers of the elm.
> O, how I love thee! how I dote on thee!

This, for all its felicities, sounds to me very much like the language of inordinate desire.

Confirmation of Shakespeare's debt comes from an earlier chapter of *The Golden Ass*, where Lucius rescues a gentlewoman who tells how she will reward him:

First, I will bravely dresse the haires of thy forehead, and then will I finely combe thy maine, I will tye up thy rugged tayle trimly, I will decke thee round about with golden trappes, in such sort that thou shalt glitter like the starres of the skie, I will bring thee daily in my apron the kirnels of nuts, and will pamper thee up with delicates; I will set store by thee, as by one that is the preserver of my life: Finally, thou shalt lack no manner of thing.

This, in general, resembles the provisions that Titania makes for Bottom, but the significant detail is that she will send a venturous fairy "that shall seek/ The squirrel's hoard, and fetch thee new nuts." Fresh nuts, as Bottom's expressed preference for "a handful or two of dried peas" indicates, are not normally fed to donkeys.

Yet there is one instructive difference between Shakespeare and Apuleius. Lucius is completely metamorphosed into an ass, whereas Bottom's translation is only partial, and this admits the possibility that the germ of the idea came from Plutarch, who, in *The Life of Theseus*, tells both of the battle with the Centaurs, which is referred to in the play, and of the Minotaur, so that there may have been a dovetailing of sources. Though it is probable that the first promptings for *A Midsummer Night's Dream* came from *The Knight's Tale*, which yielded Duke Theseus and Hippolyta, the names of Egeus and Philostrate, the rival lovers, the vows of undying friendship which turn to hate, the rites of May and one or two other details, there is a good deal of supplementation from Plutarch. It was *The Life of Theseus* which furnished the relationship with Hercules, corroborated the names of Egeus and Hippolyta and supplied those other names which Oberon uses as ammunition:

> Didst not thou lead him through the glimmering night
> From Perigouna, whom he ravished?
> And make him with fair Aegles break his faith,
> With Ariadne and Antiopa?

The mention of Hermes, Hermus and the city of Hermione affords as good an explanation as any for the name of Hermia, while that of Helena must surely have been drawn from Plutarch's extended account of the rape of the nine-year-old Helen of Troy which Theseus was alleged to have committed. Helena's beauty is emphasized in the play and if we admit the identification it adds something richly comical to the fact that she of the face that launched a thousand ships should persuade herself:

> No, no, I am as ugly as a bear,
> For beasts that meet me run away for fear.

Perigouna conceals herself in a place overgrown with shrubs and

> rushes called Stoebe, and wild Sperage, which she simply like a child intreated to hide her as if they had heard, and had sense to understand her.

Here we have precedent both for Titania's over-canopied retreat and for the human qualities which, according to Puck, the rude mechanicals attribute to briers and thorns. Titania's Indian votaress died in child-birth. So did Ariadne, and both deaths are associated with sea, ships and the wanton wind.

For the name of Lysander, Shakespeare simply turned to the life of that worthy. Demetrius the Phalerean is mentioned in *The Life of*

Theseus and, curiously, Emetrius, King of Inde, figures in *The Knight's Tale* but, as the late Terence Spencer showed,[5] the revelation that Helena's lover, like Theseus, had a savage and promiscuous past was derived from Plutarch's account of Demetrius Poliorcetes. There are, I think, other obligations to *The Life of Demetrius*. I mention, for what it is worth, that it contains graphic accounts of a couple of dreams which, at least, consort with the character of Shakespeare's play, but return to that nightmarish summer weather and the confusion of the seasons throughout *A Midsummer Night's Dream*. For it so fell out in Athens at the time of Demetrius that

> On the feast day also of *Bacchus*, they were compelled to leaue the pompe or procession for that day, it was such an extreme hard frost out of all season: and beside, there fell such a mil-dew and a great frost vpon it, that not only their vines and oliues were killed with it, but also the most part of the wheate blades which were newly sprung vp:

The consequence was that:

> . . . by the deuice of *Stratocles* it was enacted at an assembly of the city, that the moneth of March in which they were at that time, should be called and reputed Nouember . . . & afterwards againe, this selfe moneth of March which they had translatd into Nouember, became suddenly August.

Hence, says Plutarch, Phillipides wrote of Stratocles:

> Into one moneth his coming hither
> Hath thrust vp all the yeare together.

The same could have been written of the author of *A Midsummer Night's Dream*.

Certain dream-like qualities linger in *As You Like It* but there are no perceptible obligations to either Plutarch or Apuleius and the play's affinities are with *Love's Labour's Lost* rather than *A Midsummer Night's Dream*. Jaques, like Armado, begins as a traveller, and he and Duke Frederick, like Navarre, retreat to a hermitage; Orlando, like Berowne and his companions, litters the scene with love-poems; Audrey forsakes William for Touchstone as Jaquenetta deserts Costard for Armado, and the startling and significant intrusion of Jaques de Boys in the closing moments of the play is strongly reminiscent of that of Marcade. *As You Like It* also develops that kind of stylistic metamorphosis which I have attributed to Berowne. Critics have remarked on the frequent subtle transitions from poetry to prose and vice-versa

---

5. "The Vile Name of Demetrius", *MLR*, xxxxix (1954), pp. 46-8.

and it will suffice here to observe that, in the "Seven Ages of Man" speech, the verse is pitched only very slightly above the level of prose, while the stretto in V. iii., notwithstanding that Rosalind likens it to "the howling of Irish wolves against the moon," is prose which has the full impact of poetry, and very moving poetry at that. The play also adumbrates Shakespeare's late romances. The apparition of Hymen, so much more positive than the duality of Marcade and the semi-divinity of Theseus, constitutes a full theophany and his assurance:

> Then is there mirth in heaven,
> When earthly things made even
> Atone together

crystallizes that theme of reconciliation which the romances so power-fully develop. Rosalind's magical pretensions may not match Prospero's but they foreshadow Paulina's.

In *As You Like It* the several levels of pastoralism are complemented by diverse aspects of metamorphism, different from those of *A Midsummer Night's Dream* but no less significant. Mutations resulting from disguise and the like are too obvious for comment so I turn to metamorphosis of character and that of time, both of which are adumbrative. By metamorphosis of character I mean those changes of personality which are drastic, unpredictable and even inexplicable as distinct from the process which converts Katherina, Benedick and Beatrice into new and better people—a process which is not much in evidence in *As You Like It*. Oliver and Duke Frederick are the two most conspicuous instances of sudden conversion but it is pertinent to ask whether the Orlando who kills the lioness is still the same person as the one who twice turned his back. It seems to me that his nature constantly alternates between that of the lamb with Rosalind and the lion with everybody else. But his very origin is itself metamorphic and we can see what must have been in Shakespeare's mind when he converted Lodge's Rosader into Orlando and gave him a father named Rowland and a brother named Oliver. The received adjectives were "inamorato" and "furioso," both of which strike me as being applicable to Rosalind's "excellent young man."

There is, throughout the play, a voice that denounces the pastoral life, but it is not always the same voice. The note of disparagement shifts to and fro between Touchstone, Jaques, Orlando, Rosalind, Celia, all of whom, when the fit is on them, seem like allotropic forms of a single critical intelligence at variance with the complacent apologetics of the Duke and the stilted conventions of Silvius and Phoebe. That Jaques should be one of the more prominent of those voices is only to be expected, though his attitudes may not always be consistent. The view that he typifies the Elizabethan malcontent is tenable so long as it admits that mutability was proper to the species, for Jaques, in his time, has played many parts—those of traveller, libertine, courtier, moralist, jester and religious recluse—and there is nothing to suggest that this last-named role will be an enduring one. This intellectual eccentric, whose complexion shifts to strange effects, is himself a walking metamorphosis and it is appropriate that to him should be allotted the play's clearest exposition of the metamorphoses of time. But in that exposition, although it is one man who, in his time plays many parts, the parts themselves present an arbitrary sequence. The soldier is not implicit in the lover, nor the justice in the soldier, while the transformations attributed to the sixth and seventh ages admit of many exceptions—Adam, almost fourscore yet strong and lusty being one and Corin, perhaps, another.

What Jaques expounds, with modern instances, reflects that pre-occupation with time's changes which dominates the play and even verges on obsession. By my reckoning *As You Like It* goes far beyond any other play both in its treatment of time, which it makes to amble, trot, gallop and stand still, and its handling of those disparities—youth and age, past and present, old and new, spring and autumn, summer and winter—which time itself creates. The conviction that time's changes are always for the worse leads, in the end, to the *carpe diem* philosophy: "And therefore take the present time."

This notion of devouring time yields, in the final romances, to the more optimistic view that time can restore as well as destroy. It is *The Winter's Tale* which most clearly exemplifies this outlook and this is because here Time is the theophany and the personification, notwithstanding its emblematic basis, is its ultimate metamorphosis. Time, the Chorus, has all too often been dismissed as a convenient, some say clumsy, device for indicating the passage of sixteen years, but he is, by his own assertion, the controller of all that happens in the play, and, since the full title of Shakespeare's main source is *Pandosto, The Triumph of Time*, the claim is one that cannot be lightly set aside. I shall return to this, but must first attempt to relate the play to those things which I have segregated as the main ingredients of Shakespearian pastoralism.

There are, no doubt, many who would argue that *The Winter's Tale* is pastoral only in the second half, but this can be countered by posing a single question: why did Shakespeare, working with a copy of *Pandosto* open before him, transpose Sicily and Bohemia? The only plausible answer that occurs to me is that he was intent on imposing

pastoralism from the outset. That he had first-hand knowledge of
Theocritus and his disciples is, I think, doubtful but he would certainly
have known that it was in Sicily that the Dorian settlers established
their great tradition of pastoral poetry and he would also have been
aware of that island's connection with the Proserpina myth. The
Sicilian setting is, then, by implication, even by definition, pastoral
and this is underlined at the beginning of the play:

> Nine changes of the wat'ry star hath been
> The shepheard's note since we have left our throne
> Without a burden

Polixenes continues in pastoral vein when telling of his boyhood
friendship with Leontes, which, incidentally, brings to mind the
classic Sicilian relationship between Damon and Pythias:

> We were as twinn'd lambs that did frisk i'th'sun
> And bleat the one at th'other. What we chang'd
> Was innocence for innocence; we knew not
> The doctrine of ill-doing, nor dream'd
> That any did.

We then see how, through Leontes's suspicions, that pastoralism is
equivocally transformed:

> Come, Captain,
> We must be neat—not neat, but cleanly, Captain.
> And yet the steer, the heifer, and the calf,
> Are all call'd neat.—Still virginalling
> Upon his palm?—How now, you wanton calf,
> Art thou my calf?

Here, precisely, is the first stage of a stylistic metamorphosis concomitant with one of character. The imagery changes abruptly from
the pastoral to the bestial and so remains until the shepherds appear at
the end of Act III. But the overall pattern is that of a pastoral world
which lapses into tragic chaos but is restored to its former state by
the workings of Time.

Metamorphosis of character, adumbrated in *As You Like It*,
achieves its ultimate manifestation in Leontes. The transformation
is in kind, like that of Othello and, in degree, perhaps more drastic
since the gentle, courteous and magnanimous monarch turns suddenly into a "jealous tyrant." But the process is completely different,
more resembling that which alters Henry Jekyll into Edward Hyde,
though even that is given a rational basis. For the jealousy of Leontes,

as Shakespeare presents it, all that I can say is what Coleridge said of Dryden's genius, that it is "of that sort which catches fire by its own motion; his chariot wheels *get* hot by driving fast." Its sheer intensity somewhat obscures the fact that other characters too undergo sudden changes. Paulina's tempestuous denunciation of Leontes yields to compassion and the patience of the female dove with an abruptness which, when Hamlet displays it, is attributed to madness. Polixenes, who has so transparently been captivated by Perdita, turns within minutes into the abusive tyrant who threatens her with hideous punishment. Camillo, tempted by the prospect of returning to Sicily, falls headlong into deviousness.

If the sheep-shearing scene is so inordinately long, this is perhaps because Shakespeare chose to use something which, in Greene's romance, is casually presented as a ground-plot for metamorphic invention. It accommodates metamorphoses of almost every kind. Through circumstances or disguise so many of the participants are transformed into what they are not. Florizel's Ovidian catalogue of the shapes assumed by various gods presents at one level what Autolycus's ballads present at another, and in between these comes the debate about natural metamorphoses. This, though different in form and matter, accords with Jaques's meditation on the metamorphoses of time and both epitomize the wider implications of the respective plays.

In its obligations to Plutarch and Apuleius, *The Winter's Tale* harks back to *A Midsummer Night's Dream*. It seems probable that, whenever he was stuck for a name, Shakespeare turned to Plutarch and, having found something that appealed to him, used either the original form or changed it to its Italian equivalent. Occasionally he altered the original or maybe conflated two names. As I have already cited the case of Hermia, I might perhaps add that Demetrius's principal enemy was not named Lysander, but he was named Lysimachus, which save for the metrical problems that it would have raised, could have served just as well. Of the abundant Plutarchan crop in *The Winter's Tale*, Antigonus, Cleomenes, Dion, Archidamus, Autolycus, Hermione and Emilia are straightforward borrowings. So is Leontes, save that Shakespeare turns a tribal name into a personal one. Camillo is the Italian form of Camillus and Paulina the feminine one of Paulinus. The New Arden editor rightly cites Polyxenus as the source for Polixenes but there is, I think, conflation with Philoxenus, of whom Plutarch, in *The Life of Dion*, relates the not insignificant fact that, having incurred the enmity of his brother-in-law, Dionysius the Tyrant, he fled through fear out of Sicily. It is in Plutarch's *Life of Dion* that

Leontium and the Leontines are prominent and my guess is that Shakespeare owed more to it than has so far been identified.

It has been suggested that it was to Adlington's translation of *The Golden Ass* that Shakespeare was indebted for the word " fardel," but there is a more substantial obligation in the punishment which, according to Autolycus, lies in store for the Shepherd's son:

> He has a son—who shall be flay'd alive; then 'nointed over with honey, set on the head of a wasp's nest; then stand till he be three quarters and a gram dead; then recover'd again with aquavitae or some other hot infusion; then, raw as he is, and in the hottest day prognostication proclaims, shall he be set against a brick wall, the sun looking with a southward eye upon him, where he is to behold him with flies blown to death.

It has been generally supposed that Shakespeare here was availing himself of the punishment prescribed for Ambrogiuolo in Boccaccio's story of Bernabo of Genoa, which is one of the sources for the Wager plot in *Cymbeline*:

> Then the Soldane strictly commaunded, that on some high and eminent place of the Citie, Ambrogiuolo should be bound and impaled on a stake, having his naked body nointed all over with hony, and never to bee taken off, untill (of it selfe) it fell in peeces . . . the verie same day that hee was impaled on the stake, annointed with honey, and fixed in the place appointed, to his no mean torment: he not onely died, but likewise was devoured to the bare bones, by Flies, Waspes, and Hornets, whereof the Countrey notoriously aboundeth.

But this has to bear comparison with Apuleius's tale of a servant whose lecherous conduct leads his wife to kill herself and her child and whose execution is promptly decreed by his master:

> The Master taking in evill part the death of these twaine, tooke his servant which was the cause of this murther by his luxurie, and first after that he had put off all his apparell, he annointed his body with honey, and then bound him sure to a fig-tree, where in a rotten stocke a great number of Pismares had builded their neasts, the Pismares after they had felt the sweetnesse of the honey came upon his body, and by little and little (in continuance of time) devoured all his flesh, in such sort, that there remained on the tree but his bare bones.

There has been some confusion amongst the commentators. Professor Bullough suggests, perhaps rightly, that the *Decameron* passage "called up a distant memory in Shakespeare" but then wrongly asserts that the dramatist had already used "a milder version of this punishment" for Aaron in *Titus Andronicus*,[6] while Professor Tobin's recent article perpetuates the error that the servant in *The Golden Ass* was buried alive.[7] It would seem that, when it comes to the more exquisite forms of torture, the Shakespearian producers are usually a good deal more knowledgeable than the professors. But be that as it may, Boccaccio's primary form of execution is impalement on some high and eminent place of the city, ostensibly the Alexandrian counterpart to Tyburn, with visiting swarms of predatory insects, attracted by the honey, as an added refinement, whereas Apuleius and Shakespeare concur in choosing a seemingly more pastoral location where there are convenient nests over which their bound victim can be set. But Autolycus speaks of additional torments and these, too, find precedent in *The Golden Ass*. Immediately after Lucius has rescued the fair maiden who promises to feed him with fresh nuts, they again fall amongst thieves who discuss various ways of killing them. One is that the maid should be burned to death; another that she should be flayed alive. Then comes the ingenious counter-proposal that the ass should be slain and

> . . . when all the guts and entrailes of his body is taken out, let the Maide be sowne into his belly, then let us lay them upon a great stone against the broiling heate of the Sunne.

It is pertinent to add that these passages occur in those chapters of *The Golden Ass* which prominently involve both thieves and shepherds.

I have claimed that *Love's Labour's Lost* has a mythological, and partly metamorphic, hinterland in which Apollo and Mercury join forces against Cupid and win what is at least a temporary victory. The same conflict, differently structured and developed and admitting a measure of inversion, underlies *The Winter's Tale*. In the earlier acts Shakespeare is at some pains to stress the significance of Apollo, excluding his more benign functions and concentrating on his role as the bringer of sudden death to Mamillius, Antigonus and, seemingly, Hermione when angered by Leontes's repudiation of both the Delphic oracle and the Apolline precepts. Those precepts of self-knowledge and moderation are reaffirmed in the second half of the play and the principle of "nothing in excess" in particular directs Perdita's thinking in the debate with Polixenes: but otherwise the initiative passes to Autolycus, littered under Mercury, the god of

---

6. *Narrative and Dramatic Sources of Shakespeare*, pp. viii. 16.
7. *Ibid*.

thieves and vagabonds, and bearing the very name of Mercury's son by Chione. Whereas, in the earlier play, the songs and sonnets fall within the province of Apollo, here Mercury comes into his own as the immediate progenitor of eloquence and song and king of the dance. For Autolycus is nothing if not eloquent and musical. He sings all five of the play's solo songs and joins Dorcas and Mopsa in the trio with significant assurance, "I can bear my part; you must know 'tis my occupation,"—an occupation no less Mercurial than theft and cozenage—and the major inversion is that the songs of Mercury are sweet after the words of Apollo. Both gods are in alliance once again, no longer waging war against Cupid but against Time, who, with his power "To o'erthrow law, and in one self-born hour/ To plant and o'erwhelm custom," is inevitably victorious.

All in all, Autolycus embodies the same metamorphic ambiguity as Marcade and effects a similar transformation in theme and structure. The powerful impact of Marcade is due in no small measure to the extreme lateness of his appearance and the same holds for Jaques de Boys. Shock tactics of this kind are good theatre but they are not altogether difficult to achieve. Yet Autolycus, entering exactly in the middle of *The Winter's Tale*, is, thanks to Shakespeare's sheer technical virtuosity, no less startling. Had he been given a late entry what we would have lost would indeed have been "a world of fine fabling; the illusion of which is so grateful to the *charmed Spirit*," but there could, in Shakespeare's mind, have been no question of delay, since the transformation which Autolycus effects is preparatory to, and must be some distance from, the culminating metamorphosis which turns the statue into Hermione. This, as corrupting familiarity has led us to know, is not really a metamorphosis at all though, in the theatre, many of us willingly and unresistingly suspend our disbelief. What signifies, however, is that, apart from Paulina and Hermione herself, all the characters believe that the statue really comes to life, and, even more significantly, this belief was shared by the original audience. I like to indulge the fancy that in that audience there was a certain dramatist glumly reflecting, after three acts of dramatized *Pandosto*, that here indeed was just another mouldly tale like *Pericles* and chuckling with satisfaction when old Father Time came limping in to prove him right. Autolycus and all his works should have been a cooling-card for Ben Jonson. Whether, in fact, they were is another matter.

Jonson and his unities notwithstanding, the begetter of "*Tales, Tempests*, and such like *Drolleries*" revealed, in this play dominated by Time, the infallibility of his own timing. And if the titles of the pastoral comedies are anything to go by, Shakespeare's personal unity with time was virtually unique. He had given his public *As You Like It* in the year when a reflective admixture of pastoralism and metamorphosis was exactly what they liked. In his life's heyday he had dreamed *A Midsummer Night's Dream*: towards its close he told *A Winter's Tale*.

Fifteen seventy-nine and the Decline of Civic Religious Drama in Coventry

R. W. INGRAM

The dramatic as well as the pastoral world has a claim on the pivotal significance of 1579, for in that year Coventry's Corpus Christi plays—the most famous of their kind in England—were performed for the last time. The general reasons, religious and political, that led to mysteries' end have been urged by Father Harold Gardiner, and they still stand. The particular applications of these reasons to individual cities are as idiosyncratic as the geographical positions and histories of the cities are distinctly their own. Coventry's attitude towards its drama was very much its own.

The term "civic religious drama" is a valuable coinage of Stanley Kahrl which marks the particular source and controlling agent of the entertainment, its central theme and its genre. Equally valuably, it embraces the Corpus Christi plays—or cycle/mysteries/miracle plays/ Biblical cycles—saints' plays, creed plays, civic pageants of welcome, and for Coventry's purposes, traditional Hocktide celebrations and religious historical drama, under one heading.

Any commentary on the decline of civic religious drama in Coventry might reasonably be expected to take the last performance of the Corpus Christi plays in 1579 as its *terminus ad quem*. That this cannot be done is due to the Coventrians' religious feeling, civic pride, love of drama, business acumen and force of habit, in whatever mixture. In 1584 a spectacular religious historical drama of *The Destruction of Jerusalem* was staged at extraordinary cost. When popular demand for civic drama had to be bowed to in 1591, the council proposed this play and two others—*The Conquest of the*

Danes and *The History of Edward IV*—as the trio from which the citizens could choose. What choice was made is not known, but financial enthusiasm for the venture did not run strongly, as it had in 1584; official coolness was probably an influence here. Other entertainments, dramatic and quasi-dramatic, are noticed or hinted at in later civic records. The last civic play (patriotic rather than religious) dates from 1614; it was some sort of "staged" military combat performed in the city market place. The inverted commas indicate both the uncertain nature of the affair and the fading away, as it were, of civic drama in Coventry, but 1614 I take as a *terminus ad quem*.

To select a *status a quo* for this fading away is almost impossible. The impact of Coventry's unusually grim economic history during the sixteenth century, as much as the clerical changes effected by the Reformation, at first suggests itself as a likely cause of dramatic decline. Oddly enough, however, the decline of drama seems not to have been caused by Coventry's economic collapse in the early decades of the sixteenth century. *The Desolation of a City* is the title of Charles Phythian-Adams' fine study of "Coventry and the Urban Crisis of the Late Middle Ages."[1] He reckons that "Coventry's population appears to have shrunk from over 10,000 in c.1440, to between 8,500 and 9,000 in 1500. Thereafter it collapsed with appalling rapidity: to perhaps 7,500 in 1520, to about 6,000 in 1523, with the downward spiral reaching its nadir of something in the region of 4,000 to 5,000 by the mid sixteenth century" (p. 281). The textile industry and Coventry's position as a market town for importing and exporting was the city's strength; it was also the city's weakness because depressions in the textile industry affected it doubly. Not a few trades only were affected but, in one way or another, nearly all those in the city. Nonetheless, and perhaps astonishingly, throughout the long period of economic decay, the Corpus Christi plays were regularly performed. Some crafts felt the pinch more than others and this led to changes in the support of individual plays: in 1531, for instance, the Cappers (one of the very few prospering trades at the time) joined with the Cardmakers and Saddlers in keeping up the latter's chapel and pageant, both of which they took over completely in 1537; from 1532 nearly half the Weavers' expenses were met by annual payments by the Walkers and by the

---

1. Charles Phythian-Adams, *Desolation of a City: Coventry and the Urban Crisis of the Late Middle Ages* (Cambridge, 1979). At several places in this book the relationship between the economic history of the city and of the individual guilds is taken up.

Skinners.[2] In 1539, Mayor Coton made a general plea to Thomas Cromwell concerning various civic expenses, among which he cited: "At Corpus christi tide the poore Comeners be at suche charges with ther playes & pagyontes that thei fare the worse all the yeire after." He sought "some redresse . . . lettres vnto vs for reformacion of the same excessive charges:"[3] what redress or reformation he did not specify and as far as the Corpus Christi plays were concerned, he must have received none, for their performance continued with no sign in the guild (or civic records) of any retrenchment of expenses for them.

What changes were made seem to have been textual. The two surviving plays were rewritten by Robert Crow, one-time master of the Cappers' company, in 1535. Those of the Cappers, Drapers and Smiths were revised early in Elizabeth's reign as discretion may have demanded.[4] These demands were more clerical than economic or social, and were doubtless the results, to some extent, of the opposition of the crown and the church to civic religious plays as proclaimed on 16 May 1559, wherein city officials were charged to "permyt none to be played wherin either matters of religion or of the gouernaunce of the estate of the common weale shalbe handled, or treated, beyng no meete matters to be wrytten or treated vpon, but by menne of auchthoritie, learning and wisedome, nor to be handled before any audience, but of graue and discreete persons: All which partes of this proclamation, her majestie chargeth to be inuiolably kepte."[5]

This was a not altogether unwelcome doctrine to some in Coventry whose council was already inclining towards the puritanism for which the city was to become notable in the Stuart period. However, their members were not all cast in this mould and they represented a city whose attitude towards civic drama was often at variance with that of the proclamation. As a local Victorian historian forthrightly put it: "Coventry, renowned for its religious pageants, for its splendid churches, and ancient halls, was at once the home of popish bigotry,

2. CR pp. 131-3, 144-6; 134, 137 References to CR refer to my edition of "The Dramatic Records of Coventry, 1392-1642," *Records of Early English Drama*, vol 3, (Toronto, 1981).

Cappers: *Leet Book*, ed Mary Dormer Harris, EETS, 1907-13 (hereafter referred to as LB), p. 710.

3. PRO SP/1/142, ff 66-66v: CR. pp. 148-9.

4. I have discussed these changes in: " 'To find the players and all that longeth therto': Notes on the Production of Medieval Drama in Conventry," in *The Elizabethan Theatre* v. ed. G. R. Hibbard (Toronto, 1975), pp. 17-44.

5. E. K. Chambers, *The Elizabethan Stage* (Oxford, 1926), IV. p. 263.

and staunch Protestantism."[6] Put less bluntly, Coventry was as important clerically as it was commercially. However, the authority of the church—symbolized by the dominating bulk of the Benedictine priory and cathedral of St. Mary in the heart of the city—had not been unquestioned in Coventry. From early in the fifteenth century Lollardy found powerful support there. In 1519, seven Protestant martyrs were burned in the Little Park. In Queen Mary's reign one of the sheriffs was haled to the Fleet for "evyll relygion" whilst the mayor and his brethren, sent orders by the bishop from Lichfield to apprehend certain suspects for questioning, gave them warning to flee instead. The upshot was that Mary had to force a Catholic mayor on the city in 1556.[7] The reforming force continued to gather strength: in 1569 "the Register Books of St. Michael's parish were destroyed by some who were so eager to burn Popish Books, that they burned the Registers, because they had some marks of Popery in them."[8]

6. J. T. Burgess, *Historic Warwickshire*, ed. and rev. J. Hill, 2nd ed. (Birmingham, 1893), p. 79. Lollardy: J. A. F. Thomson, *The Later Lollards* (Oxford, 1967), pp. 104, 112, 245.
7. On 7 January 1556, a letter was sent to the mayor and aldermen of Coventry "to cause sum Catholike and grave man to be chosen to thier Maiour for this yere comyng, and for that the Quenes Majestie is advertised that John Fitzherbert, Richard Whestler and oone Colman . . . are Catholike and honest personnes, they are required to give thier voyces to oone of them to be Maiour" (*Acts of the Privy Council*, ed J. R. Dasent, ns vol. 5 [1892] p. 218). Fitzherbert was a mercer, involved in council affairs since 1547 and sheriff in 1553. Of Whestler I can find no mention in the records. Colman, a cooper, had played an important role in city affairs since 1539; in 1539 he was chamberlain, in 1549 sheriff. Such "Catholike and honest personnes" were very much a minority in the city (see VCH *Warwick*, VIII, pp. 217-18, 368).
   For the mayor's warning, see LB, pp. 811 n 2. In November 1553 four men were arrested "for thier lewde and sediciouse behaviour on All Hallowe Daye last passed; whereupon, and for other thier noughtie demeanour" they were committed to jail (*Acts of the Privy Council*, ns vol. 4, p. 368). One of the four was John Careles, a weaver (his name appears nowhere in the company's records for this period). Before being sent to London, where he died on 1 July 1556, he was in gaol at Coventry whence, solely on his word, he was released, "to play in the Pageants about the City with other his companions. And that being done, keeping touch with his keeper, he returned agayne into prison at his houre apppointed" (Foxe: *Acts and Monuments of Martyrs* II, 1698 ed. pp. 1920 col b—1921 col a). In a letter to a fellow prisoner and martyr, Philpot, Foxe mentions "my olde frendes of Couentry haue put the Counsell in remembraunce of me, not 6 dayes agoe, saying that I am more worthy to be burned, then any that was burned yet. Gods blessing on theyr harts for their good report. . . ." (ibid, p. 1921 col b). The martyrdom he so joyfully sought was denied him; he died in the King's Bench prison in 1556. This incident shows how the Corpus Christi Cycle continued to be performed despite the religious turmoil in the city: Careles played in it as a Protestant prisoner of Catholics who allowed the cycle to be performed. Did each see it as a tribute to their own divergent beliefs?
8. T. Sharp, *Antiquities of the City of Coventry* (Birmingham, 1871), p. 50n. A radical preacher who settled in Coventry after Mary's death (he had been in exile in Switzerland until then), Thomas Lever, writes of the mood in the city: "There have always been, since the revival of the gospel, great numbers zealous for evangelical truth; so that in the last persecution under Mary, some were burnt, others went into banishment

It is just at this time that the first evidence of direct clerical intervention in civic drama is found. The joyful play that in Coventry, since at least 1416, had celebrated the Hocktide holiday, was silenced in 1568 as the result of the pressure exerted by certain narrow-minded preachers. This firm though negative action marks out for me a *terminus a quo*.

The part taken by the church in this affair is not remarked upon until 1575 when Robert Laneham describes the many entertainments offered to Elizabeth on her visit to Kenilworth castle in July of that year.[9] One of these entertainments was Coventry's adaptation of the ancient Hocktide festivities into a celebration of a great defeat of the Danes near Coventry in which the women of the city played a vital part. As Laneham describes it the play was a rambunctious affair, like a glorified mumming play. One of the city annals (lively but unreliable lists of mayors and notable local and national events that occurred during individual mayoralties) asserts that the play was "invented" in 1416.[10] No more is heard of it until 1561 when another annal notes

together with myself; the remainder, long tossed about in great difficulty and distress, have at last, on the restoration of pure religion, invited other preachers, and myself in particular, to proclaim the gospel to them . . . vast numbers in this place were in the habit of frequenting the public preaching of the gospel . . . now for a whole year, I have preached to them without any hindrance, and they have liberally sustained me and my family" (*The Zurich Letters*, ed. H. Robinson [Parker Society, 1842] i, pp 86-87). This is understandably enthusiastic: a useful companion to such views is the essays edited by Felicity Heal in *Church and Society in England, Henry VIII to James I* (London, 1977), especially those by Imogen Luxton ("The Reformation and Popular Culture," pp. 55-77) and W. J. Shiels ("Religion in Provincial Towns: Innovation and Tradition," pp. 156-76).

9. "Robert Laneham's Letter" describing the princely pleasures presented to Elizabeth, STC 15191, pp. 32-38. Muriel Bradbrook argues for his identification with a member of the Earl of Leicester's Men, John Laneham and that the letter presents the "the common player's point of view" of the 1575 entertainments (*The Rise of the Common Player* [London, 1962], pp. 141-61). R. J. P. Kuin, however, has strongly identified him with the mercer and "Clark of the Councel chamber door" which he claims to be: "Robert Langham and his 'Letter' ", *Notes and Queries* ns 25, no 5 (1978), 426-7 which undermines Miss Bradbrook's argument.

10. The full entry reads: "The Pageants and Hox Tuesday invented, wherein the King and Nobles took great delight" (Sharp, p. 8). The "Pageants" or Corpus Christi cycle had been "invented" long before as there is a reference to the Drapers' pageant-house in a cartulary of St. Mary's Priory dated 1392. Sharp, accepting this fact, simply stated that the entry therefore meant that the Hock Tuesday play had been invented for Henry V's enjoyment. In this assumption he has generally been followed. He may be right, but the annal entry does not say that: both dramatic entertainments are linked together and, failing other evidence, both must have been "invented" in 1416. "Invented" in this case must mean "rewritten," "fabricated anew," "freshly produced." Perhaps a better solution would be to assume that "The Pageants or Hox Tuesday" was misread as, "The Pageants and Hox Tuesday"; this suggestion is supported by an annal entry for 1576 which Sharp quotes (the original now lost): "This year the Pageants or Hox Tuesday that had been laid down 8 years were played again" (Sharp, p. 12).

that it was put down. Notwithstanding, it reappears in 1566 when the city recorder, in his address of welcome to Elizabeth, boasts of Coventry's part in overthrowing the Danes: "A memoriall whereof is kept vnto this day by certaine open shewes in this Citty yearely."[11] Despite the recorder's finding the "shewes" worthy of being drawn to Elizabeth's attention in 1566, they were banned after the 1567 performance.

The ban still held in 1575 (Captain Cox, the leader of the "good harted men of Couentree" who came to perform the play, circumspectly said only that the play was "tyll noow of late laid dooun"; only a lost annal quoted by Sharpe reveals that it "had been laid down 8 years").[12] Thus, Cox took a great risk in bringing as what was more or less Coventry's "unofficial" contribution to the Kenilworth entertainments an "olld storiall sheaw" which had been put down by authority of Elizabeth's church. However, he excused its performance very astutely. He admitted that it had been put down but argued that it was longstanding; that "without ill exampl of mannerz, papistry, or ony superstition" it "did so occupy the heads of a number that likely inoough would haue had woorz meditationz." "Papistry" is cunningly slotted in, and the danger that idle minds might ponder unwelcome thoughts was one only too well known to Elizabeth. Cox then turned innocently to those who had worked against the Hock Tuesday play, inferring that their action was an aberration of otherwise commendable minds.

> The knu no cauz why [the play had been banned] onless it wear by the zeal of certain theyr Preacherz: men very commendabl for their behauiour and learning, & sweet in their sermons, but sumwhat too sour in preaching awey theyr pastime: wisht therefore, that az they shoold continu their good doctrine in pulpet, so, for matters of pollicy & gouernauns of the Citie, they woold permit them to the Mair and Magistratez . . . that they might haue theyr playz vp agayn.[13]

In weighing the intentions of zealous preachers, Cox's arguments, and her own enjoyment of the play (and that of Coventrians), against the general thrust of her government's policies about such plays, Elizabeth was hampered by no foolish consistency. Mayor Hopkins, in 1576, "caused hoc tuesday . . . to be againe set up and shewed forthe to his great commendacion and the Cities great comoditie

11. 1561: Sharp, p. 11: CR, p. 215.
1566: Bodleian, MS Top. Wark. d. 4, f 22v: CR, p. 233.
12. Laneham, pp. 32-33: CR, pp. 272-73.
13. Laneham, p. 33: CR, p. 273.

which said hoc twesday was the yeare before plaide before the Quene at Kenelworth in the tyme of her progresse by the commaundment of the Quenes Counsell."[14] Such fulsome language about a play the council had been content to have banned for eight years might have been suitable as part of a reply to the demand of the "Quenes Counsell" for a reversal of policy.

Were it not for Laneham we would not know the nature of the play nor why it was banned after 1567. Thus civic records—such as survive—may hide far more between their lines than they reveal. The whole history of this play throws a curiously revealing light on one aspect of the struggle for civic drama carried on between the citizens, the city council and the church. So far as can be told, the Hock Tuesday play ran for a century and a half after its "invention" in 1416 until it was banned in 1561. I think it likely that clerical pressure influenced this decision but the only available information is the single entry in a lost annal. When, after 1561, it was revived is not known: popular demand may have made itself felt too powerfully to be denied almost at once. Possibly deliberately, or by lucky chance, it was revived in 1566 enabling the recorder to boast its long continuity (antiquity he should have said) to Elizabeth in 1566. To boast of it at all shows some official hypocrisy, the more so as only one perfor-mance at the most was permitted after Elizabeth's official visit before it was banned again. The play's hold on the people however, is shown by Cox's taking it to Kenilworth.[15]

The history of this play also demonstrates how nice distinctions of proclaimed public policy may crumble in particular local situations. The Hock Tuesday play may not have touched upon "matters of religion" or of the "gouernauce of the estate" but civic authority with the strong backing of the church had banned it: Elizabeth simply overrode them.

However, the Corpus Christi plays which, ironically, had not been played in 1575 due to the plague, were soon to be permanently laid down. The guilds either did not know this or refused to believe it. How could what had been a great civic attraction for some two hundred years, outlasting civil wars and religious perturbation, be

14. Sharp, pp. 11-12: CR, p. 276.
15. Cox himself seems to have become something of a local hero: on 19 August 1624, Ben Jonson's *Masque of Owls* was performed before Prince Charles at Kenilworth—it was "Presented by the ghost of Captaine Coxe mounted on his Hoby-horse." A brief commentary on Cox's previous appearance at Kenilworth and his connection with Coventry is offered but, for a full appreciation of the man, the Prince and his court would have needed to know more of the 1575 entertainment than Jonson has time to tell them (Ben Jonson, ed. C. H. Herford, Percy and Evelyn Simpson, x, pp. 780-86).

ended? Guild accounts read confidently and expensively: pageant stuff and wagons were kept in better repair than ever before. The Cappers never spent more than they did in 1579 on their play. In 1572 the Smiths revised a part of their play, "The Trial, Condemnation, and Crucifixion of Christ," or added a "new pley," as their accounts call it, of Judas, it is not clear which. In 1576 the Drapers spend 88s. 6d. on their play, half as much again as they usually spent on their pageant. The high figures for 1576 may be due to the non-performance in 1575; the generally prosperous figures from the later 1560s until 1579 may represent something of a recovery from the economic slump of the first half of the century. Nonetheless, after 1579 the plays were not performed again: nor, presumably, was the Hock Tuesday play, already a suspect play and now stained with guilt by association. The annals mention several natural phenomena in the fifteenth century which were read as heavenly warnings: by whatever coincidence, one of them notices "a suddaine Earthquake which hapned the vith of Aprill 1580 almost generally throughout England it caused such amazednes of the people as was wonderfull for ye time & caused them to make there earnest prayers vnto Almighty god. . . . And this yeare was a disease all the land ouer called speedy repentaunce."[16] Only one of the nearly twenty annals records: "This year the Pageants were again laid down."

They were splendidly taken out again in 1584 when unprecedented sums for civic drama were spent to produce *The Destruction of Jerusalem*. The play was seemingly based on Josephus' *The Jewish War*. Everything to do with it was on a far larger scale than the Corpus Christi plays: for example the Drapers' costs (not itemized) came to £6 4s.; the Mercers spent £8. 9s. 6d., of which 52s. 2d. was contributed by the Girdlers; the Cappers spent 28s. 9d. on preparations for the play but split the actors' expenses of 44s. 2d. with the Shearmen and Tailors (they also received 13s. 4d. from the Walkers, the Skinners, and the Joiners and Painters); the Smiths spent £6. 6s. 9d. It will be seen from the above that the regular apportioning of plays between the guilds was altered for this production: the Girdlers and the Shearmen and Tailors had always had their own Corpus Christi play. Actors certainly doubled roles (the Smiths paid Henry Chamberlain 3s. 4d. for "playenge of Pristus, a pece of Ananus and Zilla") but some

16. Cappers 1579: Cappers' Account Book 1, ff 116v-117: CR, pp 290-2.
Smiths 1572: Sharp, pp. 36-37 and Halliwell-Phillips, *Illustrations of the Life of Shakespeare* (London, 1874), 1, p. 55: CR, pp. 260 and 264-65.
Drapers 1576: Drapers' Accounts, Coventry Record Office Acc 154, f 94: CR, p. 280.
Earthquake: Bodleian: MS Top. Wark, d.4, f 26: CR, p. 294.

of the same actors were paid by more than one company for their acting. The plays were acted on pageant wagons, but companies did not perform on a single wagon: the Smiths "paid for carryenge of our aperaill from pagent to pagent, vid."[17] The play had a Chorus, so named. The extensive musical accompaniment named included various drums and trumpets, a flute, a bagpipe, these (or some of them probably) played by the city's waits, who added their own additional incidental music to the play. A young man from Coventry who was a student at St. John's College, Oxford, esteemed for his piety and learning, received from the city "the xv^th daye of Aprill 1584 for hys paynes for writing of the tragidye" the handsome sum of £13. 6s. 8d. A certain shadow is cast upon his piety by the suggestion that he stole the play from a distinguished and elderly colleague.[18]

Such extravagance could not be sustained annually; no more could the citizens' liking for their own drama be slaked by so gorgeous a show. Celebrating the Queen's holiday—the anniversary of Elizabeth's coronation—more festively was not sufficient. In 1591 the will of the commoners was heeded and in May it was agreed by council, "that the distrucion of Jerusalem the Conquest of the Danes or the historie of King Edward the 4 at the request of the Comons of this Cittie shalbe plaid on the pagens on Midsomer daye & St peters daye next in this Cittie & non other playes."[19] The choice among three plays seems generous but the will to have did not match the will or the ability to pay. The guild payments recorded are only half to one-third of what was usually spent in the olden days: the Cappers, the Weavers and the Smiths gave 20s. each, the Mercers 33s. 4d.; payments on this scale would not finance another production (actually two productions) of *The Destruction of Jerusalem*. The council's agreement is by far the fullest item about the 1591 plays. The guild accounts merely record payments for them, either to the mayor or to Thomas Massie, who seems to have been in charge of the production.

What the second and third plays the council was willing to have performed were is also a matter of mystery. *The Conquest of the Danes*

17. Drapers' Accounts CRO: Acc 154 f 107: CR, p. 307.
Mercers' Accounts CRO: Acc 15 ff 34v-36v: CR, pp. 305-6.
Cappers' Account Book I ff 122V-123: CR, pp. 303-4.
Smith's Accounts: Halliwell-Phillipps, pp. 56-57 and Sharp, pp. 37-38: CR, pp. 307-309.
18. Chambers, *Elizabethan Stage*, III, 408-409; *Medieval Stage*, III, p. 361; W. W. Greg, *Lost Plays*, p. 137. The evidence is very slender, amounting to a clear "not proven" at worst and a "not guilty" most probably. Alan Nelson's recent discovery of what may be the Latin play which Smith 'stole' will alter this verdict and add significantly to Coventry's, and England's, dramatic history.
19. CRO Council Book A14 (a), p. 216: CR, p. 332.

could be a formal way of referring to the Hock Tuesday play. The choice of King Edward IV for a play is more puzzling. As the city lay so near to Warwick and was so strategically placed upon the road north and south (and was then in its most flourishing state), Coventry had seen much adventure during the reign of Edward IV. In 1469 he had been briefly imprisoned there: in 1471 Warwick had held the city and defied Edward's armies under its walls. When Edward came into his own again he confiscated the mayor's sword and denied the city its liberties, save by a payment of 500 marks. Eventually reconciliation came and was emphasized by the rich welcome staged for the Prince of Wales in 1474. It it unlikely that this was the dramatic entertainment sanctioned in 1591; however, the text was available because it was copied into the Leet Book.[20]

Because the texts of the songs in the Shearmen and Taylors' play (added at the end of Robert Crow's 1535 version of the play) are dated May 1591, it has sometimes been thought that this play, plus others or all the Corpus Christi plays, were revived in that year. The copying of the songs may indicate that this was hoped for, but the council's firm "& non other playes" militated against that, as did the convenient fact that Corpus Christi Day itself, the traditional play day, fell on 3 June in 1591, three weeks before the performance days chosen by council.

Unless there had been some rehearsal of a play in anticipation of council allowing a performance, the granting of such permission on 19 May left the players a mere five weeks to prepare their show. This guarded response to "the request of the Comons" is of a piece with the second part of the consent of 19 May: "And that all the mey poles that nowe are standing in this Cittie shalbe taken downe before whitsonday next [23 May], non hereafter to be sett vpp in this Cittie."

The strength of official opposition to civic drama and entertainment was growing but it could not eradicate love of them at one blow. Some installation and anniversary days were kept with rather more celebration than had been the case when the city's dramatic, religious and great civic occasions had flourished. Thus, in 1594 and again in 1596, Thomas Massie and William Showell were paid 20s. for the pains they took in arranging the celebration of the Queen's holiday.[21]

20. LB, pp. 391-93: CR, pp. 53-55.
21. The best discussion of the change in public and civic ceremonial between pre-Reformation and post-Reformation Coventry is in an essay by Charles Phythian-Adams," Ceremony and the citizen; the communal year at Coventry 1450-1550," included in *Crisis and Order in English Towns 1500-1700*, ed. P. Clark and P. Slack

Guild records show their different response to the putting down of the Corpus Christi plays. The Smiths sold their pageant house and their pageant (this may mean either the wagon or the costumes and props) in 1586. The Weavers pulled down their pageant-house and built another house on the land which they let in 1587.[22] They also record 14d. spent, "when we sold our padgent," in the same year. This must mean the wagon, as they were hiring their costumes twenty years later to Thomas Massie. The Mercers sold all their "pagant stufe" in 1588 for 59s. 8d., in five lots of "certaine parsells" and a sixth consisting of single copper chain. The Shearmen and Taylors sold their pageant-house in 1590. It was not until 1596 that the Cappers sold the fur off the players' gowns and the bishops' hoods. If they retained the rest of their pageant stuff they shared the same hopes as the Weavers and the Drapers: the latter received 4s. in 1595 for "the hyer of oure players Clothes with other such stufe."[23]

A likely customer for such hiring was Thomas Massie, a relentless proponent of civic drama. That full-scale civic drama ended in Coventry in 1579, and in 1584, and in 1591 was not for the want of his trying to have it continue. Indeed, its extensions of life probably owed something to his efforts. He is first heard of in a dramatic context as supplier of "a trwse for Judas" in 1578 for the Smiths' "new pley."[24] However, that is only the first time his name occurs; his involvement with drama must have predated 1578. He had a relatively slight part (so far as naming goes) in the 1584 production, but appeared to be director of the 1591 play.[25] By this time he had become the city's man for dramatic shows and celebrations. It was his

(London, 1972), pp. 57-85. The nature of the celebrations on the Queen's holiday is never made clear. Two clues exist, however: The first is an entry in the Wardens' accounts for 1578 (CRO: A 7(b) p 26): "Item paid to Thomas Kyllingley in the Bushop streete for a standing for maister maior & the maisters at the plays on the quees hollyedaye iiij s." The second is that Thomas Massie wished to present a play or plays for his abortive celebration of the King's holiday (see below). Massie's seems to have been planned on a grand scale—as a special occasion?—but how far the 1578 plays were unusual cannot be told.

22. Hardin Craig reckons that this shows the Weavers' hopes of a revival of the Corpus Christi plays (see *English Religious Drama* [Oxford 1955], p. 362). Certainly they retained their players' costumes, but I believe their extensive rebuilding was to erect a newer, larger and more profitable rental property, for rent it they did thereafter.

23. Mercers' Accounts CRO: Acc 15 f 45v: CR, pp. 321-2. Shearmen and Tailors' Deed of Conveyance CRO: 100/37: CR, pp. 328-31.

Cappers' Account Book 1 f 134v: CR, p. 346.

Drapers' Accounts CRO: Acc 154 f 122: CR, p. 345.

24. Halliwell-Phillipps, *Outlines of the Life of Shakespeare*, 9th ed. 2 vols (London, 1890), p. 341: CR, p. 289.

25. The Cappers, Drapers and Mercers all paid their pageant contributions directly to Massie, as did the Wardens.

misfortune to be an incorrigibly theatrical man who grew up just as civic drama was in decline. If many in Coventry were prepared to make do with the quite rich dramatic entertainments offered to them by touring companies, he was not. His dissatisfaction was to lead him into a decade of serious legal trouble.

In 1600/1 the Weavers had him pursued with a summons and arrested. The matter may have concerned theatrical affairs, for the Weavers loaned their "playres aparell" several times between 1597 and 1607 (in 1606 to Massie, he paying them 2s. 6d.).[26] Whatever his argument with the Weavers, it was as nothing compared with the fierce, long-drawn-out and costly legal-dramatic battle he carried on with the mayor and senior men of the city that began in 1604.

Not surprisingly, this long and acrimonious argument rose from a simple disagreement. Massie wished to celebrate the King's day (24 March) with some dramatic entertainment of his own devising. The mayor and his brethren, for reasons not given, said that he might not do so. The two sides of the argument are laid out in "Certain Perticulers of Thomas Massie his ill demeanor towards Mr. Richard Page, the Maior, Mr. Roger Clark, and others, truly recorded," and Massie's reply "To the Right Worshipfull Mr Maior and the rest of his Bretheren."[27]

The mayor reports that Massie made his request and was told, "such toyes (as he would sett abroch) deserved noe Contribucion." Massie then offered to produce the welcome at his own expense. The council thus neatly caught, Massie's "project and speaches were referred to the view of two Preachers, who mislyking many thinge both in subject and forme, there was an order prescribed for his proceeding, and he confined in his shews." Massie lay low until he stunned the council with the news that he had been to see Lord Harrington (Princess Elizabeth's guardian and tutor whose home, Combe Abbey, was very close to Coventry) who was to come with his ward to see Massie's show in two days' time. The authorities at once approached Lord Harrington and found this tale was untrue. They

---

26. 1600 Weavers' Rentgatherers' Book II CRO: Acc 100/18/2 f34—given a summons CR, p. 357.
1601 Ibid, f 36: CR, p. 359. "arestinge of Thomas Massie."
1604 Weavers' Account Book CRO: 100/17/1 f97: CR, p. 366. "Reseyvyd for the hier of ovr players Apparell vj s." Might this have been to Massie as part of his preparations for his intended King's day play?
1606 Ibid. f 99: CR, p. 370.
27. These two documents are interleaved in Sharp's own annotated copy of the *Dissertation* which is in the British Library (BL 43645). The "Perticulers" make up ff 39-39v, Massie's response, ff 40-40v. A full transcription is printed in appendix 6 of CR.

demanded that Massie come before them; only at a second bidding did he come. A slanging match ensued: Massie refused to take his cap off, reckoning himself better than any man present. Roger Clark, who had been mayor in 1598, he dismissed as a miller's son and, being told that comparisons were odious, replied: "That there was no more comparison between Mr. Clark and him, then between a custard a dunghill . . . their Mayraltys finished, they were noe more Magistrats but Commoners as him self, and that his ancestors kept as good men for their dogg-keepers as they were." After much more of the same, Massie was gaoled. He was released after friends pleaded his case and swore he would apologize on being released. He was set free but never apologized. Finally, it was reported that Massie had promised, once this current argument with council had been settled, to take up another suit "against Dick Page, for his promise of Charges Concerning his pajeant." "A Shew upon the Kinges daie" is also a "project and speaches," and is now a "pajeant": thus are we warned against the comfort of neat, pigeon-hole definitions of genres.

Massie's view of the matter is at once more impassioned and longer. He does not come to the question of the King's day show for some time, dealing first with the fact that he was falsely imprisoned and "raviled withall . . . for that he spake the truthe" about Roger Clark's family and his own. By his account he was gaoled with "them that had the Plague" and after fifteen days, "was thrust out of prison by violence of the Gaolers." Judge Warburton, a distinguished man of law then retired to Cheshire in a village very close to that from which Massie claimed his good family came, was sent the case to adjudicate. His verdict was in Massie's favour—£6. 13s. 4d. was awarded to him on condition he dropped his suits against Mayor Page and six others for false imprisonment. The "dramatic" matters had not been submitted for judgment, it seems, or so Massie insists: "I did never tell the Judge how Mr. Page Maior did threaten to clapp me by the heels yf I did showe any thing for the honour of the Kinges Majestie: Neither told I the Judge; how this Mr. Page Maior, did buffitt me with both his clutch ffists, manny blowes; and spitt filthily in my face, for telling hym I heard saye. The Lady Elizabeths grace was desyrous to see Coventrie." Massie acts the injured royalist, attacked for his patriotism: the extent to which he had prepared his shows is not mentioned. Only later does this emerge amid further self-justifying pleas.

Coventry had various bequests of money which formed sources of loans for Coventrians. Massie had used these funds, both for himself and, by means of standing surety, for others. The council, in their struggle against him, witheld his bonds. Massie demanded these and also recompense for "my charges I was at for the honuour of the Kings Majestie by the consent of the Mauor and his Bretheren, and for forbearing of the same. The charg came neere to xxij^{li} I have borne it long, and have ben kepte from yt; and I hope I shall not Loose yt".

This is an astonishing amount of money to have been laid out on a show/play/pageant of welcome, by one man. Even allowing for exaggeration to bolster the case, Massie spent a good deal of money. His projects were clearly far advanced and this perhaps explains why he tried in the last resolve to get them performed by springing them upon the civic authorities at only two days' notice. Certainly the image is raised of a good deal of quiet backdoor preparation of costumes and rehearsing going on without it being officially noticed. The open boldness of the request and the amount claimed is typical of Massie; so also is the amount spent and, I would venture to suggest, the essential truth of the claim. Were it a pure fabrication could not the mayor and his men have quickly discovered it? Massie was ready to go to law about it.

Understandably, Massie does not touch upon the matter of the first rejection of his project by the council, not the second one, following upon the two preachers' review of the "subject and forme" of the entertainment and its "speaches." As is so often the case, there is no record of the final outcome of this matter. Massie continued his craft as upholsterer—obviously a fine one as the council called upon him more than once to execute work on their chairs—and accepted that demise of civic drama.

Ironically, the last example of civic drama came to pass two years after what seems to have been Judge Warburton's final letter in the case of Page et alii versus Massie. In one of the annals, it is noted that in 1614:

there was an admirable Stratagem made by Master Maior consisting of a Squadron in warlike manner & being very well ordered & completely furnished contayning Englissh Scottish Irish & Spanish & divers Captaines Liueteenaantes & Ensignes. Bills Bowes Speares & gunnes, Pikes holberts & holbert diers being a very tough Skermidg & acted at the Cross in the said Citie: in which Battell death leech was fained to be slayne (being then one of the liueantes or Sergiantes Barnaby Davenport was the chief Streamer of Standardbearer And in his displaying of the Colores at the Crosse he [c73 letters erased] he acted the same with great agilitie.[28]

28. Bodley: MS Top. Wark. d.4 f 33: CR, p. 390.

As did *The Conquest of the Danes* in 1591, this exciting military tattoo seems to hark back to the Hock Tuesday play. No other mention of its exists. It should be noted, as neutrally as possible, that Henry Davenport was mayor of Coventry in 1614.

Thus the history of Coventry's own drama ends with agile acting of a wealthy son of the city in an exciting battle piece with very old-fashioned overtones as "death leech was fained to be slayne." This history had probably spread over some 250 years, lingering out its days in a last colourful outburst. Doubtless Thomas Massie made one of its audience, himself a living memorial of drama's vigour and appeal in Coventry.[29]

29. I am grateful to the masters of the Cappers' company and of the Broadweavers' and Clothiers' company for permission to quote from their companies' books. My thanks are also due to the Coventry Record Office for its continually kind attention to my requests and for permission to use its documents. I also thank the Keeper of the Bodleian Library, the Trustees of the British Library, and the PRO for access to Coventry documents in their keeping.

Urban Pastoralism in English Civic Pageants

DAVID M. BERGERON

"Cities are more alien to the pastoral and rural spirit of this world [of romance], and the tower and castle, with an occasional cottage or hermitage, are the chief images of habitation"—so writes Northrop Frye.[1] But in fact urban life gives rise to pastoral, its writers—almost all city-dwellers—reflecting on and sometimes idealizing the bucolic life. As Frank Kermode observes: "Pastoral flourishes at a particular moment in the urban development, the phase in which the relationship of metropolis and country is still evident, and there are no children (as there are now) who have never seen a cow."[2] Such a moment seems to have been the late Tudor and early Stuart period. When I first grasped the title of this paper out of very thin air indeed, I was struck primarily by the paradoxical linking of urban and pastoral. But as I have become more educated, I have realized, paradoxically, that there is little paradox here at all. The pastoral, in whatever form, has historically been associated with the city; and, at least in the era of our concern, Londoners, for example, would not have been pressed to be reminded of the country life not far from them. Such reminders are manifest in civic pageants through extensive use of pastoral elements. What I will demonstrate is the continuing presence of pastoral traditions in the pageants, though most were sponsored and financed by city governments or trade guilds. Whatever paradox there may be resolves in the unstrained blending of civic occasion with pastoral reminders. On the great stage of London—its streets—shepherds jostle with allegorical and historical figures for dramatic attention.

In a comment that reflects the time in which it was written, W. W.

---

1. *Anatomy of Criticism* (Princeton, 1957), p. 152.
2. *English Pastoral Poetry: From the Beginnings to Marvell* (London, 1952), p. 15.

David M. Bergeron

Greg notes: "The English pastoral drama had one advantage over many other literary fopperies, in that it obeyed the fundamental law of literary progress, which is one with artistic evolution."[3] We may be assured that there is no evidence of "literary progress" in the pageants. One of the problems, indeed, in studying the pastoral in civic entertainments is that the shows sustain little coherent development; that is, many different kinds of subject matter may be crammed into a single show; thus, there is no extended treatment of pastoral themes but rather momentary representations, brief tableaux. Pageant drama is drama literally on the move with all the attendant difficulties of a processional theatre. One might strain the point a bit to suggest that this lack of sustained development suits the conclusion of a number of theorists of the pastoral who assert that it is a fleeting experience: "Whether it involves a genuine sojourn in nature or a mere cohabitation with illusions, the pastoral experience is always temporary."[4]

Little has been said explicitly about pastoral elements in civic pageants. Greg cites four or five of the entertainments quite briefly, and David Young and Harry Levin also mention a few but hurriedly.[5] Hence, I welcome the opportunity to explore the subject more fully. I hope that we will end up with more than a mere calendar of shepherds. There is a nagging suspicion, no doubt, that if you've seen one shepherd, you've seen them all. In addition to whatever shepherds I can round up from the pageants, we will see, more seriously, that the pastoral appears primarily in three ways in the civic shows: in architectural structures or devices; through metaphors; and in certain characters, both realistic and mythical. Whatever the fashion or form, the pastoral reference typically serves a didactic purpose.

As the notorious E. K. has divided Spenser's *Shepheardes Calender* into three parts (moral, plaintive, and recreative), I shall arrange my discussion in three, focusing on what I see as the principal forms of civic pageants: progresses, royal entries, and Lord Mayor's Shows. Whether I will be the E. K. who occasionally illuminates Spenser's work or the E. K. who frequently obscures the issue, remains to be seen. One might observe in passing, given our commemoration of Spenser, that *The Shepheardes Calender*, with its scenic technique, its slight drama and its emblems, corresponds, in part, to a civic

3. *Pastoral Poetry and Pastoral Drama* (London, 1906), p. 339.
4. Eleanor Winsor Leach, *Virgil's Eclogues: Landscapes of Experience* (Ithaca and London, 1974), p. 47.
5. Greg, especially pp. 371-74 and 385. Young, *The Heart's Forest: A Study of Shakespeare's Pastoral Plays* (New Haven and London, 1972), p. 14; Levin, *The Myth of the Golden Age in the Renaissance* (Bloomington and London, 1969), p. 99.

entertainment. Perhaps the twelve Eclogues should be mounted on pageant wagons and be thus represented. In any event, as I work my way through the kinds of pageants, I will place the greatest emphasis on the London Lord Mayor's Shows in which Ironmongers, Skinners, Haberdashers, Drapers, or whatever the sponsoring guild might be, saw fit to include some pastoral tableaux in their distinctly urban setting.

Examining progresses first, we note that Queen Elizabeth and her successors, leaving the city behind, went on summer provincial tours, known as progresses, during which a splendid array of dramatic entertainments would be presented in the sovereign's honour. On the estates of great noblemen it took no particular leap of imagination to construe these park-like settings as a kind of Arcadia. Elizabeth was forever in danger of bumping into a shepherd, a mythological figure appropriate to the pastoral, or a wild man. Her experience was, if I may borrow a title, like "Ovid among the goats."[6] The Queen's literal retreat into this Arcadian world is, or course, only temporary, for she must return to the court and the city. Thus, one might argue, the progress offers a paradigm of the pastoral movement as it also suggests the pattern for much of Shakespeare's early romantic comedy. The park of Navarre (*Love's Labour's Lost*) or the woods outside Athens (*Midsummer Night's Dream*) are momentary places of retreat, just as were the environs of Kenilworth Castle (1575) or Elvetham (1591) for Elizabeth. One may enter the pastoral world, but one does not remain there.

Describing the setting at Kenilworth and part of the pageant, Robert Laneham (if that is his name) notes the deer roaming freely, the arbours "that with great art, cost, & diligens wear very pleazauntly appointed: which also the naturall grace by the tall and fresh fragrant treez & soil did so far foorth commend, az *Diana* her selfe might haue deyned thear well enough too raunge for her pastime."[7] And so she did in the person of Elizabeth. Laneham also points out that "Captain Cox" who performs with the citizens of Coventry in their historical show is a learned man; among his accomplishments in reading is "the Sheperdz kalender" (p. 35)—perhaps a reference to Spenser's work four years before publication? Mythological gods and goddesses leave

6. Alice V. Griffin, *Pageantry on the Shakespearean Stage* (New York, 1951), pp. 134-49, a consideration of progress pageants and some plays.
7. *A Letter: Whearin, part of the entertainment vntoo the Queenz Maiesty, at Killingwoorth Castl, . . . iz signified* ([London, 1575]), p. 4. For discussion of the Kenilworth show see my *English Civic Pageantry 1558-1642* (London and Columbia, 1971), pp. 30-35. All the pageants discussed in the paper are included in this book.

David M. Bergeron

gifts; the Lady of the Lake and Arion on a dolphin greet Elizabeth; and there is a bear-baiting incident, graphically described by Laneham, who can report casually: "It waz a sport very pleazaunt of theez beastz . . . " (p. 23). Bear-baiting in Arcadia? Nothing reinforces the point more clearly that the pastoral world is a place of conflict and contrasts, that it is not sentimentalized ruralism.

As these halcyon days at Kenilworth draw to a close and Elizabeth departs, George Gascoigne, at the request of the Earl of Leicester, impersonates Sylvanus and speaks to her, sometimes running alongside her horse. (At one point Elizabeth stayed "her horse to favour Sylvanus, fearing least he should be driven out of breath by following her horse so fast.")[8] Trying to restrain her, Sylvanus offers what he can: "I will intreate Dame Flora to make it continually spring here with store of redolent and fragrant flowers. Ceres shall be compelled to yeelde your Majestie competent provision; and Bacchus shall be sued unto for the first-fruits of his vineyards"(Nichols, I. 518). The voice of Deepe-desire," coming from a hollybush, echoes the plea of Sylvanus, noting, for example, that "Pan would pipe his part such daunces as he can:/ Or els Apollo musicke make, and Mars would be your man" (I. 522). A charming song and a final speech by Sylvanus close the entertainment. The pastoral world clearly has its allures, but the Queen moves out of that world and back toward London.

Constructing a special crescent-shaped pond at Elvetham for the elaborate progress pageant there in 1591, the Earl of Hertford unintentionally reminds us that pastorals are artificial. During the entertainment a fierce battle rages at the pond between the sea gods led by Nereus and the wood gods led by Sylvanus, himself strikingly costumed: ". . . from the middle downewarde to the knee, in kiddes skinnes with the haire on; his legges, bodie, and face, naked, but died over with saffron, and his head hooded with a goates skin. . . ."[9] While Elizabeth, seated under a green satin canopy, looks on, the battle continues until the combatants recognize her presence "as alwaies friend to Peace, and ennemy to Warre" (III. 115). As in many other pastorals, Elizabeth here has the power to reconcile the conflicting forces.

In a dramatic episode that may recall the April Eclogue of *The Shepheardes Calender*, one specifically in praise of the Queen, a Poet greets Elizabeth when she arrives at Elvetham with full praise, acknow-

8. John Nichols, *The Progresses and Public Processions of Queen Elizabeth*, new edition (London, 1823), I.517
9. Nichols, *Progresses*, III, 113-14, 115.

ledging that all nature responds: "Thee, thee (sweet Princes), heav'n and earth, and fluds,/ And plants, and beasts, salute with one accord. . ." (III. 107). Six Virgins surround this Orpheus-figure, and they busy themselves removing stumbling blocks presumably left by Envy. They are the Hours and Graces, the latter singled out in Spenser's eclogue, and described thus at Elvetham: "They were all attired in gowns of taffata sarcenet of divers colours, with flowrie garlands on their heads, and baskets full of sweet hearbs and flowers upon their armes" (III. 108). The Virgins go before Elizabeth "strewing the way with flowers, and singing a sweete song of six parts," an echo of Hobbinoll's report in the April Eclogue (ll. 127-53) where the virgins (shepherds' daughters) are urged to strew Eliza's path with various kinds of flowers. After such recreation there is the plaintive plea at the Queen's departure, voiced by the Poet and sung by various characters. Elizabeth, a veritable goddess of the Arcadian world, is called "faire Nature's treasure," the "sweete lively Sunne," the "worlds star-bright eye" (III. 121). Hobbinol's emblem at the end of the April Eclogue seems also appropriate to the Elvetham pageant: "O dea certe!"

In a brief show at Lady Russell's estate at Bisham in 1592, Elizabeth encounters Pan who yields all the flocks of the field to her and promises to break his pipe "which Apollo could never make me doe. . ." (Nichols, III. 135). Ceres is also present "with her Nymphes, in an harvest cart"; she surrenders her deity in the presence of the Queen. Echoing a familiar pastoral theme, the old Shepherd who greets Elizabeth at Sudley Castle in 1592, insists on shepherds' simplicity: "we carry our harts at our tongues ends, being as far from dissembling as our sheepe from fiercenesse. . . " (III. 136). Walking in the gardens at Wanstead in 1578, Elizabeth suddenly finds herself in the middle of a pastoral debate, Sidney's quasi-dramatic The Lady of May. The May Lady must choose between the virtues of Espilus, a shepherd, and Therion, a forester. The conflict has its physical dimension: "ther was hard in the woodes a confused noise and fourthwith there came oute sixe shepheardes, with as many fosters halinge and pullinge, to whether side they should Drawe the Ladie of maye. . . ."[10] As an "actor" in the pageant, Elizabeth finally renders a judgment in favour of the shepherd, Espilus, finding him the worthier of the two. The natural landscape and the landscapes of the imagination in the progress pageants readily provide a pastoral world in setting and in dramatic episodes. Arcadia seems fully alive during the summer tours.

10. Robert Kimbrough and Philip Murphy, "The Helmingham Hall Manuscript of Sidney's The Lady of May: A Commentary and Transcription," Renaissance Drama, NS 1 (1968), 109.

David M. Bergeron

Elaborate preparation, sometimes months of planning, and always considerable expense characterize royal entries, the official welcome of the sovereign into a city with spectacular display and dramatic tableaux. Coronation activities give rise to the richest of these civic pageants, planned and financed by city governments with generous assistance from the guilds. The construction of a garden tableau with the resulting metaphor and the representation of rural and mythical figures evoke the pastoral world in the royal entry shows. Symbolizing the union of the York and Lancaster houses is a genealogical tree, garnished with red and white roses, the first pageant device to greet Elizabeth on her entry into London, 14 January 1559. The last tableau offers Deborah, ancient ruler of Israel, behind whom is a tree "in curious, artificiall maner," "bewtified with leaves as grene as arte could devise";[11] it is a palm tree, symbolizing peace. At the Little Conduit in Cheapside in the same pageant two hills contrast the distinction between a flourishing and a decaying commonwealth. The northern hill is barren and decaying, but the hill on the south is "fayre, freshe, grene, and beawtifull, the grounde thereof full of flowres and beawtie, and on thesame was erected also one tree very freshe and fayre . . ." (p. 47). This bucolic hill represents the future, implying the hopes that rest with Elizabeth; its idealized, artificial form is at one with the construction of many pastorals.

Involving the dramatic talents of Jonson, Dekker and Middleton, the delayed, but incomparable, royal entry of James I took place in London on 15 March 1604, enhanced by the construction of seven triumphal arches, located throughout the city. The suggestion of a garden in the 1559 pageant gets full treatment here. Reminiscent of Elvetham, the arch at Soper-lane end, entitled *Nova Faelix Arabia*, includes the Graces and Hours. Dekker describes their costumes as follows: the Graces, ". . . the one had a Chaplet of sundry Flowers on her head, clusterd heere and there with the Fruites of the earth. The seconde, a Garland of eares of Corne. The third, a wreath of Vine-branches, mixt with Grapes and Olives"; the Hours, "attyred in loose Roabes of light cullours, paynted with Flowers: for so *Ouid* apparrels them."[12] A song likens London to a summer arbour: "*Troynouant* is now a Sommer Arbour"; "*Troynouant* is now no more a Citie" (II. 280). All of this is but a prelude to the pageant device of a garden.

Near the Cross in Cheapside, Sylvanus suddenly confronts the

11. *The Quenes Maiesties Passage through the Citie of London*. ed. James M. Osborn (New Haven, 1960), p. 53. All quotations are from this fascsimile edition.
12. *The Dramatic Works of Thomas Dekker*, ed. Fredson Bowers (Cambridge, 1955), II, 277-89. All quotations from Dekker will be from the Bowers' edition.

King, "*Syluanus* drest vp in greene Iuie, a Cornet in his hand" (II. 282).
He is himself a "prologue," having been dispatched by his mistress
Eirene (Peace) at the next arch, called *Hortus Euporiae*. Sylvanus
requests: ". . . I humbly execute her pleasure, that ere you [James]
passe further, you would deigne to walke into yonder Garden" (284).
The decorations on the arch are rich in pastoral suggestion: "The
garnishments for the whole Bower, being Apples, Peares, Cheries,
Grapes, Roses, Lillies, and all other both fruits and flowers most
artificially molded to the life" (285). Pomona, "the goddesse of
garden fruits," and Ceres, "crowned with ripened eares of Wheate"
(286), join other figures who accompany Peace and Plenty, themselves costumed so as to suggest fertility and abundance. Carrying a
weeding hook and a grafting knife, Vertumnus, "the maister Gardner,"
is the chief speaker, his brows "bound about with flowers, out of
whose thicke heapes, here and there peeped a queene apple, a cherie,
or a peare" (288). The "tenor" of his speech is, as Dekker says, that
the fruitful Cynthian garden has been drooping, but now "on the
sudden by the diuine influence" it is "apparelled with a fresh and more
liuely verdure" (288). Echoing the sentiments of another garden, that
in *Richard II*, Vertumnus says that the leaders of London "carefully
pruine this garden, (weeding-out al hurtful and idle branches that
hinder the growth of the good)." The Gardener offers to James "this
Arbor, the bowers and walkes" (289). If London is indeed no longer a
city but an arbour, then the allegory of this pageant device is clear: the
King is to assume the role of gardener, binding up dangling apricots
and pruning away troublesome weeds. Speech, structure and metaphor coalesce in didactic purpose.

Near the end of our historical period, Charles I on 15 June 1633
made a royal entry into Edinburgh where he had gone to be crowned.
The entertainment shares many characteristics with the pageants in
London, including arches and pastoral references. On the Cross in
Edinburgh, for example, is a show of Bacchus with Silenus, Sylvanus,
Pomona, Venus and Ceres "in a straw coloured mantle, embrodered
with eares of Corne."[13] There is also Mount Parnassus, complete with
Apollo and the Muses, perhaps reminding us of Spenser's June
Eclogue. But the chief pastoral figure is Endymion who emerges "from
out a Verdant Groue . . . apparelled like a Shepheard . . .; hee had a
wreath of flowers upon his head . . .; in his hand he bare a Sheep-
hook" (p. 18). An innocent and somewhat naive shepherd, he

---

13. *The Entertainment of the High and Mighty Monarch Charles* (Edinburgh, 1633),
pp. 13—27. All quotations are from this original text.

wonders in his speech if this place is heaven, for figures representing the seven planets are also present. Each speaks, forecasting Charles's bright future. Venus, for example, wishes for the blessings of Flora and Pomona (p. 24). Endymion ends the tableau presentation, asserting that the mountains, floods, and all "shall observe, and serve this blessed King" (p. 27). The idealizing impulse of the pastoral is apparent in Edinburgh. Royal entries, dramatically realized in cities, frequently seek some other place, some other time as a frame of reference, as a means of praise and instruction for the sovereign; and the pastoral is a likely means of achieving those purposes.

Since medieval times English artisans, craftsmen and traders had organized themselves into guilds ("mysteries") and had been involved with the production of drama, notably the Corpus Christi drama beginning in the fourteenth century. A pastoral flair can be observed in the justly famous *Second Shepherd's Play* in the Wakefield cycle, for example. Through the mid-seventeenth century appears an unbroken lineage of the guilds' support of drama, seen in the latter part of the period in the presentation of Lord Mayor's Shows. These pageants, presented each 29 October at the inauguration of the new mayor of London, begin in the mid-sixteenth century and become, in part because of their frequency, the principal form of civic pageantry. The mayor was chosen from one of the twelve major guilds of London, and his company set out to provide an appropriate entertainment for his installation, the result being a keen sense of competition involving great expense and the talents of some of the best-known dramatists.

From the time of the first show for which we have speeches (1561) to the last pageant (1639) before the theatres close, we have thirty printed texts of mayoral pageants, plus two with speeches included in guild records. Of these pageants in the seventy-eight-year period, nearly two-thirds contain some kind of pastoral element, though Greg cites only two. In England's largest city, with urban guilds as sponsors, why all this reliance on pastoral in their civic entertainments? Part of the answer rests, of course, with the predilections of the particular dramatists, and another part may derive from the guilds producing the shows. Most pageants with pastoral references have as their sponsor the following guilds: Drapers, Clothworkers, Haberdashers, Merchant Taylors, and Skinners—all connected in some way with the cloth trade and its obvious dependence on wool or furs, hence their reliance on country products. In addition, the Drapers and Clothworkers have on their heraldic crest a golden ram, the Merchant Taylors, a lamb, and the Haberdashers, goats as supporters to the arms.[14] There is, therefore, a practical explanation, a kind of self-advertisement, to join the more esoteric and literary ones in accounting for the presence of pastoral.

No hostility occurs between city and country; for the pageant dramatists frequently envision London as some variation or extension of the fragrant countryside, London being thus idealized by use of pastoral. In the first Lord Mayor's Show for which there is a text, Peele's of 1585, the presenter, a Moor riding on a lynx, says: "The honest Franklin and the Husband-man/ Layes downe his sackes of Corne at Londons feet,/ And bringes such presents as the Countrie yeeldes."[15] And a figure called "the Cuntry" asserts: "For Londons aide the Cuntry gives supplie,/ Of needfull things, and store of every graine:/ . . . had never Towne lesse cause for to complaine" (p. 211). The explicit link between rural and urban life manifests itself in the pageants in three broad categories of pastoral: some variation of the garden, shepherd characters and mythical figures. The discussion that follows pursues these three topics.

In his first mayoral pageant (1609) Anthony Munday includes a device of an island which has on it "a golden Feild or Garden, imagined of the nature of *Hesperides*, where all the Trees and Fruites are of pure golde."[16] If not precisely pastoral, the device at least establishes a metaphor to be explored in the pageant speeches by St. George and St. Andrew; for the garden has appropriate allegorical figures in it, such as the Graces and Tranquility, "attired in Carnation, . . . a branch of Palme in one hand, and a fayre Chaplet or wreath of Floures in the other" (sig. B1ᵛ). The island with the garden becomes a symbolic statement about England. Thomas Campbell, the new mayor in 1609, had as a successor twenty years later his son, James; Dekker prepares the pageant (*London's Tempe*), drawing a connection to the earlier show. He, too, constructs a garden complete with trees, flowers, fruit, "Intimating that as *London* is the best-stored Garden in the Kingdome . . .; So, on this day it is the most glorious Citty in the Christian world."[17] Addressing the mayor, Titan assures him that Flora, Ceres and Pomona leave their gifts to enhance the garden that is London. In the previous year Dekker in his *Britannia's Honor* (1628) also has a

---

14. See John Bromley, *The Armorial Bearings of the Guilds of London* (London and New York, 1960).

15. *The Life and Minor Works of George Peele*, ed. David H. Horne (New Haven, 1952), pp. 209, 211. All quotations from Peele are from this edition.

16. *Camp-bell: or The Ironmongers Faire Feild* ([London, 1609]), sig. B1. All quotations are from this fragmentary text.

17. Bowers, *Dekker*, IV, 110.

garden, this time "Sun's Bower," in which the Seasons accompany the Sun; and beneath them on the pageant structure is a wilderness, full of the beasts that produce fur. Sol speaks in praise of the peace that England knows, symbolized in the tranquil, pastoral garden.

Rather like the 1604 royal entry, two pageants by Middleton and Heywood explore the garden motif as a commentary on the political state. In *The Triumphs of Health and Prosperity* (1626), honouring the Drapers, Middleton begins with a device called "the Beautiful Hill or Fragrant Garden, with flowery banks, near to which lambs and sheep are a-grazing."[18] Flowers and fruit garnish the structure by which Middleton intends "the most pleasant garden of England, the noble city of London, the flowers intimating the sweet odours of their virtue and goodnesses, and the fruits of their works of justice and charity" (p. 404)—by which he refers to the accomplishments of the guild. The sheep give the dramatist an opening for briefly commenting on the "noble mystery of ancient drapery." Apparently referring to the previous year's plague in which there was no pageant, the speaker notes that the former cloud of grief hanging over the city has now given way to a new freshness: "The garden springs again . . ./ Fruit overlade their trees, barns crack with store." But such rejoicing prompts a question: "what's requir'd?" The answer, not surprisingly, refers to the necessary balance in the commonwealth, just as there must be harmony in the garden: "That which in conscience ought to be desir'd;/ Care and uprightness in the magistrate's place,/ And in all men obedience, truth, and grace" (p. 405).

When a few years later Heywood picks up this theme, he seems to recall Elizabeth's 1559 royal entry. Within the shadows of St. Paul's, Heywood in *Londons Ius Honorarium* (1631) places the first land pageant, "a greene and pleasant Hill, adorned with all the Flowers of the spring" and containing a "faire and flourishing tree" full of fruit.[19] A creature, "apparrelled like Summer," embodies the motto, "a City well governed" (sig. B2-B2ᵛ). The Theological Graces accompany her, and labels hang from the tree, indicating those attributes that cause a city to "flourish and prosper" (an echo of the 1559 show). Interpreting the symbolism, Time asserts that if such qualities are adhered to, then "*Cities, shall like perpetuall Summers bee*" (sig. B3). Countering the idyllic beauty of the garden, Time picks up "a leafe-lesse & withered branch" (B3ᵛ), observing that it is a symbol of a city

18. *The Works of Thomas Middleton*, ed. A. H. Bullen (London, 1886), VII, 404-405. All quotations from Middleton are from the Bullen edition.
19. Thomas Heywood, *Londons Ius Honorarium* (London, 1631), sig. B2.

"ruind, and trod downe." He enumerates the qualities that bring about such decay. A citizen of London, standing in the narrow, dirty, perhaps cold streets of Cheapside to watch the show, would have noted the gap between present reality and pastoral tableau. But through the "landscape of the mind," as Richard Cody would call it, the pastoral writer provides a vision of the other world, one capable of being idealized so that pageant writers can use the garden, for example, to comment symbolically on *respublica.*

Shepherds in the mayoral pageants seem to serve two primary functions: to advertise the guild and to provide a metaphor. The first has the virtue of celebrating the interdependence of urban and pastoral life. Honouring the Drapers, Munday in 1614 includes a Shepherd seated by a golden ram (emblem of the guild). Somewhat testy and realistic, the Shepherd blurts out: "Why gaze yee so vpon me? am I not a man, flesh, bloud, and bone, as you are? Or in these silken sattin Townes, are poore plaine meaning Sheepheards woondred at, like Comets or blazing Starres?"[20] This leads to his discourse on the tradition of Cotswold shepherds' bringing "the very fairest Ram" (B4) as an offering to the mayor. And putting the whole matter rather bluntly, the simple Shepherd says: "no Lambe, no Wooll: no wooll, no Cloth: no Cloth, no Draper (B4ᵛ)." In Munday's fictional world this shepherd seems realistic; at least he raises actual issues. He is at the same time pastoral and slightly anti-pastoral. Something of the same may be said about the Shepherd in Heywood's *Porta Pietatis* (1638), who is appropriately costumed and surrounded by his flock. He suggests that it is not possible for poets and artists fully to express the virtues of sheep, so he gives it a try in an extraordinary encomium on behalf of sheep. We might, for example, admire the peacock, but we do not wear its feathers. Search *"the wide Universe, the Earth, and Skie."* the Shepherd says, *"Nor Beast nor Bird can with the Sheepe comply."*[21] It is, in addition, an emblem of Patience and of Profit (sig. B2ᵛ), he suggests, an observation not wasted on the sponsoring guild, the Drapers.

The shepherd figure in Peele's *Descensus Astraeae* (1591) becomes a means of evoking the myth of the Golden Age, a common theme in some pastorals. Astraea, by whom Peele means Queen Elizabeth, is a shepherdess; she says in her only speech: "Feed on my flocke among

20. Anthony Munday, *Himatia-Poleos: The Triumphs of Olde Draperie* (London, 1614), sig. B3ᵛ. All quotations from this text.
21. Thomas Heywood, *Porta Pietatis, or, The Port or Harbour of Piety* (London, 1638), sig. B2. Greg says this show is Heywood's only use of the pastoral tradition, but I obviously think otherwise.

the gladsome greene/ Where heavenly Nectar flowes above the banckes" (p. 215). Accompanied by the Graces and other figures, Astraea embodies the peace that has come to the land. As the opening speaker puts it simply: "O happie times/ That do beget such calme and quiet daies,/ Where sheep and shepheard breath in such content" (pp. 214-15)—a pastoral world at its idealistic best. The presence of sheep in Middleton's 1621 show leads the character Aries to suggest that they represent the magistrate's subjects: ". . . not unfit,/ Since kings and rulers are, in holy writ,/ With shepherds parallel'd" (VII. 347). Unintentionally the statement is a gloss on Peele's method.

If the sovereign can be metaphorically linked to a shepherd, so can the new mayor of London; and that is the purpose of the first land pageant in Heywood's 1633 entertainment, honouring Clothworkers. Not only does the Shepherd have all the appropriate implements, but also the dangers a shepherd faces are apparent in the presence of a wolf "ready to cease vpon his prey."[22] The shepherd with his hook ("a Symbole of his care and vigilancy") must stand ready to meet the threat "with a bold spirit and wakefull eye" (sig. B1ᵛ). In his speech Heywood's Shepherd drives home this point, making the obvious application to the mayor. His rhetorical formula is, "As I, so you." After singing the praises of woollen cloth, he closes with instructions for the mayor: "Make much Sir of your great Charge, 'tis not mine,/ Y' are the true Shepheard, I my place resigne" (sig. B2ᵛ). Biblical and pastoral traditions converge in the metaphor, one readily apprehended by the original street audience.

The pastoral invades London's streets in the pageants by one final means, the use of figures traditionally associated with the bucolic world. By their simple, brief representations they may set off a chain of associations; Spenser's Shepheardes Calender is, of course, rich with such persons. The first that I mention is one distinctly English, namely, Robin Hood. He had appeared in an entertainment for the sovereign in 1515, and in a show, devised by Thomas Campion, for Queen Anne during her travels in 1613.[23] Given his two "Robin Hood" plays at the end of the sixteenth century, it is not surprising to see Munday including this figure in the 1615 Lord Mayor's Show. Richard Cody reminds us that "outlaw scenes also spell English

---

22. Thomas Heywood, Londini Emporia, or Londons Mercatura (London, 1633), sig. B1ᵛ.
23. See Sydney Anglo, Spectacle Pageantry, and Early Tudor Policy (Oxford, 1969), p. 119; for the latter, see my English Civic Pageantry, p. 98.

pastoral."[24] We need only recall Shakespeare's Forest of Arden or Ben Jonson's *The Sad Shepherd* to recognize the validity of that assessment.

In Munday's pageant, *Metropolis Coronata*, heavy with emphasis on the guild, the Drapers, Robin Hood appears presumably because he is son-in-law to London's first mayor, Henry Fitz-Alwine, also represented. Without pausing to wonder how Munday reached such a conclusion, we note the description in the pageant of Robin Hood and his men, "all clad in greene, with their Bowes, Arrowes and Bugles, and a new slaine Deere carried among them."[25] As the activities of the pageant wind down, this group confronts the new mayor at day's end and celebrates the pastoral life that they represent. This is made obvious through the dialogue between Robin Hood and Friar Tuck and by the final song. They have come "*from the Forrest of merrie Shirwood*" (sig. C1^v) in order to join the festivity in honour of the mayor; and, at Friar Tuck's insistence, they agree to serve the mayor "*When any occasion shall require*" (C2^v.) Standing in the streets of London, they nevertheless sing a charming hymn in praise of the greenwood where they live, "For there is neither City nor Towne,/ That likes them halfe so well" (C3^v). Quite simply, one may live in Sherwood, the song says, "As pleasantly as a King a"; life there "is so pleasant a thing a" (C3). Robin Hood thus epitomizes the pastoral retreat of both time and place.

As there are a number of classical mythical figures in Spenser's pastoral, so in the pageants. Apollo with the Muses sits on Mount Parnassus in John Squire's *The Triumphs of Peace*, the Lord Mayor's Show of 1620; two of the Muses sing in the mayor's honour. We have already noted the appearance of Endymion in the 1633 royal entry. He also performs in the 1634 mayoral pageant, John Taylor's *The Triumphs of Fame and Honour*, where he suddenly confronts the mayor in Cheapside, explaining who he is: "I am *Endimion*, that of yore did keepe/ Upon th'Arcadian hils my harmeles sheepe."[26] Offering something of a testament to the staying power of Spenser's work, Endymion claims: ". . . for my sake the Swaines doe still prefer/ The booke ycleap'd the shepherds Kallender" (B2). Riding on a golden ram (emblem of the Clothworkers), he praises the guild and woollen cloth and wishes for the mayor "prosperous windes, and happy tides" (B2^v). The Endymion episode closes with a dance of shepherds.

24. *The Landscape of the Mind: Pastoralism and Platonic Theory in Tasso's Aminta and Shakespeare's Early Comedies* (Oxford, 1969), p. 100.
25. Anthony Munday, *Metropolis Coronata: The Triumphes of Ancient Drapery* (London, 1615), sig. B3. All quotations are from this text.
26. Taylor, *The Triumphs of Fame and Honour* (London, 1634), sig. B2.

David M. Bergeron

The mythic figure of most importance is Orpheus. As Cody suggests, "The invocation of his name in an appropriate context of love, landscape, and poetry can be said to signalize the Renaissance pastoral mode."[27] Not surprising, then, that Spenser invokes him in the October Eclogue, one greatly concerned with poetry. Orpheus appears in the London royal entry of Philip and Mary in 1554; and he has a role in three different Lord Mayor's Shows, nicely ranging from the first one with speeches (1561) to the last one of the era (1639). He symbolizes harmony, and he provides instruction for the new mayor. In the 1561 show, sponsored by the Merchant Taylors, he accompanies several other figures all associated with the power of the harp and music—David, Amphion, Arion. Orpheus refers to his power, noting the rivers that give attentive ear to his music; and he plays on the name of the mayor, William Harper: ". . . how greate a ioye it weare/ our harper in this towne, the sworde of power to beare."[28] The pageant device also carries a picture of Orpheus, "playeng vpon his harpe, and Trees Rivers Mountaynes, as Daunsinge & harkeninge" (p. 44). More extensive is the treatment of Orpheus by Middleton and Heywood.

For the Skinners in 1619, Middleton wrote *The Triumphs of Love and Antiquity* in which the first device on land is a wilderness, presided over by Orpheus. "great master both in poesy and harmony" (VII. 318). Two basic points inform Orpheus' long speech to the mayor: he should perfect his personal virtues, and he must control the city. Relying on the idea of Orpheus as artist, the mythic figure says in reference to the encouragement of virtue, "That's a great work to perfect" (319). The wilderness in which Orpheus stands becomes a metaphor (rather like the garden structures elsewhere) for the political world: "Just such a wilderness is a commonwealth/ That is undrest, unprun'd, wild in her health" (320). But by fair example, musical grace, and harmonious government the mayor may tame the wilderness; for "Every wise magistrate that governs thus,/ May well be call'd a powerful Orpheus" (320). Gardener, shepherd, and now Orpheus, all images emanating from the pastoral mode, serve as metaphors that help delineate the approach of a ruler, sovereign or mayor, to the task of governing.

With unintended irony Heywood celebrates the theme of peace in the 1639 show as unknowingly the country stands on the verge of civil war. In historical retrospect there is a special poignancy to Heywood's

27. *Landscape of the Mind*, p. 14.
28. *Collections* III: *A Calendar of Dramatic Records in the Books of the Livery Companies of London 1485-1640*, eds. Jean Robertson and D. J. Gordon (Oxford, 1954), pp. 42, 44.

142

pageant. Honouring the Drapers, the dramatist has as one of his principal emblems of peace the figure of Orpheus, "seated in a faire Plat-forme, beautified with pleasant Trees" with beasts and birds of all sorts, "all imagined to be attentive to his Musick."[29] Orpheus rehearses his accomplishments, his charming of all opposing elements of nature, so that, for example, lions and lambs are now "*coucht in love*" (sig. B3ᵛ). There is, however, a harmony greater than that achieved by Orpheus: that "*of unanimous hearts; plenty, increase;/ With all Terrestriall blessings waite on peace*" (B4). Such an accomplishment would be a "*Devine Concordancy*," a music sweeter "*than e're Orpheus made.*" Echoing Middleton, this Orpheus says to the mayor: "*You are that Orpheus who can doe all these*" (B4). In the poetic imagination, the landscape of the mind, it is possible to conceive of the ideal Orpheus, presiding over some government, whatever the reality may be.

But the harmonious voice of Orpheus fades in the presence of acts of Parliament that shut down theatres and warring forces that tear apart a country. Having symbolized peace, Heywood turns in his pageant to a final device that graphically portrays the horrors of war, as if he has some premonition. Arcadia is, of course, not a place devoid of strife; we recall that the name "Arcadia" was the code word for a World War Two conference that helped plan joint allied strategy.[30] Pageants with their pastoral characters and themes are but momentary escapes from present reality; the insubstantial pageant does indeed fade. For the moment, though, we may be lifted by poetic skill out of the limitations of our urban world to perceive something grander and richer than our lives afford. When poets or pageant dramatists achieve such moments, they are themselves Orpheus-like. It is the poet who can take the brazen world of nature and make gold out of it. Doubtless Londoners needed such gold, for lurking among their streets after the shouts have died out is the sombre recognition of the difficulties of city life. I know of no more telling note of the intrusion of reality into the celebrating, festive, pageant world than the simple account in the Grocers' records for 1640: "their is noe publike show eyther wth Pageats or vpon the water" (*Collections* III, p. 131).

---

29. Thomas Heywood, *Londini Status Pacatus: or, Londons Peaceable Estate* (London, 1639), sig. B3. All quotations are from this edition.
30. Noted by Harry Levin, *Myth of the Golden Age*, p. 98.

The English Masque and the Functions of Comedy

EUGENE M. WAITH

Thanks to a number of distinguished critics, it has become a staple of comment on masques to note the crucial importance of the occasions on which they were performed. They are, in fact, perfect examples of occasional art, not intended to endure, but praiseworthy in so far as their creators found or devised suitable forms. This is not to say that when a masque was performed it was appreciated in exact proportion to what we would recognize as its degree of formal coherence. We know how often the very opposite was the case. But now that the applause for the unique performance has long since died down, or the lack of applause has been largely forgotten, there is still some interest in appraising the ingenuity of those early creators in adapting various kinds of available material to their uses. If the results were sometimes a rather haphazard sequence of numbers, as in many a twentieth-century revue, they were sometimes remarkably shapely and strikingly apt.

My aim is to call attention to some of these successes and to suggest they they were due, at least in part, to the appropriation of some of the functions traditionally assigned to comedy. Two of these have for centuries been taken as distinguishing features of the genre: first, to ridicule the defects of ordinary people (to "sport with human follies, not with crimes," as Jonson put it); and secondly, to enact the ultimate surmounting of obstacles by the sympathetic characters. The first of these functions is part of the classical distinction from tragedy, in that the characters of comedy are assumed to be less than illustrious and their misdeeds less than criminal. This function thus establishes certain expectations not only about the characters but about the plot. The second function could be described as a structure or, in Frye's terms, a *mythos*: the movement from a society dominated by blocking

characters to a new and freer society, favourable to the desires of the
hero and heroine.[1] Sometimes the change is the result of successful
trickery; sometimes it is closer to transcendence. With each function
is associated a repertory of forms, some of which closely resemble the
forms of other genres. Some ways of ridiculing folly bring comedy
close to satire, while some happy endings resemble those of romance.
One of the virtues of Frye's scheme is the clarity with which it shows
these generic relationships, in which the masque also became involved
when it borrowed from comedy.

The usual occasion for a masque, as for the diverse entertainments
out of which it grew, was a feast day, a bethrothal or marriage, an
important event in the life of the ruler, or the visit of a distinguished
guest, and the inevitable function was to celebrate the occasion. So it
was natural that the comic mythos and laughter at the expense of
fools should have been found appropriate; but we know that the
devisers of these shows experimented with many other forms, some
inherited from the Middle Ages, some derived from the newly redis-
covered classics. Banquets, dances, jousts and processions (sometimes presented as *trionfi*) were all suitably festive, as was the performance of a play. Best of all, in any case, was an entertainment
explicitly tied to the occasion or to the distinguished person or to
both. Hence borrowed forms must be adapted to serve not only their
original functions but this new one as well. The discovery of the great
usefulness of comedy did not take place immediately.

Since the history of courtly entertainment has been so well covered
by D'Ancona, Reyher, Prunières, Welsford, Orgel[2] and others, we
are free to choose examples arbitrarily here and there with no attempt
at representing the development as a whole or even the mainstream.
We can concentrate, instead, on a number of solutions to the problem
of suiting form to function. Among the earliest Renaissance court
entertainments none has been more frequently discussed than
Poliziano's *Orfeo*, and rightly so, since it can claim to be the first
serious secular play in the Italian vernacular, the first pastoral drama,
and the first step toward opera. For my special purposes it makes an
unusually good point of departure.

Poliziano, temporarily at odds with his patron, Lorenzo de' Medici,
wrote *Orfeo* in 1480 at the request of Cardinal Francesco Gonzaga

1. Northrop Frye, *Anatomy of Criticism* (Princeton, N.J., 1952), p. 163.
2. Alessandro D'Ancona, *Origini del teatro italiano*, (Turin 1891); Paul Reyher, *Les Masques anglais* (Paris, 1909); Henry Prunières, *Le Ballet de cour avant Benserade et Lully* (Paris, 1914); Enid Welsford, *The Court Masque* (1927; rpt, New York, 1962); Stephen Orgel, *The Jonsonian Masque* (Cambridge, Mass., 1965).

to be performed at Mantua, probably as an entertainment to celebrate two Gonzaga betrothals.[3] Like the *sacre rappresentazioni* which it resembles in so many ways, it opens with a messenger announcing the subject of the play. Instead of an angel it is Mercury, described as "annunziatore della festa," and the action concerns a pagan, not a Christian, martyr: when Eurydice dies fleeing from Aristaeus, Orpheus visits the underworld to rescue her; he loses her and meets death and dismemberment at the hands of the maenads. The enactment begins with a brief pastoral dialogue in which Aristaeus reveals to two other shepherds his love for Eurydice and then leaves to pursue her. It may be that the spectators were to see her cross the stage from the side where the country landscape was presumably represented in part of a simultaneous set.[4] No sooner have Eurydice and Aristaeus disappeared than Orpheus appears with his lyre on a mountain (that conventional piece of medieval scenery put to different use), and descends singing some Latin verses, not for the edification of the flora and fauna, but in praise of Cardinal Francesco Gonzaga. He is interrupted by the news of Eurydice's death brought by a shepherd, moves to the other side of the stage, where the underworld was represented (shades of the hellmouth), charms Pluto and Proserpina, and begins the trip back. In the space of only a few lines he makes his fatal turn, laments his fate, and after inveighing against the disastrous consequences of love for a woman, meets the Bacchae. Most of the remainder of this brief drama is given over to their festive song as, holding the head of their victim, they honour Bacchus.

At first sight the murder of Orpheus by a rout of drunken women might not seem to be the ideal fable for a double betrothal, but there is a broader view, much broader. For Richard Cody "The *Orfeo* is a love rite, composed by the Laureate of Ficino's academy, in which the passion of the founder of poetic theology is celebrated."[5] This is part of the author's argument that Platonism opens up a prospect on "the landscape of the mind" in pastoral poetry, and even though Ida Maïer is probably right in denying that Poliziano loads his playlet with the full weight of humanist interpretation of the myth (p. 395), *Orfeo* could hardly have failed to suggest to some of the audience at the Gonzaga court the relationship between an ideal love and the power of music and poetry, or perhaps even the power and perils of the con-

3. See Ida Maïer, *Ange Politien; la formation d'un poète humaniste* (Geneva, 1966), pp. 387-90.
4. See Maïer, pp. 403-4.
5. *The Landscape of the Mind: Pastoralism and Platonic Theory in Tasso's Aminta and Shakespeare's Early Comedies*, (Oxford, 1969), p. 31.

templative life. As Cody says, "an Orpheus poem should be hermetic," and he may not be extravagant in suggesting that "with the scene of his playing the lyre, Orfeo enters upon a ministry which reveals him as Apolline prophet and Bacchic man of sorrows" (p. 40).

The scene of Orpheus's first appearance, singing his Latin eulogy of the cardinal, troubles many critics, as does most encomiastic poetry in an age which often brands such writing as purely venal and relegates it to the same category as television commercials. Yet here the evidence of a kind of Platonizing is the clearest. Here, if anywhere, the audience is invited to see into or through the visible manifestation to an ideal form. The mythic Orpheus addresses the patron of the feast as a prince who cares for poets and poetry with the exemplary generosity of Maecenas and the imagination of Virgil.[6] It is the longest of Orpheus's speeches, and serves the vital function of relating the entertainment to its host as well as, more generally, to the court where it is being given. If it is, in a sense, Platonic, it is also essentially courtly— a combination that Daniel Javitch has fruitfully treated in his *Poetry and Courtliness in Renaissance England.*[7] In Poliziano's *Orfeo* the connection is cemented by the assignment of the role of Orpheus to a Florentine gentleman, Bartolomeo (or "Baccio") Ugolini, an associate of Lorenzo de' Medici's. As Orpheus descended the mountain the audience was to see the mythic dimension of its host as it also recognized an eminent Florentine visitor in the guise of the mythic hero. We customarily praise an actor for totally becoming the character he impersonates, but in a courtly entertainment there is a special interest in detecting the person beneath the mask. It is important that both the actor and the princely object of the encomium should be perceived with double vision, losing neither the contemporary man nor the mythic figure for whom he stands.

If Poliziano related poetry and courtliness in the choice of his principal actor and in his compliment to the cardinal, he did so too in the tone of his comments on the play in a prefatory letter published with the first edition. There he says that he wrote *Orfeo* in two days in the midst of continuous tumult, and professes to wish that his ill-formed little entertainment might have been exposed, like a defective Spartan baby, and left to die instead of being preserved in print (*Poesie*, p. 19). Surely Castiglione would have found this a superb example of *sprezzatura*, very proper for a courtier-playwright.

It is peculiarly ironical that we cannot be sure whether or not the

6. Angelo Poliziano, *Poesie italiane*, ed. S. Orlando (Milan, 1976), pp. 116-18.
7. Princeton, N.J., 1978.

feast for which *Orfeo* was so knowingly tailored ever took place (Maïer, p. 390), but the description by De Sanctis of the hypothetical occasion shows a keen appreciation of the way the play might have been received. Comparing it to a medieval joust he says:

> Just as the burghers, dressed up as knights, reproduced the world of chivalry, these new Athenians reproduced the world of the ancients, and certainly must have thoroughly enjoyed watching each other parade in the costumes of the older days. There was enormous enthusiasm when Baccio Ugolini, dressed as Orfeo and holding a zither in his hand, came down the mountainside singing the praises of the Cardinal in magnificent Latin verses, *"Redeunt saturnia regna."* The ancient days of Athens and Rome seemed to have come back again.[8]

An attitude similar to this becomes a defining characteristic of the entertainments we are considering.

Generically *Orfeo* is an anomaly. Originally called a *favola* or *fabula*, in the neutral sense of "dramatic poem," it was later somewhat altered, divided into five acts, and called *Orphei Tragoedia* in certain manuscripts discovered in the eighteenth century.[9] Although students of Poliziano do not now attribute this reworking to him, it provides for a useful comparison. Destined for a later occasion at Ferrara, it properly omits the eulogy of Cardinal Gonzaga, the prominent centrepiece of the *favola*. But it ends, even in this "tragic" form, on the festive note of the ecstatic chorus of Bacchantes. To call it comic would be excessive, but in neither version is there the emphasis on loss found in even so celebrative a tragedy as *Tamburlaine*:

> My body feels, my soul doth weep to see
> Your sweet desires deprived my company,
> For Tamburlaine, the scourge of God, must die.[10]

There is none of this in *Orfeo*. The end, however ironic it may seem, is dance, intoxication and song, with the repeated "Bacchus, Bacchus, evoe." Perhaps we should think of the final destination of the head and of the transcendent survival of the Orphic voice. In any case, the requirements of the occasion seem to have exerted a shaping influence on the material.

Given the nature of the desired response to courtly entertainment,

8. Francesco De Sanctis, *History of Italian Literature*, tr. Joan Redfern (1931: rpt. N.Y., [1960]), I, 383.
9. See Maïer, p. 392; Poliziano, *Le Stanze, l'Orfeo e le rime*, ed. G. Carducci (Bologna, 1912), pp. 393-507.
10. *Complete Plays of Christopher Marlowe*, ed. I. Ribner (N.Y., 1963), p. 174.

classical mythology was an obvious source of inspiration. Suggesting not only the return of a great period in western history but also an ideal world beyond this one, it conferred upon the courtier-actor and upon his audience the very qualities to which they aspired. Nothing is less surprising than the large number of intermezzi, ballets de cour and masques which revived or refashioned Greek and Roman myths. The gods and godlets of mountains, woods, fields and streams had the special appeal that both underlay and then was reinforced by pastoral poetry. Bacchus, his foster-father Silenus, Pan, and their attendant fauns, satyrs, nymphs, oreads, and dryads were all, at one level of interpretation, expressions of the natural forces which any courtier extravagantly admired as the antithesis of the effete court, while doing his best to avoid them. Cinthio chose precisely this mythological milieu for his pastoral drama *Egle* in 1545, performed at the author's house in Ferrara twice in the presence of Duke Hercules II and his brother Cardinal Ippolito d'Este. Paid for by the university law students, the entertainment celebrated no happy event other than Cinthio's attempt to revivify the satyr-play, but like more precisely courtly entertainments, it was presented to the best people, had music specially written for it and scenery specially designed. A gentleman named Sebastiano Clarignano da Montefalco, whom Cinthio considered the Roscius of their time, was the principal actor.[11] But the most compelling reason for mentioning *Egle* in a study of the forms adapted for masques is that Cinthio, taking the *Cyclops* of Euripides as his model, produced in fact a predecessor of pastoral tragicomedy, and in so doing devised a kind of action which would be most useful to the authors of masques. In a brief essay on the satyr-play he says that it differs from comedy and tragedy, "partaking of the pleasantness of the one and the gravity of the other."[12] Here he comes close to anticipating Guarini, who wrote that "He who composes tragicomedy takes from tragedy its great persons but not its great action . . .; from comedy laughter that is not excessive, modest amusement, feigned difficulty, and above all the comic order."[13] The combination of great persons and a comic order was just right also for the masque.

The comic action was very simple: Egle, the mistress of Silenus,

11. *Egle, Satira di M. Giovanbattista Giraldi Cinthio* (s.l.n.d.), fol. 5, and see D'Ancona, II, p. 414.
12. "Discorso sulle satire atte alle scene," *Scritti estetici di G. B. Giraldi Cintio*, in *Biblioteca rara*, LIII (Milan, 1864), p. 135; see also Marvin T. Herrick, *Tragicomedy* (Urbana, Ill., 1955), p. 10.
13. *Il Pastor fido e compendio della poesia tragicomica*, ed. B. Brognoligo (Bari, 1914), p. 231; translation altered from Allen H. Gilbert's in *Literary Criticism: Plato to Dryden* (New York, 1940), p. 511.

undertakes to help the sylvan deities prevent the Olympian gods from taking away the nymphs with whom they are all in love. After an unsuccessful attempt to reason with the nymphs, Egle devises a trick which goes disastrously wrong for the sylvan deities. When they rush unexpectedly on the nymphs, who have been lured into dancing with seemingly harmless little satyrs, Diana frustrates the would-be rapists by transforming her followers into fountains, rivers and trees; Pan's Syrinx becomes a reed. Instead of fooling a wicked Polyphemus, as in the *Cyclops*, Silenus and his merry men are routed by the superior power of chaste Diana. Only for her nymphs can the ending be considered happy, and only then if total identification with the landscape is seen as desirable. Still, salvation by transformation has its own Ovidian attraction, which was not lost on later court entertainers. Equally ripe for future exploitation were the incidental laughs provided by the drunken satyrs.

Silenus, satyrs, nymphs and also Bacchantes had already appeared in some intermezzi performed for the wedding of Cosimo I in Florence in 1539. The similarity of the source material makes all the clearer the very different plan which underlay this sort of entertainment. *Orfeo* and *Egle* were little plays; the Florentine intermezzi of 1539 were spectacular *divertissements* performed before and after a play and between its acts. What Guarini called "the comic order" was unmistakably present in the play by Antonio Landi, which was modelled on Roman comedy, but the design of the evening's entertainment as a whole was a baroque elaboration of comic design. The intermezzi served in part to emphasize the play's temporal unity: before the first act dawn was presented by a rising sun and an impersonation of Aurora; after the third act, when it was noon, a drunken Silenus was shown drowsing in a grotto; aroused, and asked to sing, he complied with praise of the Golden Age; after the fourth act eight nymphs in hunting costume appeared as if returning from the hunt "to show that evening was coming,"[14] and after the last act Night, dressed in black silk, sang to the accompaniment of four trombones; finally ten satyrs in hairy breechclouts danced with ten Bacchantes and chanted "Evoe" like the Bacchantes of *Orfeo*, though to very different effect.

The intermezzo following Act I was related to this scheme in that it contained a hymn to the sun, but more important than the sun were the singers, who were twelve shepherds. More obviously pastoral than

14. Pier Francesco Giambullari, *Apparato et feste nelle noze dello illustrissimo Signor Duco di Firenze* . . . (Florence, 1539), p. 143; and see Alois Nagler, *Theatre Festivals of the Medici 1539-1637* (New Haven, 1964), pp. 10-12.

the other intermezzi, this one was characteristic of them all in presenting a sharp contrast with the urban setting of the comedy. The stage represented the town of Pisa with its famous tower and baptistry, various "bizarre and capricious" palace façades, and street perspectives (Nagler, p. 9). Apparently these remained in view all evening, even when country shepherds, nymphs or gods appeared in the intermezzi. In the shepherds' scene, as Alois Nagler points out, "Closeness to nature was stressed in their rustic costumes: two shepherds wore costumes of bark, another pair appeared in red goatskins, and a third wore a bird's costume" (p. 10). He speculates that for the intermezzo with Silenus "a grotto set piece . . . was simply rolled into the Pisa decor" (p. 11), and we know from Pier Francesco Giambullari, who described the festivities, that the huntress nymphs walked across the urban set (p. 143). Thus an implied or very simply suggested mythic landscape was periodically imposed on the comic world of neighbouring Pisa. The contrast foreshadowed one often used in the masque.

The intermezzo after the second act brought the contrasting worlds of court and country together in a significant way. Scantily dressed sirens and nymphs emerged from a canal at the front of the stage, seeking the bride, Eleonora of Toledo, who had left Naples to become Duchess of Florence. The sirens, lamenting her desertion of the sea for the Arno, made her seem for the moment a kind of sea-goddess, out of her native element. It was the only instance in that evening's entertainment of outright courtly compliment.

With its classical time-scheme and divisions into five acts, Landi's comedy provided a logical structure for a sequence of spectacularly mounted "numbers" which had little to do with each other and which, in theory, were there to embellish the play. From the attention given to them by Giambullari, however, we may guess that the guests were at least as interested in the elaborate ornaments as in the edifice which they adorned.

That the intermezzi, important precedents for the masque, often swamped the plays with which they were performed is well known. A striking instance was a seventeenth-century performance of Tasso's *Aminta*, a pastoral play only tangentially related to the development of the masque, but so generally influential that it must be mentioned, if only briefly. It was first performed for the court of Ferrara in 1573 by the Gelosi, the famous company who acted plays and *commedie dell' arte* in both Italy and France.[15] The story is one of misfortune avoided.

15. See Giosuè Carducci, *Su l'Aminta di T. Tasso* (Florence 1896), p. 80; Prunières, p. 80.

Silvia, saved by Aminta from the brutal advances of a satyr, refuses to reward her faithful lover. In his despair he gets a false report that she has been killed by a wolf (for the wolf, too, is in Arcadia). By the time that Silvia's friend Dafne has found out that Silvia is alive, Aminta has gone to commit suicide. Silvia now repents of her cruelty, and after supposing her lover dead, finds that he too is alive. The end is reconciliation. It is, of course, the kind of plot that became a pattern for tragicomedy.

Highly regarded as the *Aminta* was and still is, it did not hold the attention of the audience at a gala performance in Parma in 1628 honouring a Medici-Farnese wedding. What everyone commented on, as Nagler remarks (pp. 143, 152), was the intermezzi, or, more truly, the spectacular staging of the intermezzi. Had Tasso been alive he might have complained as Jonson did of Inigo Jones. The intermezzi were not even related to the *Aminta* except in the very general way that many of them dealt with love. They presented Bradamante and Ruggiero, Dido and Aeneas, a dispute between the Olympians over love and chastity, the story of the Argonauts, and a joust between the gods led by Pluto and Jupiter respectively. A high point was the moment when Jupiter's knights, *mounted on their horses*, were lowered in a machine to the stage—*equi et equites ex machina*.

If the 1628 *Aminta* represents a centrifugal extreme to which such entertainments might fly, the famous *Ballet Comique de la Reine* of 1581 is a counter-example of a varied entertainment which incorporated in a coherent action some of the most successful features of its predecessors. More spectacular than *Orfeo* or *Egle*, and having more of a story than the intermezzi, it was more thoroughly integrated into the occasion than any of these by presenting the Queen, some of her ladies, and several courtiers as performers. Thus it also absorbed the tradition of the masquerade, in which not only disguising but declamation, song, and dance were expected features.[16] The result was dramatic ballet, and the dramatic model was comedy of a rather special sort, closely related to mythological plays, satyr-plays, pastoral drama, and tragicomedy.

To celebrate the marriage of his sister-in-law to the Duc de Joyeuse, Henry III of France arranged a number of festivities. The Queen, seeing all that was planned in her sister's honour, asked an Italian violinist and *valet de chambre* at the court, Baltasar de Beaujoyeulx (or Belgiojoso), to devise a further entertainment to outdo them all. He was in touch with the activities of the new Académie de Musique et de

16. See Prunières, pp. 58-94.

Poésie and apparently familiar with what had recently been written at the Italian courts. Prunières speculates (p. 80) that he may have seen a performance of the *Aminta* by the Gelosi in Paris, since the gallant tone of the dialogue in the ballet recalls Tasso's pastoral. Beaujoyeulx responded to the Queen's request with plans so elaborate that they could not be executed until three weeks after the other festivities, but his ballet was none the less their high point and was recorded in a profusely illustrated little book published the next year.

In an address to the reader Beaujoyeulx explains the combination of forms which constitutes his brilliant invention.[17] He says that he called it a "ballet comique" to do honour to the dance with the first word and to indicate by the second more "the beautiful, tranquil, and happy ending" than the rank of the characters, who are almost all gods, goddesses or other heroic personages (rather than the everyday folk of classical comedy). Having mixed comedy and ballet, he could not call the hybrid "ballet" without wronging comedy "distinctly represented in acts and scenes," nor call it "comedy" without prejudice to the ballet, which he says "honors, enlivens, and fills out with harmonious speeches the fine idea of the comedy."

The ingenious structure that Beaujoyeulx devised is made up of alternating "acts" and what he refers to as "intermèdes," the equivalents of intermezzi, already familiar in French entertainments. But here the mixing of comedy and ballet is such that although the "acts" present the major developments of the story, the "intermèdes" are progressively drawn into it.

Since both the comic action and the related intermèdes were precisely calculated to fill the space in which they were performed, I must remind you of the often-reproduced illustration showing the hall of the Petit Bourbon on the night of the performance. You will recall that at one end of the long room one sees the backs of the King, his mother, Catherine de' Medici, and their entourage. At the opposite end is the garden of Circe beneath an over-arching trellis, with two smaller trellises to the right and left. In the garden, behind a parade of animals headed by a stag and an elephant, is the enchantress herself, holding her magic wand, and behind her a castle gate, over which can be seen a tower, part of what Beaujoyeulx describes as a "town in perspective" (fol. 6v). It is not entirely fanciful to see in the royal dais and Circe's garden polar opposites comparable to heaven and hell in a medieval religious play, for despite the Renaissance perspective, the

17. *Balet comique de la royne* (Paris, 1582), sigs, e3ᵛ & e4; see facsimile, ed. G. A. Caula (Turin, 1962).

Figure de la Salle.

PLATE I *Balet comique de la royne*, sig. A4, from facsimile cited in notes.

staging of this ballet owes much to the old simultaneous set. To the right and left of the hall, half-way between the two ends, are two more localities: a wooded grotto where Pan sits (actually veiled by a curtain at the beginning of the ballet) and a golden vault concealing many musicians.

The action begins with a rapid movement from Circe's end of the hall toward the King, as a fugitive gentleman (played by a courtier in the service of the Queen Mother) escapes from the garden and asks King Henry for help against the enchantress. Circe then rushes out of her garden in pursuit, but is unable to see her victim, kneeling at the King's feet. After uttering an angry complaint she goes back through her garden and leaves the room. Beaujoyeulx says that the spectators marvelled at these two "acts" (fol. 10). They must have marvelled far more at the ensuing intermède, which seems at first to be as unrelated to the story of Circe as any Italian intermezzo. It is essentially a spectacular parade of marine creatures, followed by a magnificent fountain-chariot, on which are seated, amongst sculptured nereids, tritons and dolphins, Glaucus and Tethys, impersonated by the composer and his wife, and twelve naiads, impersonated by the Queen and other distinguished ladies of the court. To the accompaniment of instrumental and vocal music the procession approaches the royal dais, and Glaucus and Tethys sing a song in which he asks her help against Circe, who has transformed his beloved Scylla. But Tethys replies that she has given her power to the chief naiad, Queen Louise. So the parade is, after all, tied to the story and to the courtly audience. Once the procession has made the circuit of the hall and disappeared, the naiads leave the chariot and reappear to dance the first entry of the ballet.

Circe brings the intermède to an abrupt end when she again comes out of her garden in a fury, and with her wand turns the dancers into statues as she silences the music. Her attack not only involves the characters of the intermède more thoroughly in the main action, but introduces the chief complication of that simple plot. All the rest of the ballet consists in moves and countermoves by Circe and her enemies.

It is not necessary to tell all the rest of the story once again, but only to comment on certain distinctive moments. The low point in the fortunes of the naiads comes when Mercury, who has freed them from the spell, is himself overcome, and Circe leads them all captive into her garden. The naiads disappear, Mercury lies helpless on his back, and Circe diverts herself with a procession of animals into which she has transformed her previous victims. The space at the King's end of

155

Figure de la Fontaine.

PLATE II *Balet comique de la royne*, sig. D2^v, from facsimile cited in notes.

the hall is empty while the magic garden seems to be the sole locus of power.

The second intermède begins a renewal of the forces opposed to Circe, as various rustic divinities enter the action. A song by satyrs, a moving wood, and an address to the King by dryads from the wood precede the unveiling of the remaining fixed location, Pan's wooded grotto. Responding to the appeal of one of the dryads, he agrees to fight against the enchantress.

The third intermède joins the four virtues and Minerva to the woodland gods, and leads to another adress to the King, in which Minerva says that the castle of Circe is the only one in France still unconquered by the King, the wielder of Jupiter's sceptre. She claims to have responded to the King's call for help, and promises to overwhelm Circe. Though she now prays to her father Jupiter, it is clear that both of them are acting as a favour to the King of France. The inevitable end is the humbling of Circe, who is led to the heavenly end of the hall and made to sit at the King's feet. Finally the disenchanted naiads come out of the garden, left empty at last, and dance the main ballet before the King.

Although the final episodes recall earlier entertainments in which a castle was besieged and finally captured, Beaujoyeulx was not wrong to call his design comic. Circe, enemy of the dance, is a blocking character *par excellence*, if that is not a paradox. Sometimes, like Medusa, paralysing, sometimes transforming, she always demeans and reduces her victims. The society which triumphs over her is one in which human beings mysteriously partake of the nature and power of the divinities who rule the sea, the woods and the heavens. For the privileged persons who inhabit this special world the ending will always be happy. Or so, at least, the ballet leads one to suppose.

A comic action of this sort, concerning illustrious rather than ordinary characters, became an invaluable, though by no means the sole, resource of the English masque, giving its poetry, dance, and spectacle a clear and simple shape. As the catastrophe of classical comedy, which, as Donatus says, "is the change of the situation to a pleasant outcome,"[18] came to be rendered in the masque mainly by means of spectacle and dance, the function of the comic mythos was subordinated to the principal function of the masque, to honour the occasion and its participants. The moment of comic triumph became a kind of apotheosis of the masquers.

18. "A Fragment on Comedy and Tragedy," in *Theories of Comedy*, ed. Paul Lauter (New York, 1964), p. 30.

We may note more than one kind of comic action. In one of Jonson's earliest masques, *The Masque of Blackness* of 1605, the plot falls in that part of the comic gamut closest to romance. It is the long quest of the Daughters of Niger for a land where their complexions may be miraculously blanched. The masquers, in black face and elegantly exotic gowns, were Queen Anne and her ladies. Of their quest we see only the moderately happy ending—their arrival in Britannia, described as "a world divided from the world,"[19] where they receive the promise of transformation the following year. *The Masque of Beauty*, in which the promise is carried out, was delayed for two years, by which time four more fugitives had joined the expedition, and all sixteen had been transformed by the power of Albion, or James I. The brief but spectacular masque shows the arrival of these beauties on a floating island, their thankful dances, and their greeting by Albion's deputy January, lord of the Twelfth Night feast, enthroned in the middle of the hall. Notice that if Jupiter did favours for Henry III of France, England's king was a sufficient deity in himself on these occasions to perform the necessary miracles.

A quest again provides the structure for Davenant's *Temple of Love*, written for Queen Henrietta Maria, who impersonates Indamora, Queen of Narsinga, and reinstates the Temple of Chaste Love on her Indian island. Hearing of it, noble Persian youths set out to find it. Despite the efforts of certain magicians to sidetrack them, the Persians, played by courtiers, arrive and dance their dance, but the true climax is the arrival of the Queen of Narsinga and England with her ladies in a chariot drawn by sea-monsters. When they have finished their dances, the Queen is seated on the state with the King as, for the first time, the Temple of Chaste Love to which she has come is fully revealed on the stage facing the royal dais. In earlier sets it has been seen at a distance or in clouds, but now it is in the foreground of a space which is India and Whitehall. The temple is a reflection of the throne, as we see when Chaste Love and the priest and priestess of the temple move out to the state to sing the closing apostrophe to Charles and Henrietta. For the quest must end in the banqueting house, whether it be called Britannia or Narsinga.[20]

Jonson's *Love Freed from Ignorance and Folly* (1611) has a more standard comic action, in which Love, at first frustrated, manages to

---

19. *Masque of Blackness*, l. 218 in Ben Jonson, *The Complete Masques*, ed. Stephen Orgel (New Haven, 1969), from which all quotations from the masques are taken. See Orgel's note on this line, p. 473.
20. The text of *The Temple of Love* will be found in editions of Davenant's dramatic works and in *Inigo Jones: The Theatre of the Stuart Court* (London, 1973), II, pp. 600-4.

outwit his captor, the Sphinx, release the Daughters of the Morn, and bring about the marriage of the eldest to Phoebus, enthroned in the west. Love, appropriately enough, is here the clever trickster, who guesses the sphinx's riddle, assisted, to be sure, by the priests of the muses. He has been told "to find a world the world without" (1. 147). If he had seen *The Masque of Blackness* he would not have needed anyone to tell him that Britain was this special world. Once he knows this he is freed from ignorance and folly and able to carry out his mission. Queen Anne is again reunited, for the moment at least, with her James.

Anyone familiar with English masques will readily think of other scenarios that constitute comic actions; Reason and the Powers of Juno end the strife of humours and affections to bring about reconciliation and wedding; Love is rescued from the wiles of Pluto; Mercury is vindicated from the alchemists at court; Juno puts an end to the jealous Cupid's interruption of the rites to Chloris. Again and again obstacles are overcome and society renews itself; again and again the ending not only fulfills the aims of the protagonists but becomes a celebration of the forces they represent. The Platonizing which Cody sees in pastoral operates here to push comedy in the direction of ritual.

The world in which these comic actions take place is more remote than familiar—a world of gods and heroes, "a world the world without"—and yet in certain ways familiar to the select audience of the court both because the masquers themselves are known and because of the devices which involve the King in the action. In fact the ambiguity about the world of the masque is part of what makes it effective panegyric. Orgel speaks of every masque "transforming the courtly audience into the idealized world of the poet's vision" (*Complete Masques*, p. 2), and one might add that this transformation, which affects both the masquers and the audience, is an analogue of the comic action, in which a superior power transforms a bad situation into a good one.

In all these comic actions there are opposing forces, blocking characters, to whom we must finally give some attention. They come in varying degrees of effectuality. While Circe in Beaujoyeulx's ballet is relatively formidable and active, the only opposition in *The Masque of Beauty* is Night, whose attempt to delay the Daughters of Niger has already failed by the time that we are told of it. In *The Temple of Love* the magicians have several threatening speeches, but give up with very little struggle. The Sphinx of *Love Freed from Ignorance and Folly* is more troublesome, but even she is more foolish than criminal,

159

Eugene M. Waith

as befits a comic antagonist. Thanks mainly to Ben Jonson, the opposing forces in the English masque came to be treated as the objects of satire and presented to be laughed at in an antimasque. Before this development there had been lighter moments and bits of grotesquerie in courtly entertainments in England and on the continent. Where the setting was pastoral the satyrs and Silenus were natural choices for this sort of diverson, as in *Egle* or the Florentine intermezzi of 1539, but other "antics" also appeared, and hence the term "antic-masque" enters confusingly into the history of the antimasque. Jonson describes the dancers of his "antimasque of boys" in *The Haddington Masque* as "twelve boys most anticly attired." They do "a subtle capricious dance to as odd a music, . . . nodding with their antic faces, with other variety of ridiculous gesture, which gave much occasion of mirth and delight to the spectators" (*Complete Masques*, pp. 112, 123). The famous antimasque of witches in *The Masque of Queens* is similarly antic. The achievement of these early antimasques, however, was not the introduction of laughter or of new material but the establishment of a clear function for this sort of comic moment and of a firm structure into which it could be placed. I could even suggest that when the popularity of antimasques led to their notorious multiplication their function was not lost and the structure was not destroyed.

The nature and function of the antimasque appear with great clarity if we compare Beaujoyeulx's *Circe* with its refashioning by Aurelian Townshend and Inigo Jones as *Tempe Restored*. The *Ballet Comique* was not funny unless Circe herself made her tantrums so, as some of Beaujoyeulx's descriptions may suggest. He describes her on one occasion, for instance, as returning to her garden like a victorious captain (fol. 23), which might have been made into an amusing moment. It is also possible that the parade of her victims transformed into animals was played for laughs, though nothing in the text tells us that it was. Here Townshend and Jones elaborate by turning her brief self-entertainment into a series of antimasques "consisting," we are told, "of Indians and Barbarians, who naturally are bestiall, and others which are voluntaries, and but halfe transformed into beastes."[21] Perhaps this does not sound hilarious, but the satirical intention of the antimasques is unmistakable, especially in the fourth, consisting of "3 Apes. An Asse like a Pedante, teaching them Pricksong" (Townshend, p. 88). These are presumably some of the "voluntaries," the willing victims of the enchantress, who are thus

21. *Aurelian Townshend's Poems and Masks*, ed. E. K. Chambers (Oxford, 1912), p. 87.

160

held up to ridicule. At the same time Circe becomes somewhat less sinister and more of a humour character, when Townshend's chorus sings about "*the distemper'd Heart, /Of sullen Circe, stung with Cupids dart*" (p. 87). The blatant racism of his comment on the antimasques suggests a standard comic point of view which is turned to a special use in the masque; the point of view from which we seem to see a total difference between "us" and "them." If Indians and Barbarians hardly share a common humanity with the spectators in Whitehall, it is equally evident that the willing victims of an enchantress share none of the spectators' wisdom and self-discipline. Thus the distance, or refusal of sympathy, which we know to be a precondition for satirical laughter becomes another means of glorifying the participants in one of these great occasions.

It is entirely characteristic of Jonson that he often defines this distance as a contrast between folly and wisdom. In addition to the Sphinx, who represents ignorance and folly, one thinks of Merefool in *The Fortunate Isles* or the "Curious" in *Time Vindicated*, "ignorant admirers" of the unprincipled poet Chronomastix. Sometimes the demonstration of folly constitutes what Orgel calls "a tiny comic drama" (*Jonsonian Masque*, p. 73), very similar to a scene in one of the comedies, and he rightly says that for Jonson the antimasque "served to give meaning to the masque," to explain it, to make the audience understand (p. 93). These last comments are part of Orgel's discussion of the poetic Cook of *Neptune's Triumph*, who defends antimasques against the disapproving Poet. The Cook insists that the understanding must be approached by way of the senses, and forces the Poet to grant that "even a Triumph likes fun" (11. 40-47, 220-23). Yet even here, where the Cook is allowed to score against the purism of the Poet, the fun of the antimasque, like the fun of Jonsonian comedy, is at the expense of the foolish. If Jonson delights in their portrayal he leaves no doubt about the judgment he passes on them, and in the masques the distance between ridiculed and sympathetic characters is more absolute. The Cook's *olla podrida* of foolish court characters helps us to understand the noble masquers only by being totally different.

In *The Temple of Love* Davenant goes a step further by allowing one character in the antimasque to make fun of some of the masquers. A "Persian page" leaps on the stage after the preceding entry of the antimasque, warning the ladies of Narsinga (and England) that they may be disappointed in the noble Persian youths who are just arriving,

> For I must tell you that about them all
> There's not one grain but what's Platonical. (ll. 319-20)

161

As in his play *The Platonic Lovers*, Davenant dares to laugh at the cult made fashionable by the Queen and honoured in this masque. For this irreverence he has precedents in the anti-Petrarchan moments of Petrarchan poetry and the anti-Platonic jibes of other works devoted to Platonic love, but the device is exceptional in the masque. And even here no real adjustment of point of view is demanded. There is nothing laughable about the noble Persian youths when they arrive, and chaste love is an easy victor onstage and in the Whitehall of that evening.

The pastoral masque *Pan's Anniversary*, performed at Greenwich for King Jame's birthday, June 19, 1620, shows how the comic action itself may be little more than the acting out of a contrast between the foolish and the admirable—the *aristoi*. The scene in Arcadia, where nymphs, encouraged by an old shepherd, are strewing flowers for the "yearly rites" of Pan, as his alter ego King James looks on from the state in the midst of the hall. Then the scene opens to reveal a "fountain of light," around which are seated the masquers (Prince Charles and certain lords), accompanied by musicians in the guise of priests of Pan. Here the celebration is interrupted by the arrival of a foolish Fencer, ushering in "certain bold boys of Boeotia . . . to challenge the Arcadians at their own sports." The Boeotians, whom the Fencer describes before they dance the antimasque, are a Tinker of Thebes, a tooth-drawer, a juggler, a corn-cutter, a maker of mousetraps, a tailor, and a clerk. If it were not for the mention of Thebes, one might well think this motley crew belonged in London. Several, indeed, seem to have come from Bartholomew Fair. In the presence of "the best and bravest spirits of Arcadia" they offer their rival entertainment, for which, according to the old shepherd, the best they can expect is forgiveness. Their diversion belongs to everyday Smithfield (or Thebes); the solemn hymns and dances that follow are appropriate to the Arcadian holy day of Pan's annniversary and the birthday of King James. The contrast is between the trivial and the significant, between the world of city comedy and that of courtly entertainment, between a band of self-deceived fools and what the old shepherd calls a "true society." The distinction between "them" and "us" could not be more plain— except to the fools, who "perceive no such wonder in all that is done here," and return to offer another rival show. This time they appear as sheep, but what looks at first like a successful adaptation to environ-ment turns out to be a different sort of proof of folly. They have only the stupidity of sheep, which they are told to take back to Boeotia. "This is too pure an air for so gross brains." The masque then concludes with a prayer to Pan, addressed, one may suppose, to the throne. The happy ending is quite simply the expulsion of folly from the true society headed by the king.

Pan's Anniversary is a slight and unpretentious masque in comparison with many that were mounted at this time, but it was well suited to Greenwich in the summer—a more pastoral location in 1620 than now—and in it Jonson and Jones made very adroit use of the traditions we have been considering. It is not only a pastoral, but a comical-satirical-mythical-pastoral masque.

A Greater Power
Than We Can Contradict:
The Voice of Authority in the
Staging of Italian Pastorals

JAMES J. YOCH

They shall choose judges of not less than fifty years of age, who shall make the selection . . . taking into their counsel poets and musicians . . . but explaining to them the wishes of the legislator in order that they may regulate dancing, music, and all choral strains, according to the mind of the judges; and not allowing them to indulge, except in some few matters, their individual pleasures and fancies."

> Plato. *Laws* 7.802, in *The Dialogues of Plato*, trans. B. Jowett (1892; rpt. New York, 1937), II, p. 557.

I

Commentators from Jonson to the present have resisted the appeal that spectacles such as intermezzi and masques provided for Renaissance courts. Only in the last twenty years has there been a substantial change in the attitude which J. A. Symonds stated so clearly: "The habit of regarding scenic exhibitions as the adjunct to extravagant Court luxury, prevented the development of a theatre in which the genius of poets might have shone with undimmed intellectual lustre."[1] Aristotle seemed on the side of such critics when he noted that the production of scenic effects lies more in the province of the "costumer

---

1. *Renaissance in Italy* (1881; rpt. New York, 1964), II, p. 124.

and stage-manager" than of the poet and is the "least artistic" of dramatic elements.[2]

Yet rather than complain of the poetic loss or admire the stubbornness of Jonson in his struggle with Inigo Jones, I propose to look at some of the successful collaborations of poet, musician and designer. There were many. Stephen Orgel summarizes Renaissance justifications for such shows: "Purists scorned the practice, but many Renaissance theorists defended it, pointing out that Aristotle himself recommended the use of spectacle to produce the wonder that is required in drama."[3] Noting the political dimensions of splendid productions, Sidney called them "the armour or ornament" of the monarch.[4]

If we relinquish the notion that emotion is always part of rebellion (part of a "purely sensual and pagan paradise"[5]) and that it is somehow an inferior way of arguing, we can find many reasons to admire the successful ways poets and producers craftily directed emotion to create a useful political effect: awe of the prince's power. In the *Discourses* (3.6) Machiavelli discussed the importance of the gut effect which pomp provides in the defence of the prince. He recalled the story of how a slave, sent to kill Marius in prison, was unable to do so because he "was so overcome by the presence of this great man . . . how much more is to be feared from a prince who is free, and clothed in all the pomp and ornaments of royalty, and surrounded by his court?" Machiavelli summarized his argument: "All this pomp is calculated to inspire fear." Similarly, Evarchus knowing well "a secreat of government," in Sidney's *Arcadia*, staged the difficult trial with "pompous ceremonyes" in order to win the support of the people.[6] Rather than excursions into delicious, forbidden worlds that invite escape from the tedium of court, such entertainments showed how unsatisfactory secret lusts in the woods were and concluded with an affirmation of the courtly world, its place and its ruler.

This paper argues that there is a rigid and prevailing rhetoric in court performances which contain pastorals and what De Sommi called the fantasies of the intermezzi.[7] By reductions of old stories and mocking portraits of outsiders, by the contrast of styles and the

---

2. *Poetics*, in *Aristotle*, ed. Philip Wheelwright (New York, 1951), p. 299.
3. *The Illusion of Power* (Berkeley, 1975), p. 35.
4. *Arcadia*, ed. A. Feuillerat (1912; rpt. Cambridge, 1968), II, p. 167.
5. W. W. Greg, *Pastoral Poetry and Pastoral Drama* (1905; rpt. New York, 1959), p. 43.
6. *Discourses*, in *The Prince and the Discourses*, ed. Max Lerner (New York, 1940), p. 425; *Arcadia*, II, p. 167.
7. *Dialoghi*, in Alessandro D'Ancona, *Origini del teatro italiano* (1891; rpt. Rome, 1971), II, p. 421.

use of machinery, intermezzi and masques displayed the court's well-being and authority. The productions represented disorder, no matter how attractive and wild, to show how neatly and awesomely prince and art controlled it within their greater powers. The Italians implied the power of the prince through analogies with Amor, Jove, Providence. The English designers were more blunt and factual, for courtiers and monarchs took roles in the performances, and the propaganda for the crown was literal and explicit.

In this paper, the first section focuses on how the intermezzi of *Seicento* Italian plays contributed to this political design; the second part looks briefly at a few of the changes the English court introduced into these formulas. My chief example is the extensive descriptions of the intermezzi published with Antonio Ongaro's pastoral play, *L'Alceo*, (Ferrara, 1614).[8] This edition represents fully the intended contrast in the production between power and gracious style framing and dominating evil, inept and passionate action. The authors changed their sources in order to degrade the non-courtly world by humour and folly and thereby accentuated the prince's power.

Witty tension is the stuff of these productions. The Italian pastoral dressed rude peasants in gorgeous costumes and trees in silken leaves;[9] Ongaro parodied Tasso's *Aminta*; in the revival of Ongaro's play, intermezzi provided heroic and mythological stories that interrupted the action of shepherds; in the published edition not only descriptions of the performance but also long critical and moral essays further embellished the text and diminished the importance of the drama by shifting attention to the courtly and academic milieu observing it. Although less complex in framing devices, the English masques developed similar contrasts between the clumsy and ordinary, who became stylishly eccentric foils to the grace and light of the court itself. The last Caroline masque, *Salmacida Spolia*, is an example of the way English artists borrowed and adapted Italian materials.

There was never a question about which mode of life was superior in the *agon* between the court's elegance, imaged in the staging, and the rest of the world. Perhaps one explanation for the extraordinary success of the pastoral at courts across Europe is not because it provided a simple alternative to their style but because its simplicity

8. Listed by Louise Clubb, *Italian Plays (1500-1700) in the Folger Library* (Florence, 1968), p. 174.
9. See, for example, De Sommi, *Dialoghi*, in *A Source Book in Theatrical History*, ed. A. M. Nagler (1952; rpt. New York, 1959), pp. 105-107. Lodovico Zuccolo, *L'Alessandro, ouero della pastorale* (Venice, 1613) presented a discussion in which it is assumed that shepherdesses look like queens (p. 8ᵛ).

provided a ready vehicle for delivering clearly the message that power mattered.[10]

Indeed, power was overwhelming. The combination of intermezzi and pastoral drama helped bring resonant, sacred vocabularies into support of princely policy. As D'Ancona showed, the *pompe sceniche* and intermezzi which had long been a part of *sacre rappresentazioni*[11] from the date of Politian's *Orfeo* also appeared in secular drama.[12] So adapted, they continued to support passive themes of wonder, temperance and humility. Louise Clubb has pointed to the similarities between Guarini's and Tasso's use of human error beneath the unperceived designs of providence, which the *Pastor Fido* recognizes: "Eternal gods, oh, how different are those high, inaccessible paths by which your grace descends to us from the erring and wrong ones by which our thoughts ascend to heaven (5.6. 1207-11)."[13] Guidobaldo Bonarelli ended his famous *Filli di Scyro* (1607) with the observation: "That he alone can see these sacred things / Who shuts his eyes, and trusts what heaven brings."[14] Sidney sharply presented a similar idea: "In such a shadowe, or rather pit of darkenes, the wormish mankinde lives, that neither they knowe how to foresee, nor what to feare: and are but like tenisballs, tossed by the racket of the hyer powers."[15] This sense of futility before unassailable power provided useful imagery for the courts of absolute princes by stressing the wisdom of submission and the distance of power from actual life.

Thus in Italy these shows separated the frenzied action of the pastoral from the audience, helped modulate by extravagant cost and labour from the simplicity of rustic life to the elegance of the theatrical scene of the watching court,[16] illustrated with mythological

10. Symonds, *Renaissance*, claimed that the ideal of the Italian Renaissance is "the Golden Age," when no restraints were placed on natural inclination (II., p. 454).

11. D'Ancona, *Origini*, I, pp. 515-21.

12. D'Ancona saw this control as ruthlessly exercised by princes who needed to dominate the Florentines with the "arts of tyranny, a tinselled and ornamented corruption" (*Origini*, II, p. 163). Duke Ferdinand ordered that Coppola's *Le nozze degli dei* (1637) should include "spectacular scenes of the Heavens, the Seas, and the Infernal Regions" (Clubb, *Folger*, p. 83).

13. "The making of the pastoral play: some Italian experiments between 1573 and 1590," in *Petrarch to Pirandello*, ed. J. A. Molinaro (Toronto, 1973), p. 65.

14. *Filli di Sciro*, trans. J.S. (London, 1655), sig. Q4^v.

15. *Arcadia*, II, p. 177.

16. Lily Bess Campbell, *Scenes and Machines on the English Stage During the Renaissance. A Classical Revival* (1923; rpt. New York, 1970), noted the boastful contempt of cost in the spectacles (p. 41). Reporting on the production of Cardinal Bibbiena's *La Calandria* at Urbino in 1513, Castiglione admired the incredible absorption of labor and skill in the preparations: "an octagonal temple in low relief, so well finished that it seems hardly possible that it could have been built in four months even if one considers all the potential workmanship which the state of Urbino can muster" (In *A Source Book*, p. 71).

and natural figures the theme of restraint, and, like the architecture of the proscenium, framed the events of the drama within heroic poses of sporting cupids, naked *colossi*, lolling goddesses and gods. Similar figures and architecture surround actual paintings of the landscape on the walls of villas such as at the Villa Trissino at Cricoli or in the famous murals by Veronese for the Villa Barbaro at Maser. Besides the translation of the native scene into one classical—with ruins, like the quotations in the pastorals, to tie the visual contemporary world to that of Theocritus and Virgil—frames, columns, *grotteschi*, full-scale figures established the countryside, its tasks and antique gods as distant background to the riches and organization of aristocratic life.

In the theatre comic action and the representation of the final, stunned awe of the non-courtiers put enemies in place: the performance proved them controllable and separated not only by style but even scenery from the court, as in *Salmacida Spolia*, where "craggy rocks and inaccessible mountains" divided the ordinary world from the place of honour. Developing the delicate implications that humility had advantages in the Italian pastorals and intermezzi, the English masques made subservience to secular authority an explicit part of the plot's design. In *Oberon*, for example, Silenus orders the rowdy satyrs to quake before the King and ordains a dance that, like perspective, aims dutifully at the King: "then let your nimble feet / Tread subtle circles that may always meet / In point to him."[17]

II

Seicento Italian designers had a long tradition of productions that supported the use of intermezzi to explicitly state the theme of the triumph of order. These shows splendidly framed dramas about oafs and peasants who display the folly (and dangers) of alternatives to the court. As Castiglione's descriptions made clear, the first Urbino production of Cardinal Bibbiena's *La Calandria* emphasized the folly of Plautus's characters from the *Menaechmi* and inflated the intermezzi, which move from the desperate story of Jason to the serene ones of Neptune and Juno; Cupid as commentator made sure the audience understood the allegory. Peruzzi's production in Rome provided scenes whose fame further diminished the importance of the drama by providing important ordered urban vistas as alternatives to

17. *Salmacida Spolia*, ll. 278-79; *Oberon*, ll. 290-92, in *A Book of Masques* (Cambridge, 1967), 61, 355.

L'ALCEO
FAVOLA PESCATORIA
D'ANTONIO ONGARO,

Fatta recitare in Ferrara dall'Ill.mo S. Enzo Bentiuogli mentre la feconda volta era Principe dell'Accademia degl'INTREPIDI,

Con gl'Intramezzi del Sig. Caualier Batifta Guarini.

Defcritti,e dichiarati dall'ARSICCIO Accademico Ricreduto.

Aggiuntici appreffo alcuni Difcorfi del medefimo Arficcio fopra ciafcheduno Intramezzo.

Dedicati all'Ill.mo & Reu.mo Sig.'

CARDINAL SERRA.

In Ferrara . Per Vitt. Bald. Stamp. Cam.
Con licenza de' Superiori 1614.

1. Antonio Ongaro, *L'Alceo* (Ferrara, 1614), title page. (My copy).

2. G. A. Fasolo, Central Hall, Villa Caldogno Pagello at Caldogno. Giants and gods in support of aristocratic life. (By permission from Giuseppe Mazzotti, *Palladian and Other Venetian Villas* (London, 1958), plate 140.)

3. Unknown artist, restored mural of a seated nobleman in front of a landscape, Villa Godi Valmarana at Lonedo. Violence (Jupiter carrying off Ganymede) does not disturb the calm aristocratic pose. (By permission from Giuseppe Mazzotti, *Palladian and Other Venetian Villas* (Rome, 1966), plate 162.)

4. Paolo Veronese, Stanza del Cane, Villa Barbaro at Maser. The domination of the frames makes the picture incidental and shows how many modulations are necessary to move from the simplicity of the scene to the opulence of the noble world. (By permission from Paolo Ojetti and others, *Palladio, Veronese e Vittoria a Maser* (Milan, 1960), p. 114.)

5. Vista through doorways to a *trompe l'oeil* scene, Villa Barbaro at Maser. Multiple, playful, indolent rhythms leading to an illusion of life. (By permission from Ojetti, *Palladio*, p. 87.)

173

it.[18] In like manner, in Guarini's *Pastor Fido*, the intermezzi move from earth to sea, air and finally heavenly music.[19]

The contrast between drama and intermezzi is like that between the wildernesses, grottoes, *nymphaea* of the gardens and the neat geometries of the main avenues which provide ultimate architectural structures. Excursions into the pleasures of the shaded, the mysterious, the overgrown, the subterranean were part of a plotted experience which ultimately led the observer to appreciate the comfortable images of order.

In 1613, in his dialogue on the pastoral, Lodovico Zuccolo specifically answered the charge that the pastoral might be a political threat by encouraging anarchy and self-indulgence. He argued that rather than proposing examples of plots to change laws and similar customs, the pastoral showed lusts only in the "scum of the crowd," and "in those minds either lacking in experience in the management of affairs or short in common sense."[20] Moreover, the style of presentation showed the power of the court. Zuccolo argued that mere shepherds leading their sheep and doing other country tasks "in a style unadorned, base, familiar" were fit only for comedy. He described with contempt the actual peasants of major Italian districts: for example, those of Siena, "rough and boorish" and of Apulia "awkward and foolish and stupidly innocent of the ways of the world."[21] In answering the query of how such characters, "for this is the way most actual shepherds are,"[22] come to appear so elegant

18. Campbell, *Scenes*, summarized the surviving descriptions of the first Urbino and Rome stagings of *La Calandria* (pp. 49-51).

19. Printed with the text of the play in L. Fassò, *Teatro del Seicento* (Milan, 1956), pp. 319-22. In Cesare Cremonino, *Le pompe funebri* (Ferrara, 1590), the intermezzi have as their theme the Reform of the Kingdom of Love.

20. *L'Alessandro:* "non sia à gli essempli accennati delle riuolutioni del viuer ciuile, e della trama degli huomini intorno il cangiamento delle leggi, e dei costumi somigliante. Vi si aggiunge, che si fatti appetiti sono molto ristretti, & cadono per lo più nella feccia del volgo, & ne gli ingegni ò manco esperimentati ne i maneggi delle cose, ò manco di natura giudiciosi" (pp. 10-10ᵛ· Beatrice Corrigan, "Tasso's Erminia in the Italian Theatre of the Seicento," *Renaissance Drama*, 7 (1964), reviewed a *dramma musicale* presented in Rome in 1633; the scenes moved from the rocks, "the pleasing deceptions of the machines" and the military camp to a conclusion where "Apollo with a lovely company of Zephyrs, in a chariot sparkling with brilliant lights, brought to our ears music of indescribable melody" (p. 140).

21. *L'Alessandro:* "Tuttavia con stile più riposato, più basso, più famigliare, con sentenze meno auuertite, con costumi manco affettati procede la Commedia, che non fa la Pastorale" (p. 7); those of Siena "sono huomini rozzi, zotichi, & quasi stupidi . . . & della Puglia . . . li vedremo huomini goffi, semplici, e quasi di niuna esperienza" (p. 8). Shepherds had long been the stuff of comedy in the *sacre rappresentazioni* (D'Ancona, *Origini*, I, pp. 601-31) as well as on the medieval English stage.

22. *L'Alessandro:* "E tale à punto faranno tutti, ò con poca eccettione quegli huomini, che siano propriamente pastori" (p. 8).

in pastorals, so that mere shepherdesses dress like queens, the speaker proclaims that such changes are necessary to fit the scene to the taste of the hearers.[23] Thus, rather than luxurious, these embellishments are necessary to make, as pastoral writers do, the rustic well proportioned.[24] Such transformations, he said, resemble those accomplished by Ariosto and Boiardo who amplified, arranged, adorned and rendered in magnificent form the short and badly designed stories they inherited. In like ways, modern architecture took the narrow, low, dark and poorly made ways of the past and turned them to the lofty, grand, bright, sumptuous buildings of the present.[25] These improvements were part of the court's consistent demonstration of its power over the past, over ordinary citizens, over local myths and classical stories.

This argument in support of power based on splendour, more moving and obvious because of the insignificance of the base material of shepherds, has one of the most complete records in Ongaro's *L'Alceo*. An itinerant humanist from Padua and settled in Rome, Ongaro, at 21, turned Tasso's *Aminta* into a seaside story for a performance at the Colonna palace, the Castello Nettuno. Baptized by Italian critics the *Aminta bagnato*, the play went through seven editions in the generation following its first performance and at least as many more again before 1800. For an intended revival in 1612, Ottavio Magnanini replaced Ongaro's intermezzi with five new ones.[26] This production was postponed, so he presented the intermezzi with the tragedy, *Idalba*, instead. However, for publication in 1614, the publishers joined to Ongaro's play these intermezzi, which the title page claims G. B. Guarini wrote for it.[27] Magnanini, writing here as l'Arsiccio Accademico Ricreduto, provided descriptions of the intermezzi as though they were staged with Ongaro's pastoral. He added philosophical essays that develop themes illustrated in the production and critical comments justifying and praising the machinery, songs and design of the intermezzi. Just as style and rules made even shepherds worthy of the court, the publisher explained that the

23. *Ibid.*, "Poiche comparisce in Scena con habito, e con ornamenti più tosto da Reina, che da pastorella, ò ninfa boscareccia. Ma se la misuriamo poi dal gusto degli vditori, che dee essere vno scopo, onde il Poeta non mai, ò di rado leui l'occhio, vedremo, che più assai piace liscia, e pomposa" (p. 8ᵛ).
24. *Ibid.*, p. 24ᵛ.
25. *Ibid.*, p. 25.
26. Lione Allacci, *Drammaturgia di Lione Allacci accresciuta e continuata fino all'anno MDCCLV* (1755; rpt. Turin, 1961), pp. 22-24; Clubb, *Folger*, summarizes Allacci's conclusions (p. 174).
27. Vittorio Baldini, in *L'Alceo* (Ferrara, 1614), p. 3.

"noble and grave" material of the descriptions made the book more suitable for the eminence of the lord cardinal Serra, to whom the edition is dedicated.[28] Thus, decorum justified ornamentation and deflated, even buried, the action of the play within more than three hundred pages of commentary.

The play itself is self-conscious and partly shifts the audience's attention to an appreciation of the parody of Tasso as well as the increased sentimentality and dramatic representation of the action. Ongaro's changes in diction and structure expanded the humorously bathetic as well as enforced greater symmetry on the architecture of the play. He thus separated even more obviously the world of the court from the foolish characters outside it.

The language seems often to bring out the comic possibilities of the translation to the seashore and of the play from *favola boscareccia* to *favola pescatoria*. Tasso's original lines in which Dafne attempts to get Silvia to give in to Aminta were already parodies of a passage from Achilles Tatius' novel, *Clitophon and Leucippe*. Ongaro added remarkable shifts of diction that make the humour even more obvious. For example, Alcippe lists the creatures who love and whom she offers as models for the young girl: "The skate loves the angel-shark, the cuttle-fish the cuttle-fish, the mullet the mullet, the perch the saddled-bream, and for its dear beloved, the swift dolphin moans and sighs."[29]

Similarly, Ongaro's variations on the original plot emphasized the humour. In the *Aminta*, Silvia resists the boy, Aminta, until his attempted suicide by throwing himself off a precipice convinces her of his love. The brief narration of the fifth act describes her kisses which revive him. The play ends with the promise of their marriage, and a final chorus sensibly hopes for a little less trouble in its own love affairs. Ongaro doubled the suicide attempts, for Alceo twice dives into the sea when Eurilla refuses him. The attempted suicides of such

---

28. *L'Alceo*: "con Dichiarazioni, e Discorsi sopra gl'Intramezzi di rendere il Volume, non con la grossezza, ma con le materie nobili, e graui, all'eminenza di Vostra Signoria Illustrissima piu corrispondente" (p. 2ᵛ).

29. *Ibid.*:　　La Raia ama lo Squadro,
　　　　　　　La Sepia ama la Sepia,
　　　　　　　La Triglia ama la Triglia,
　　　　　　　Il Persico l'Occhiata,
　　　　　　　E per la cara amata
　　　　　　　Il veloce Delfin geme, e sospira. (p. 27)

Ongaro's purpose here was hardly to describe the sea and its creatures but to spoof conventions. Theocritus' *Idylls* 21 and Sannazaro's *Piscatory Eclogues* looked more closely at the actual sea. See Antonio Belloni, *Frammenti di critica letteraria* (Milan, 1903), pp. 118-19.

lovers, as Angelo Ingegneri wrote in his commentary on the pastoral in 1598, bring smiles not tears to the eyes of spectators.[30]

Besides increasing the sentimental and comic folly of the lovers by diction and plotting, Ongaro also strengthened the architecture of the plot. Although Tasso worked on the *Aminta* for almost twenty years before its authorized edition in 1591, the fifth act seemed strangely truncated: only 158 lines out of the total 1905 lines of the play. Egidio Menagio complained that the narration of the lovers' kisses was not sufficiently visual for the audience; when Abraham Fraunce translated and expanded Tasso's play he wrote a new scene showing the lovers together.[31] Ongaro expanded the act to three scenes of closely related panels. In the first, Timeta curses Love and describes the arrangements for Alceo's splendid funeral: hymns, garlands of flowers, an ornamented casket. The second shows the resurrection from death and the reversal we expect. Now there is praise for Love's miraculous works and the imitation of Tasso's lines, "O through what unknown ways do you conduct your followers to joy." Glicone tells how seamen picked up Alceo in their nets, brought him in although he wished to die, and how Eurilla revived him. Here, as elsewhere in the play, shifts in diction jar the listener and prevent revelling in the passion: Glicone observes the lovers, "joining their spirits with kisses, as new cuttlefish or squid."[32]

The third and final scene opens with another prayer to Amor and symmetrically reverses the earlier curses by now calling him most just and merciful. In what Carrara called an idyllic duet,[33] the lovers review their mistakes and misunderstandings; in this way, they put the action of the whole play in a new perspective of their great affection and their resolves to serve each other. Finally, in contrast to the plans for the funeral procession with which the act began, Timeta's ceremonial speech in the high style of a hymn describes the triumph of fishermen and sea deities who march together to celebrate the festive day, not only of the lovers but also of the patrons who arranged the performance. The concluding lines modulate, like moulding from walls to

30. *Della poesia rappresentativa* (Venice, 1598), sig. E4.
31. Menagio, *L'Aminta con gli annotationi* (Paris, 1655), sigs. Uu-Uu2; France, *The Countesse of Pembroke's Yvychurch* (London, 1591), sigs. F-F^v. Less interested in such symmetries, Greg, *Pastoral*, complained of Ongaro's additions: "The last act is spun out to three scenes in accordance with the demand for greater regularity of dramatic construction, but gains nothing but tedium thereby" (p. 213).
32. *L'Alceo*: "l'opre tue miracolose"; "O che per occulte strade i tuoi seguaci / A la beatitudine conduci" (p. 230); "Che si legano l'anime co i baci, / Quasi nouelle Sepie, ò Calamari" (p. 234).
33. Enrico Carrara, *La poesia pastorale* (Milan, 1908) p. 351.

James J. Yoch

ceilings, from the stage to the palace where the play is put on. Timeta even compares the play's closing festivities to the paintings on the walls of the Colonna palace.[34] The clear, symmetrical structure of this act establishes a comfortable final order in contrast to the desperate manoeuvrings of the characters and their whimsical passions.

The intermezzi, providing even more definite designs of stability and princely magnificence, showed confidence in the ruling powers to order the chaos of emotional life. In the planned revival, the intermezzi would have seemed all the fresher and more vigorous played within a play which was already a generation old and which used parody to diffuse the importance of the action and the characters. The designer even added an intermezzo after the final act of the play. He apologized for the inadequacy of the term intermezzo but used quotations from Aristotle and Scaliger to argue that the concluding show suited an architecture more important than the mere play.[35]

Magnanini, posing as L'Arsiccio to comment on the intermezzi, began with an essay explaining their political importance. He summoned Demosthenes, writers from both Republican and Imperial Rome, and, most importantly, Plato (Laws, 7) to support his arguments on the advantages of spectacle to the prince and particularly its usefulness in impressing and controlling the people: "There were deeply respected in all times and among all the most savage peoples both spectacles and public games, since by these means they thought no less to praise and to revere their false gods than to please the subject peoples. And no less with games did they think to placate the wrath of Heaven, than to buy the favor and good will of men."[36] Magnanini then showed the advantages of spectacles over the arena's games, which encouraged men to behave like animals. Instead, "stage presentations, which purge from souls every barbarous spirit, and every cruel thought, conserve men in their humanity, and that sweet and native pleasantness, which the hand of the divine and most clement Eternal Maker impressed in them, as more suitable to our

34. *L'Alceo:*
    Hoggi in somma si celebri vn trionfo
    Simile à quel, che si vede dipinto
    Nel Palagio real dei duo fratelli,
    Splendore, (p. 238).
35. *Ibid.*, pp. 239-40.
36. *Ibid.*, "FVRONO in tutti i tempi, e presso tutte le piu barbare nazioni gli spettacoli, ed i giuochi pubblici in venerazione grandissima, poichè con sì fatti mezzi, e'si credean non meno di lodare, e di riuerire le loro deità bugiarde, che di piacere a i popoli soggetti: E non meno co'giuochi pensauano di placar l'ira del Cielo, che di comprarsi l'aura, e la beniuoglienza de gli huomini" (p. 9).

178

nature, [these shows] much more ardently and with greater pleasure deserve to be admired."[37]

Accordingly, the intermezzi show, like the play, intense emotions contained within the explicit designs of a plot which leads from Medea's hysteria and cruelty in the first intermezzo to Jove's settled court in the last. In the first, in an exchange of arias, Medea abandons a lamenting Jason. She summons her car, a golden chariot drawn by a dragon, then pauses as she moves across the heavens to sing a final, scorning reproach to Jason, and disappears into the clouds as Jason, despairing, enters the burning city of Corinth. The second and third intermezzi come from Tasso's *Gerusalemme Liberata* and show Armida's palace and pleasures in the second, Rinaldo and Ubaldo parting from her in the third. The fourth and fifth tell the story of Proserpina: the first panel shows her rape and then the grief of Ceres, in the second the designer greatly expanded the part of Jove, who reaches his temperate decision after hearing arguments from Juno, Cynthia, Venus, Mars and Minerva. Symmetries interlock these spectacles: both Medea and Armida finish their scenes by summoning a monster to carry them from the stage; the stories of Armida and Proserpina are both in two movements in which the first displays the problem of passion and the second the triumph of reason. In the plot of the whole sequence, revenge, cruelty, lust, hatred give way to Jove's decision, which turns the wrangling of the gods to a harmonious song: "O worthy and wise decree of great Father Jove."[38]

These intermezzi flattered the audience by showing them dimensions well beyond the ken of shepherds, whose actions become even less significant and whose passions seem even sillier within the great architectural frames on which gods and heroes pose. Although the gods do not mix in the play (except for the surveying power of Amor), the audience could readily have recognized the connection between the triumphal procession within the shepherd world, the stately procession in which Jupiter leads the performers from the stage, and the ways in which these happy images resemble the prince who will lead his audience from the theatre after the applause. Thus river gods, shepherds, Jove and his court, the prince and his people all join in

37. *Ibid.*, "Ma i Scenici, che purgando da gli animi ogni barbaro, ed ogni crudele pensiero gli huomini conseruano nell' umanità loro, ed in quella dolce, e natia piaceuolezza, che in loro impresse la man diuina, e clementissima del Fattore eterno, come alla nostra natura piu confaceuoli, assai piu cupidamente, e con diletto maggiore meritano d'esser vagheggiati" (p. 10).
38. *Ibid.*: "O del gran Padre Gioue / Degno decreto, e saggio" (p. 251).

final, flattering marches that ornament and arrange into classical patterns the lives of the observers.

Within these controlling designs, each intermezzo developed its scene with a combination of witty parody of its sources, cleverly devised machinery and vigorous sensuality. Modern readers have often responded most enthusiastically to the emotionalism of these productions without duly regarding controls on it. Magnanini worked to increase and focus passions in his intermezzi. In the third, for example, he presented what seem an awesome number of incidents from book sixteen of the *Gerusalemme:* Rinaldo dressed like a woman and revelling in the pleasures of love, the garden of Armida, the labyrinthine palace, the entwining and seductive words of Armida, Ubaldo's revelation of Rinaldo's dishonour, Rinaldo's shame, Armida's pleas and curses, Rinaldo's exit, the entrance of the hydra, which Armida mounts to fly from the scene. Magnanini concentrated the passion of Tasso's material by combining cantos and reducing Armida's lines into short arias. The commentary shows that he was pleased with his success, for he recorded the audience's reaction: "O how many hearts soften, how many sighs exude from breasts."[39]

But the intensification of sighs and tears is not the only achievement of his changes and commentary. Tasso's poem made explicit the obligations of duty and the dangers of passion. Magnanini interrupted his presentation of passion in action and Rinaldo's recovery from it with disquisitions on the reversals of emotions from love to hate (with justifications from Dante and Aristotle), descriptions of how the singers performed, appraisals of Tasso and reviews of applicable criticism.[40] This added material shifts attention from the subject of the presentation to the style of it. There is a heavy traffic of authorities in the commentary, for the author was aware that many critics, observers, the prince and other writers would be asking questions about the method of presentation.

There is, of course, in the choice of old stories a direction to the audience to appreciate the *maniera* of the presentation. Magnanini's most important changes come at the end of the canto. To suit his announced theme of having the intermezzi show the necessity of softening hard feminine hearts, he eliminated some of Armida's pitiful confusion in Tasso's version: "What shall I say, or how renew

---

39. *Ibid.:* "O quanti cuori s'intenerirono; o quanti sospiri a molti trasse del petto" (p. 106).
40. *Ibid.,* pp. 107-9. To the intermezzo the commentator joined essays on the loss of liberty (that is, the loss of reason) and how to get it back (pp. 109-13).

my speech" (16.58) as well as her fainting when Rinaldo rejects her (16.60). Instead, the intermezzo concludes with her wrath and departure. Yet in the arrangements for her exit, Magnanini showed that he was willing to shift attention from the emotional point to technical ingenuity, which his commentary encouraged the reader to appreciate. On Armida's cue line of "O hellish demons," a great hydra flew into the sky above the stage, breathed fire (composed of sweet perfumes) over the audience, did a full turn to demonstrate the designer's skill, allowed Armida to get on his back, flew halfway back up and paused for her to sing a concluding aria, and finally disappeared into the clouds with "easy grace and the applause of the spectators."[41] This conclusion called attention to the technology of the production, the witty, musical and mechanical variation on Tasso, which, like the rendering of a book into a movie, partly affirms the power of artistry and the present over the past. The designers set Ongaro's play within the intermezzi as Magnanini claimed he put Tasso's lines, like a rich ruby set among other jewels.[42]

Each intermezzo concluded with a dramatic mechanical feat or triumph that embellished the gods and heroes of the past to suit a contemporary plot. In this way the court and the academy showed their control over the stuff of even the grandest romances as well as the simple lives of the peasants. All these fragments of experience become, through hyperbole and parody, song and machinery, the decorations for an entertainment. Tasso's lines and Ongaro's plays are like the pieces of antique marbles stuck on the façades of the Villa Medici and the Villa Borghese; their old contexts lost, they support the new advertisements for princely style.

Magnanini even added a third series of frames to the action of the drama by providing numerous essays on themes related to the intermezzi. These essays have a plot and move from private problems, such as suicide and the conflict between reason and appetite, to discussions of communal concerns such as providence and the necessity of counsel. Here again, the argument, now supported by philosophy and literature, is that wisdom should properly restrain violent emotion. Nothing is extraordinary in these essays, which provide a context of comfortable and obvious doctrine to the demonstrations

---

41. *Ibid:* "Particolarmente ne' petti femmili [sic] destar souerchia pietade, e tenerezza" (p. 46). The English translation is *Jerusalem Delivered*, trans. Edward Fairfax (New York, 1963), printed as 16.57. *L'Alceo:* "O spiriti infernali" (p. 108); "con infinita leggiadria, e applauso degli spettatori, disparue" (p. 109).
42. *Ibid.:* "che ha posta una cura particolare in far risplendere tra le sue gioie preziose, i viuaci carbonchi del Tasso" (p. 102).

of vigorous action in the drama and spectacle.[43] For example, the commentator added a five-page discussion on suicide to the intermezzo about Medea, and he concluded his essay with a quotation from Euripides' *Medea:* "Visitations of love that come / Raging and violent on a man / Bring him neither good repute nor goodness."[44] In a similar way, the second intermezzo ends with a procession of cupids celebrating the delights of love; the attached essay contrasts the sensitive and the reasonable faculties and shows the errors of Armida's love. Thus, the exhibition of sensuality is part of a plan ultimately illustrating the advantages of traditional morality.

Right rule is consistently a theme of all these essays and not just, as we might expect, those on providence, free will and the advantages of counsel. For example in his essay on reason and passion, Magnanini ran the familiar comparison between the person and the state. The proper order of the soul is when the passions obey the commands of reason as the son respects the father.[45] From this domestic pattern, he moved quickly to a political one where his fears of popular power and revolt inform the remainder of the images in the discussion of the organization of the self. Disaster comes "when passion, taking insolently the yoke from its collar, not only refuses to obey, but recklessly seizing the golden and heavy sceptre, wishes even to do the job of legislator, even that of a monarch, administering everything according to its mind." The essay then proceeds to the dangers in such a world, where licentiousness and confusion follow rebellion to reason, portrayed now as a "poor queen."[46]

Thus, Ongaro's parody of Tasso's *Aminta,* the intermezzi and their descriptions, as well as the essays that accompany them all argue for

---

43. There is nothing arcane in this practical moral philosophy. Only one of the twenty-five discourses considers the moral and philosophical allegory of the fable (pp. 187-93). The essays do not have what Jean Seznec called the "pedantry" and "laboured hieroglyphics" of the usual Florentine and Roman mannerist commentaries (*The Survival of the Pagan Gods* (1940; rpt. New York, 1953), p. 304.

44. *L'Alceo:*
Amores nimij, & immoderati
Venientes, neque honestum nomen
Neque virtutem conciliant
Mortalibus (p. 52)

The English translation is *Medea,* ll. 572-74, trans. Philip Vellacott, in *Medea, Myth and Dramatic Form,* ed. James Sanderson and Everett Zimmerman (Boston, 1957), pp. 29-30.

45. *L'Alceo:* "Dunque perchè suo proprio uficio, è d'ubbidire a gli imperi della ragione, sì come del figliuolo è il riuerire il padre" (sig. K).

46. *Ibid.:* "quando il senso, trattosi insolentemente il giogo dal collo, non solamente ricusa d'ubbidire, ma, dando temerariamente dipiglio allo scettro d'oro, e pesante, vuol anch'egli far del legislatore, anzi del Monarca, ogni cosa amministrando a suo talento" (sig. K); "pouera Reina" (p. 74).

the dangers of the assertive will and the disadvantages of lust whether for bodies or power.[47] The wit, the machines, the splendid sets and costumes are part of a rhetoric following literary models of irony, symmetry and repetition. An appreciation of the moral, literary, architectural patterns here, and of their analogies to the political system, confirms the audience in its superiority and emphasizes the limitations of the characters, so wittily tampered with and so unaware of the complex dimensions of their actions and words.

III

This final section considers briefly how the English masques accomplished similar tasks to those of the Italian spectacles: celebrating authority and contrasting it with rustic and inept alternatives, such as the satyrs and other bumblers, thieves and rapists of the anti-masques. Thus, for example, Inigo Jones opposed the house of fame to the tree of baboonery.[48] Within the reason of authority, the Italian designers set the emotionalism and sensationalism of passion. The English, working with different traditions, focused on the difference between the graceful movement of the masquers and the clumsiness of their opponents.

The masques show the audience how to be good subjects. In this, the English productions resemble the Italian pastorals which showed the docility of the characters at the end and the inferiority of the pastoral to the intermezzi in order to affirm the power of the prince. Just as Ongaro's play celebrated the day on which it was performed and the house that staged it, so too the masques aim their conclusion at recognizing the value of the present. At the end of *The Golden Age Restored* (1615), Astraea concluded the play by looking about and claiming that she now doesn't want to leave, for the place "is become a heav'n on earth." In *Pan's Anniversary* (1620), the chorus sings a

47. Other commentaries on pastorals argued the same point: G. B. Guarini, *Il pastor fido* (Venice, 1602), sig. Hh4; Zuccolo, *L'Alessandro*, suggested that the pastoral "gently reprehended vice" (p. 19). Even the audience's unassertive reaction to the performance demonstrated its superior rank and contact with antique custom: "rather than the whistling, yelling and noisy applause of the insolent mob, worthy men, unlike office clerks, proved their perfect appreciation of the whole production by a religious and communal silence" (". . . delle rappresentazioni, non con fischi importuni, ne con pazze gridate, ne con gli applausi strepitosi, della plebe insolente, si faceua il giudizio, ma sì come a valentuomini n'era commesso l'ufizio, così con silenzio religioso, e commune, gli spettatori lasciauan loro perfettamente tutta la fauola sentire" *L'Alceo*, pp. 147-48).
48. *Middle Temple and Lincoln's Inn Masque*, ll. 410-26, in *Inigo Jones, The Theatre of the Stuart Court*, ed. Stephen Orgel and Roy Strong (London, 1973), I, p. 259.

James J. Yoch

hymn to the King as "Great Pan, the father of our peace and pleasure."[49]

The last performed masque, *Salmacida Spolia*, condenses the ingredients of the traditional entertainment, deflates the passionate and energetic into foolish subjects, and thus repeats the formulas supporting the images of authority used in the Italian productions of pastorals. One of the major problems with *Salmacida Spolia* has been that the twenty-nine antimasques seem to run away with it. G. E. Bentley thought that they revealed the "degeneration of the form" and provided an example of "funny but barely relevant variety turns."[50] His judgment resembles that about the idyllic passions of the Italian intermezzi and pastorals: such spectacles seem expressions of a taste for luxury and anarchy. Yet the noise, antics and confusion of the antimasques, like that of passionate shepherds in the pastoral, make more attractive the stable power of the masquers who monopolize lights, machinery, splendid sets and costumes.

Salmacida Spolia established early in the text and the viewers' minds the control of virtue. In the interpretation of the title and the well of Salmacis, Jones made a radical alteration from Ovid's luxurious scene of "enervating waters" that "weaken and soften" to a story in Vitruvius's *De architectura* (2.8.11) of a natural theatre of hills where there was a fountain, by which "fierce and cruel natures were reduced of their own accord to the sweetness of the Grecian customs."[51] The change from the poet to the architect, from private to political issues, from ancient to modern theatre, indicates the designer's concern to demonstrate control over the public world.

Jones intensified the architectural restraint by means of a proscenium arch with twenty allegorical figures. This surpassed earlier frames such as the two statues of Numa and Minos and the "hieroglyphics of Peace, Justice and Law" in *The Triumph of Peace*, the simple "arch of agreeable workmanship" in *The Spring's Glory*, or Humanity, Cheerfulness and Readiness in *Lovers Made Men*.[52] The figures in *Salmacida Spolia* provide a framing vision of the gods, who constantly set the perspective and control the distance of the action. The images here are pacific virtues to suit the King's policy: Reason embraced by Intellectual Appetite, children taming a lion with reins and bit, the

49. *The Golden Age Restored* (l. 214); *Pan's Anniversary* (l. 225), in *Ben Jonson, Selected Masques*, ed. Stephen Orgel (New Haven, 1970), pp. 148, 199.
50. G. E. Bentley, *Book of Masques*, pp. 11-12.
51. ll. 70-87, *Book of Masques*, p. 349.
52. *Triumph of Peace*, ll. 158-59; *The Spring's Glory*, l. 1; *Lovers Made Men*, l. 6, *Book of Masques*, pp. 286, 324, 215.

bird of Pallas "figured for Prudence." In the frieze were a series of children expressing forgetfulness of injury, commerce, felicity, prosperous success, innocence, affection for country. The description summarizes the meaning of the frontispiece, "consisting of picture qualified with moral philosophy, [that] tempered delight with profit."[53]

In this final masque, the English designers are much more specific and individual in their description of the antitheses of power than in the more generalized forms that shepherds take in Italian court pastorals. Vandergoose adds five recipes to his nine French originals and many of his include pretenders threatening established credentials: a neophyte courtier, a poor man at a rich man's table, a linguist who hasn't travelled, a diet using only the "fricassee of confederacy; will make ignorants in all professions to seem and not to be."[54] Also changed in the direction of immediacy and realism, the characters of the antimasques are no longer the satyrs and witches from mythology nor the chimney-sweeps and beggars from the bottom of the social system but instead many ordinary citizens, turned into a joke and brought into visual subjection to the monarch. The antimasques display such figures as old men, young soldiers, a nurse with children, an Irishman, a Scotsman, an old-fashioned Englishman, an Italian mathematician and teacher, a farmer and his wife, a country gentleman and his wife. Even the fashionable in the audience might have had relatives who lived like those scorned.

Yet rather than sympathy, the production emphasized discrepancies in rank and style and between the one and the many. Besides the distance between courtly masquers and the other citizens of the spectacle, the designers brought out in their descriptions of the antimasques the humour of disproportion by which courtly lads played eccentric, non-courtly figures, whose costumes were discordant with their rank or out of date: for example, the old-fashioned gentleman and his mistress in "old habits . . . clinquant and rich."[55] These differences flattered the court and prince, who saw imaged the superiority of the aulic style. The outsiders, so deflated, were necessary; Magnanini quoted Maximus Tityrus: "The prince rules when the people serve."[56]

Salmacida Spolia aimed directly at the current political situation and tried idealistically to provide a solution suitable to the taste of the

---

53. II. 19-56, *Book of Masques*, pp. 347-48.
54. II. 214-16, *Book of Masques*, p. 353.
55. Note to ll. 234-35, *Book of Masques*, p. 367.
56. *L'Alceo*, sig. K.

crown. The rhetoric of this entertainment, nourished by the practice of Italian courts and borrowing from them designs of scenery as well as language, was not idle: a "gay series of vaudeville turns" to help the audience forget "the trouble of the times."[57] On the contrary, the rhetoric was most earnest. The King and his agents were trying desperately to hold off civil war and chose a familiar and tried device, the spectacles which commentaries said successfully entertained the subject populaces of Rome and Italy.

Perhaps because of their fears and insecurities, English court artists made power literal and explicit: King and Queen played in them and citizens bowed before them. By making the imagery so specific, so identifiable, so limited and exclusive of those outside the court, the masque displayed the myopia which spoiled the crown's decisions in other theatres. Hostility and domination came close to the surface in these productions, for the masques turned fantasy into fact. At the conclusion of *Salmacida Spolia* the Chorus sings to the King and Queen: "All that are harsh, all that are rude, / Are by your harmony subdued."[58] The English made opposition clear by such blunt statements of power.

On the other had, the pastorals and intermezzi of the Italian court stage provided alternatives to facts by presenting dreams and fancies.[59] Thus they extended the world and its contexts beyond the limits ordinarily imposed by the flesh and the unities. These productions defined the place of the court by implication and analogy through the presentation of the peasants and gods with whom the aristocrats shared the world. Power that in practice may have been ruthless found images that gently bound the world together in a mixture of separate spheres that only smiles and tears bridged. Rather than opposition, these designs relied on analogy and symmetries, which united diverse worlds in happy orders for the conclusion.

Ingenious and fresh in their variations on classical and vernacular motifs, musically and technologically elegant, all these shows presented more order than the simple indulgence in emotion and separation into parts that critics have proposed for them. In Ongaro's adaptations from Tasso, in Magnanini's rendering of Armida's parting from Rinaldo, in Davenant's and Jones's rich frontispiece and masque apparition, the sensuality, variety and energy of the presentation contribute to the aesthetic order of those who enjoy it

57. T. J. B. Spencer, *Book of Masques*, p. 341.
58. ll. 455-56, *Book of Masques*, p. 361.
59. De Sommi, in D'Ancona, *Origini*, II, p. 421.

and see through its "pleasing deceptions." Perhaps decadent in their private lives, these courts were emphatically organized and communal in public. Even the seating, architecture, staging of the theatre gave a final frame to productions that recalled Roman power and provided examples of successful control over the unruly. These spectacles showed command over rhetorical skills to organize an elaborate system of images in support of authority, which alone could provide for and unify so many through splendour.

The Contributors

DAVID M. BERGERON, Professor of English, University of Kansas. Author of *English Civic Pageantry 1558-1642*, and many articles.

JAMES BLACK, Professor of English, University of Calgary. Editor of Nahum Tate's *King Lear*, and author of numerous articles on Shakespeare.

A. C. HAMILTON, Professor of English, Queen's University. Author of *The Structure of Allegory in 'The Faerie Queene'*, *The Early Shakespeare*, and numerous articles.

R. W. INGRAM, Professor of English, University of British Columbia. Author of *Music and Poetry*, *The Production of Drama in Medieval Coventry*, and several articles.

ANNE LANCASHIRE, Professor of English, University of Toronto. Editor of Lyly's *Gallathea* and *Midas*, and of *The Second Maiden's Tragedy*; author of various articles.

† J. M. NOSWORTHY, sometime Professor of English, University College of Wales, Aberystwyth. Author of *Shakespeare's Occasional Plays*; editor of *Cymbeline* and *Measure for Measure*.

G. M. PINCISS, Professor of English, Hunter College. Editor of *The Faithful Friends*; author of several articles.

EUGENE M. WAITH, Professor of English, Yale University. Author of *The Herculean Hero*, *The Dramatic Moment*, *Ideas of Greatness*, and many articles; editor of Jonson's *Bartholomew Fair*.

JAMES J. YOCH, Professor of English, University of Oklahoma. Author of 'Renaissance Gardening and Pastoral Scenery in Italy and England', and other articles.

Index

191